SURETY
TITLE
AGENCY
INC.

1010 Leader Building
526 Superior Avenue East
Cleveland, Ohio 44114-1401
216-589-8399   800-442-8399   Fax 216-589-4826
www.suretytitle.com   e-mail: info@suretytitle.com

HERITAGE
Italian-American Style

Best regards,
Leon... Radaile
7/5/00

HERITAGE
Italian-American Style

By

Leon J. Radomile

Brief quotations may be used in critical articles and reviews. For any other reproduction of this book, illustrations and photographs, including electronic, mechanical, photocopying, recording, or other means, written permission must be given by the publisher.

Published by Vincero Enterprises
  490 Marin Oaks Drive
  Novato, California 94949

Cover design by Greg Brown
  Abalone Design Group
  Sausalito, California

Interior layout by Kay Richey
Electronically created camera-ready copy by
  KLR Communications, Inc.
  POB 192
  Grawn, MI 49637
Art illustrations by Greg Brown

HERITAGE Italian-American Style / by Leon J. Radomile
Italian-American - History

ISBN 0-9675329-0-9

Dedication

I would like to dedicate this work to my wonderful wife Lanette, and my equally beautiful daughters, Lea and Alexandra; to my loving and always supportive mother, Emma Toschi, and my step-father, Joseph V. Toschi; and to the memory of my beloved father, Leo Radomile, a gentle and loving man who passed away, too young at 64, the victim of a sudden heart attack. Thank you, Dad, for all the things you taught me about Italy. It is also dedicated to all the relatives I have found over the last two years in the United States, Italy, Australia, Brazil, and Venezuela; and finally to the good sisters, brothers, and priests who guided me along the intellectual—as well as spiritual—path during my school years. God bless you all!

Leon J. Radomile
September 1999

Introduction

"Io sono fiera di essere Italiana!" This simple sentence, shouted by *Madonna* at a Turin concert, sent 65,000 fans in the audience into a frenzy. When I read that comment in Steven Spignesi's excellent work, *The Italian 100,* during the course of my research for this book, I literally became one giant goose bump.

This book of questions about Italy contains nearly 70,000 words, yet cannot convey my Italian pride any better than those six Italian words. What *Madonna* proclaimed with passion, says it all: **"I am proud to be an Italian,"** and this book offers a fascinating compendium, with 1492 reasons why you, too, can feel a proud connection to thousands of years of art, science, history, literature, food, and music.

In 1985, indignant at finding the Italian culture always trivialized into pizza and spaghetti or stereotyped as Mafia mobsters, I determined to find a way to promote Italian culture in a positive light. I began by categorizing and listing some of the accomplishments offered to the world by Italians and Italian-Americans. Since the game *Trivial Pursuit* was in vogue at the time, I decided to create a board game that used a similar format, but devoted the questions to the history and culture of Italy. One year later, *The Italian Heritage Game* was published and, in just a few weeks, two thousand games were sold through mail order advertisements across the country.

In 1987, John Lisanti contacted me about redesigning the game and marketing it on a grand scale. We formed a company and, with the help of an enthusiastic and financially supportive group of Italian-Americans in our area, launched our newly redesigned and beautifully packaged board game. In 1988, we produced 10,000 games and proceeded to market them across the country. Though the game won critical acclaim for design and graphics and sold all 10,000 sets, several unforeseen manufacturing glitches occurred that kept the game from being profitable.

This endeavor was not accomplished through the means of a large publisher with a room full of collating machines and a shipping department—my friends, family, and the parents club from our daughter's grammar school helped collate four million game question cards by hand, in addition to putting all the parts of the board game together. Friedrich Nietzsche, the German philosopher said, "What does not destroy me, makes me stronger," and after that experience, I was ready to enter the weight-lifting competition at the Olympics. Exhausted and frustrated after two years of the game business, I was happy to return to my quiet retail health food store located in Mill Valley, ten minutes north of San Francisco's Golden Gate bridge.

This business has sustained my family and me for twenty-two years. I've kept a copy of the *Italian Heritage Game* in the store for sentimental reasons. Several months ago, almost ten years to the day that I ceased operating the game company, two of my good customers and friends, Bart Ingargiola and Carlos Zayas, came in and spotted the game behind the counter. I briefly explained its history, and they became enthusiastic and offered to help me bring it to market again. I laughed and told them I would think about it, but secretly decided I'd rather take a header off that famous jumping bridge just ten minutes down the road.

But then something in my head asked, "Why not turn the old game into a book?" The more I thought about it, the more confident and excited I became. Perhaps this time around, I could make it less work and more play. Certainly the lessons learned from my past experiences were deeply and painfully burnt into my memory banks, and I didn't have to make those mistakes again.

I began to get excited about the project. I put aside the historical novel I had been working on for the better part of a year, and decided to devote all my discretionary time and energy to this new project. The Renaissance period adventure novel that I have been working on was inspired by my genealogical research on my family origins in Italy, so I had a wealth of new information about Italy and Italians ready and waiting for a format. I think the novel has a great story to tell, but it can wait a few months.

(Stay tuned for future news on that front.)

I began the day after the conversation with my friends to rewrite, revise, and update material from the game, putting it in a format that would be reader-friendly by generously sprinkling "multiple choice" and "hints" among the questions. I feel like this new, updated material will have a broader appeal than the previous game material which, as I look back, was perhaps a little too difficult to really enjoy in a game setting.

For the past three months my daily schedule has been to get up at 5 AM and work on the book until 9 AM every morning during the regular work week then rush off to the store and work from 10 AM to 6 PM. In the evening I put in one or two additional hours, and the weekends gave me another 20 or more hours to spend on the book.

In August, I found a production editor, printer, and graphic artist. Things were finally taking shape and it looked like the three months I had given myself to complete this project would prove correct.

In working on the design and title for the cover of the book, many friends have suggested that I use the word "trivia" somewhere on the cover or in the title. I have steadfastly refused to consider the use of this word for the simple reason that there is nothing trivial about this material. The definition of the word trivial means "of little importance or significance, ordinary and commonplace." I can assure you that there is nothing ordinary or commonplace about the achievements brought to light in this book by the essence of Italian genius.

What does it really mean to be an Italian-American? For me, it is the feeling of kinship I have for an astronomical number of people. There are an estimated 26 million people of Italian descent in the U.S., and they all feel like relatives. As a group, we have many things that bind us together and my family history has, I am sure, many similarities to tens of thousands of other Italian-American families.

In the following pages, you will read about the great accomplishments Italians and Italian-Americans, throughout history, have achieved in a staggering number of areas. The common thread through all these pages are the concepts of hard work, perseverance, and innovation. What our people have accomplished, they have earned by combining their creative talents with a vigorous work ethic. Ever since I can remember, I have had a love affair with things Italian and I have always been very proud of my Italian heritage. In high school, I began using the Italian pronunciation of my last name. **Ra-doe-me-lay** (Radomile) rather than the anglicized

Rad-doe-mile.

My father's father, Attilio Radomile, married my grandmother, Lucia Ciampoli, in her town of Ortona a Mare in the region of Abruzzi in February of 1910. He like the previous seven generations, was born in the nearby town of Villalfonsia (near Vasto). On June 10, 1910, they arrived in the United States and settled in Philadelphia. My father was born in Philadelphia in 1913, and was one of six children. He was the surviving twin and was named Leo which signified strength—as in lion. Soon after World War I my grandfather decided to return the family to the coastal city of Ortona, were they lived until returning to the U.S. in 1932. However, my uncle (Anthony, born in 1912) returned to the U.S., in the late 20's, followed by my father, to help support the family back in Italy.

Along came World War II and both my father and his younger brother Galileo proudly joined the United States Army. Both were shipped out to the South Pacific and fought in New Guinea. On leave in Sydney, Australia, they asked the local USO if there were any Italian families in the area where they could perhaps have an Italian dinner. They were given the address of a successful green grocer, Giuseppe Costa, who would eventually be my grandfather.

In 1919, Giuseppe Costa had married Giuseppina Ruggera in the town of Lingua on the island of Salina in the Lipari island group. This small island, in the renowned crystal blue waters off the coast of Sicily, is near the provincial capitol city of Messina. My mother was born on the island in 1927, and moved with her family to Sydney, Australia in 1929 when my grandfather, who had learned from relatives that Sydney offered many business opportunities, decided to move his wife and four children to this new land of opportunity down under.

Under the strictest supervision of Sicilian courting customs, my parents met, corresponded by mail, and were married immediately after the war ended in 1945, which made my mother a war bride. She arrived in San Francisco in 1946 and proceeded by train across the country, with hundreds of other Australian war brides, to Philadelphia to be reunited with my father. She was eighteen years old and my father was thirty-two.

In 1955, when I was six years of age, my father decided to embark, in the tradition of the great Italian explorers, on a journey to circumnavigate the globe.

Boarding an ocean liner in New York, my parents and I crossed the Atlantic to the port of Naples. From there we were driven by a hired car to my father's childhood town of Ortona a Mare. After six weeks of visiting with cousins, we returned to Naples to begin the second leg of our journey. This took us from Naples and the Mediterranean, through Port Said and the Suez Canal, into the Arabian Sea, and on to the capital of Ceylon (now called Sri Lanka); Colombo. After several days there, we began again with brief stops in Djakarta, Indonesia and Fremantle, Australia, arriving at Sydney in eastern Australia and my mother's family in 1956. We had been on board ship thirty days from Naples to Sydney, during which time my father formed a friendship with the novelist, Robert Ruark.

I attended first grade in Sydney, where my parents seriously considered staying permanently. However, as a barber, my father felt he could do much better financially in America than in Australia. During World War II, he had passed through the San Francisco bay area on his way to the war in the South Pacific, and had fallen in love with The City. They decided to move there. We left Sydney in late '56 for the final leg of our world cruise. I have fond memories of a large, pink hotel on Honolulu's Waikiki Beach. In 1956, that pink Royal Hawaiian Hotel was *the* grandest hotel in the area.

We settled in San Francisco and set about our new life. My father got his barber's license and bought a barber shop across the street from San Francisco's impressive city hall. My mother, who began as a hairdresser in Australia at the age of fifteen, studied and received her cosmetology license in 1960.

I did poorly in the city's public schools, so my mother enrolled me into the fifth grade at St. Vincent de Paul Catholic School in 1961. This was the starting point of my real education. Two years later, my parents purchased a home in Mill Valley. The property had a beauty salon downstairs from the house, and this became my mother's business from 1963 until she retired in 1983. From here I attended Sacred Heart High School, an all male high school in San Francisco, administered by the Christian Brothers, graduating in 1968. Four years later I graduated from the Jesuit's University of San Francisco with a degree in History.

While working as a real estate agent in 1974, something wonderful happened to me that would change my life forever: a blind date with an elementary school teacher. Two months later, on Christmas Eve, I proposed, and Lanette and I were married on June 8, 1975, and we are still enjoying each other now, nearly 25 years later. Lanette is 100 percent 2nd generation Romanian. If you remember your history, Romania was the Roman province called Dacia. The people identified so closely to Rome that they continue to speak a Romance language based on Latin, and named their country after Rome—hence Romania.

Lea Linda Radomile arrived in October 10, 1976, and Alexandra Marie Radomile whom we call Lexi, arrived on May 10, 1982. A father could not have asked for two more loving or beautiful daughters, or a more special partner. My wife and I have truly been blessed.

Acknowledgements

My wonderful wife Lanette, along with my two daughters Lea, and Alexandra, have been most indulgent, helpful, and supportive during this "summer of work" with no time for vacations. Even my parents pitched in to proofread several categories. (When my mother commented that she had a tough time putting the material down at night, I knew I was on the right track.)

I want to take this opportunity to thank a long list of people who have witnessed and supported this idea from its early board game stage to its culmination as a book.I would like to start with those proud Italian-Americans who stepped forward and not only spoke of their pride in being Italian-American, but were willing to invest their money to make the *Italian Heritage Game* a reality. I have not forgotten the support and encouragement of Lee and Eva Ceccotti, Iris Campodonico Pera, Leroy Cheda, Mr. & Mrs. Mario Ghilotti, James Pedroncelli, Mr. & Mrs. Rodi Martinelli, Romano and Maria Della Santina, Bob Valentino, Steven Campagno, Martin and Velia Bramante, James Campodonico, Dr. Diana Parnell and Dr. Francis Parnell, Richard and Ingrid Kerwin, Terry and Gloria Aquilino, Gerald Donnelly, Elma Cirutti Hearle, Dr. Paul and Mary Ann Ferrari, Ralph and Jacquelyn Giovanniello, Gary and Patricia Aquilino, Joe Stillwell, Emma Toschi, Dr. Mario Pieri, Angelo Turrini, and Edward Massa. Also to my former partner, John Lisanti and our legal council, George Silvestri and his wife, Valerie.

I owe a huge debt of gratitude to my text editor, Necia Dixon Liles, an editor and published author, who has been instrumental in helping me mold this book into a work of which I can be proud. She really knows her stuff and I thank the day I found her. I also would like to thank an inanimate object: my computer. Without it, this rewriting project would have taken three years instead of three months. Other people I want to thank include, Brian "the genius" Jennings, my computer consultant who saved me a great deal of time and headaches; Kay L. Richey, my production editor in Michigan; Greg Brown, for his great book cover design; Richard Orwell, my internet consultant and web page designer; my wonderful sister-in-law, Linda Lupear, for her marketing expertise; old college friends who helped proofread: Gary Polizziani and Greg McCollum, and friends Dr. Dave Epstein, Patti Piazza-Phillips, Don Phillips, and Dr. Tony Sabatasso. If I left anyone out, you will be thanked again personally and included in the next edition.

Contents

FOOD, MUSIC, & ENTERTAINMENT

Food, Music, and Entertainment

1) *This Italian* made his film debut in 1939 and rapidly became one of the leading romantic stars on the Italian screen. His first Hollywood appearance was in *Little Women* (1949), but it was not until *The Barefoot Contessa* that he established himself as a Hollywood star, specializing in continental lovers and aristocrats. He is perhaps best known for his performance in *South Pacific.* ***Name this debonair actor.**

2) *In 1993, this young tenor* from rural Tuscany embarked on a career that has led him to international stardom. From playing piano to pay for his singing tuition fees, he became one of the most popular artists in the world, achieving tremendous chart success. His range enables him to sing great operatic arias and classical popular love songs.
*Identify this electrifying singing sensation.

3) *According to tradition,* this Italian violinist and composer was a supreme virtuoso in technical accomplishment. He wrote concertos and many other pieces for the violin which were later transcribed for the piano in studies by Liszt and Schumann, and were the source of themes for piano variations by Brahms and Rachmaninoff.
*Who was this musical genius?

4) *She was born Anna Maria Louise Italiano* in the Bronx, New York, in 1932. She won an Oscar in 1962 for Best Actress for her performance in *The Miracle Worker*, for which she previously won a Tony and the New York Critics Award. She has a long list of critically

17

acclaimed, award winning roles. (Hint: She is married to writer director Mel Brooks.) ***Name this actress.**

5) ***Born Ermes Effron Borgnino,*** this actor began his movie career as a villain. He gained attention as the sadistic sergeant in *From Here to Eternity* (1953), and a tough guy in *Bad Day at Black Rock* (1955). His portrayal of a lonely Bronx butcher in the movie *Marty*, won this Italian-American a Best Actor Oscar in 1956. (Hint: Best known for his role on popular TV comedy, *McHale's Navy*.) ***Who is he?**

6) ***What fortified wine,*** flavored with aromatic herbs, invented in the Italian region of Piedmont, is enjoyed around the world?

7) ***From the court of Savoy and Piedmont*** came this most famous of all Italian puddings. ***Identify it.**

8) ***During the sixteenth century***, a Venetian merchant ship returned home with a cargo of gold, oriental carpets, perfumes, and other treasures. Included in its hold was a sack of corn, the first to be imported into Italy. It had come from America, discovered by Columbus only a few years earlier. When the corn was brought to market to be sold, it caused a sensation. It was in Venice, that this popular Northern Italian dish was first made. ***What was it?**

9) ***This critically acclaimed movie director*** was born in Palermo, Sicily in 1897 and came to the United States at the age of six. He was a four-time president of the Academy of Motion Pictures, and three-time president of the Screen Director's Guild. Of his many movies, *It Happened One Night* was the first of the three Oscars he received for Best Director. His other movies include, *Arsenic and Old Lace, Mr. Deeds Goes to Town, You Can't Take It with You, Lost Horizon,* and *Mr. Smith Goes to Washington.* ***Who was this legendary director?**

10) ***This Italian directed*** over twenty five films, four of which won Oscars as Best Foreign Language Film. (Hint: His Oscar winning films were: *Shoeshine, The Bicycle Thief, Yesterday, Today, and Tomorrow,* and *The Garden of the Finzi-Continis.*) ***Name this Italian director.**

11) ***The NBC Symphony Orchestra*** was founded in 1937 under the baton of what famous Italian-American conductor? (Note: The orchestra survived into the television era, but after his retirement in 1954, it was disbanded and serious music all but disappeared from commercial television.)

18

12) **By the age of fourteen,** this popular Italian-American singer owned his own three-chair barber shop. He later went on to sign a twenty-five million dollar contract (a record at the time), with NBC-TV. His variety show was known for its easy-going atmosphere.

*Name this popular singer.**

13) **The internationally popular Italian film** star Giancarlo Giannini starred in many award winning movies *(Seven Beauties)* under the direction of what female Italian film director? (Hint: First woman to be nominated for an Academy Award for directing.)

14) **What respected movie actor** was typecast as the dashing villain in his early career? His movie credits include, *Oceans Eleven, Assault on a Queen*, with Frank Sinatra, *House of Strangers, Brothers Rico, The Greatest Story Ever Told*, and the role of Don Barzini in, *The Godfather.*

*Name him.**

I5) **Synonymous with Turin**, Napoleon called them Les petits batons de Turin. In Italian they call them Grissini.   **What are they?**

16) **Born Vito Rocco Farinola** in Brooklyn, New York, he was once heralded by Frank Sinatra as the world's greatest singer. This popular vocalist, with his smooth style is still captivating night club and TV audiences. (Hint: Former wives include actresses Pier Angeli and Diahann Carroll.)   **Who is he?**

17) **Absolutely the most important** Italian opera composer of the 19th century, he was an ardent nationalist associated with the struggle for Italian independence.   **Who was he?**

18) **Singer, actor, songwriter,** television and night club entertainer, this Italian-American was born Walden Robert Cassotto. Once called "the angry young man of show business," he exuded a dynamic flair which electrified audiences and made him a very popular entertainer until his premature death.   **Who was he?**

19) **The characters of this work** by Puccini are said to be fairly accurate portraits of artists and others of the Latin Quarter in Paris who were friends of Henri Murger during his youthful days as a struggling writer.   **Identify this popular Puccini opera.**

20) **Those familiar with Milanese cooking** know that many of its dishes are colored with what herb?

21) *In the 1960's,* this beautiful blonde emerged as a glamorous leading lady of international productions, particularly romantic comedies. Her U.S. films include, *The Secret Of Santa Vittoria, Not With My Wife You Don't,* and *How to Murder Your Wife.* (Hint: Born Virna Pieralisi in 1936.) ***Who is she?**

22) *In 1949, Arturo Toscanini* and Time magazine declared this tenor, "The Voice of the Century. He was the first classical artist in the history of RCA Victor Recordings to sell a million copies of a single disc: *Be My Love.* Two thousand people once paid admission simply to hear him rehearse. (Hint: Born Alfred Arnold Cocozza in Philadelphia in 1921.) ***Who was this singing legend?**

23) *For many years* this actress's name remained a synonym for beauty and glamour. Some of her U.S. films include *Strange Bedfellows, Solomon and Sheba*, and *Buona Sera, Mrs. Campbell.* She retired from the screen in the early 1970's to pursue a career as an executive with fashion and cosmetics firms. ***Who is she?**

24) *The people of this Italian city* concede with exuberant pride that their songs belong not to their city alone, but to the world. Many translations of these popular melodies exist in other languages, but they sound most expressive when performed in the rich, vibrant dialect of this city, a language Italians from other regions must bend an ear to understand. ***What are these popular songs known as?**

25) *It is said that this cooking fat* was first used in a small town several miles from Milan, and that Julius Caesar is thought to have been the first great man to appreciate its culinary value. Until then, the Romans had used it for greasing their bodies before sporting competitions and battles. ***Identify this substance.**

26) *Born Vincento Eduardo Zoino*, he played a popular TV doctor for five years. At the shows height, his no-nonsense bedside manner captivated as many as 32 million viewers.
*Name this Italian-American actor and the character he portrayed.

27) *Living and Loving, Her Own Story* (1979) is an autobiography of what star?

28) *Born in Philadelphia,* this teen singing idol was a millionaire by the time he was eighteen. Unhappy with his singing career, he bought out his contract and headed west to launch a career in the motion picture

industry. (Hint: His film credits include: *North to Alaska*, with John Wayne, and *Mr. Hobbs Takes a Vacation*, with Jimmy Stewart.)
*Who is he?

29) *For many years* he was considered one of the world's leading film personalities, and enjoyed universal popularity as a prototype of the modern-day urban European male. ***Name this Italian leading man.**

30) *In the early 1950's,* this son of a Neapolitan pasta manufacturer formed a production company with Carlo Ponti to produce a number of major films, including Fellini's *La Strada* (1954), and *The Nights of Cabiria* (1956) both winners of Best Foreign Language Film Oscars. During the 1970's and 80's he produced many popular and recognizable films, including: *Serpico, Three Days of the Condor, King Kong, Flash Gordon, Conan the Barbarian,* and *Dune.* ***Who is he?**

31) *In the early years* after World War II, this Italian director burst upon the international scene as a leading figure in the neorealism movement that suddenly made Italian films the rage among intellectual audiences the world over. His love affair and marriage to actress Ingrid Bergman and the scandal that ensued led to an unofficial boycott of his films in America and other countries. (Hint: Their daughter is the beautiful Isabella.) ***Name this director.**

32) *Born Anthony Papaleo,* this well known movie actor won an Academy Award nomination for his starring role in *A Hatful of Rain.* Other films include, *The Long, Hot Summer, Naked Maja,* and *Wild Is the Wind.* He was also featured in several popular television series'. ***Name this talented and handsome Italian-American.**

33) *What Milan opera house* is one of the largest and most important in the world?

34) *Her hit record,* Who's Sorry Now, sold over a million copies and her distinctive vocal style is very popular among many Italian-Americans. (Hint: Her first movie was *Where the Boys Are,* 1963.) ***Name this talented singer who was born Concetta Franconero.**

35) *Stockfish* or sun dried salt cod is used for what Italian dish?

36) *This Italian-American actor* has been very successful in all segments of show business. On Broadway, his credits include, *Cat on a Hot Tin Roof* and *A Hatful of Rain* ; in television, the series' *Arrest and Trial* and *Run for Your Life*; and in motion pictures, *Anatomy of a Murder,*

The Young Doctors, A Rage to Live , and *Bridge at Remagen*. Identify this actor, born of Sicilian immigrants, who grew up in New York's tough lower east side. (Hint: A recent film: *The Thomas Crown Affair*.)

37) *Verdi regarded this Italian* as the most talented composer of his time, and in the first quarter of the century, his popularity rivaled that of Verdi himself. ***Who was he?**

38) *He was the choreographer* and a dancer for many popular TV shows. Among his Broadway shows were *Kiss Me Kate, Guys and Dolls, Bells Are Ringing,* and *West Side Story.* ***Who is this talented dancer?**

39) *There were 60,000 entries* in a contest sponsored by the Prince Company, the largest independent pasta manufacturer in the US, for a new pasta design. ***Identify the winning name:**
a) Nudeles b) Melody-roni c) Umbrellas

40) *Butter,* sliced onions, bone marrow, dry red or white wine, rice, boiling meat stock, soaked saffron, and grated Parmesan cheese are the ingredients for what culinary legend of Milan?

41) *This Italian motion picture director* enjoyed an international reputation. Besides being an innovative theater and opera director, he was credited with the development of Maria Callas as an operatic superstar. Some of his memorable films include *Boccaccio '70, The Leopard,* and *Death in Venice.* ***Who was he?**

42) *Among his hit records are* *Mule Train, Jezebel, I Believe, My Heart Goes Where the Wild Goose Goes*, and his first big hit, *That's My Desire.* Born Frank Paul Lo Vecchio, he has worked in almost every form of entertainment, from nightclubs and stage to movies and television. (Hint: He sang the hit theme song for the TV western, *Rawhide*.)
*Who is he?

43) *Identify the word,* now used in the English language meaning, drama set to music and made up of vocal pieces with orchestral accompaniment and orchestral overtures and interludes.

44) *Candelabra always graced his grand piano.* In 1954, 192 TV stations carries his syndicated show. He appeared in several motion pictures including a starring role in *Sincerely Yours* (1955). (Hint: Known by his last name.)
*Identify this flamboyant concert-hall, ballroom, nightclub, and television entertainer.

45) *The people* of this Italian city claim to have invented the table napkin and the fork at a time when most people were still eating with their fingers. (Hint: Famous port city.)

*Identify the people who make this claim.

46) *After leaving* his very successful comedy/singing act, this Italian-American went on to establish himself as a leading recording star, headlining night club performer, and a star of over fifty motion pictures. He also had an extremely popular TV variety show (1965-74). (Hint: Member of the famed "Rat Pack.") ***Who was he?**

47) *What Italian singer* is considered the finest heroic tenor Italy has produced in the twentieth century? He was especially known for his interpretations of Puccini and Verdi.

48) *Born Vincente Scognamiglio* in Naples in 1922, this well-known character actor received an Oscar nomination for his role in *Bang the Drum Slowly* (1973), and a Tony for his Broadway performance in *The Prisoner of Second Avenue.* He is perhaps best remembered for his role in *Moonstruck* (1989). ***Who was he?**

49) *His reputation* is that of an endlessly creative motion picture director. He has adapted his talents to all types of movies from dramas, like *Lust for Life* and *Tea and Sympathy,* to musicals, like *Gigi* (Academy Award 1958), and comedies, like *Designing Woman*, and *Father of the Bride.* (Hint: Daughter's first name is Liza.) ***Name this director.**

50) *What traditional sauce* of Genoa is made of fresh, sweet basil, garlic, ewe's milk cheese, pine nuts, and olive oil?

51) *Born in Wayne, Pennsylvania,* this soprano won acclaim in concert halls as well as the operatic stage. After studying and performing at La Scala and touring Europe, she debuted in 1959 with the Metropolitan Opera Company as Violetta in La Traviata. ***Name her.**

52) *He was nominated* for an Oscar for his 1956 performance as a troubled youth in *Rebel Without A Cause*, and in 1960 for his supporting role in *Exodus.* His other movies include *The Gene Krupa Story, Greatest Story Ever Told, Giant,* and *Somebody Up There Likes Me.* (Hint: 1976 homicide victim.) ***Who was he?**

53) *What Italian word,* now incorporated into English, means a musical composition in a brisk lively manner?

54) *This talented daughter* of famous parents made her own way in show business. At 19, she became Broadway's youngest Best Actress Tony winner for her title role in *Flora, the Red Menace*. She received an Oscar nomination for her role in *The Sterile Cuckoo* and was a critical Broadway success in *Cabaret*. In 1972 she starred in the movie version of Cabaret for which she won the Oscar for Best Actress.
*Identify this extremely talented performer.

55) *A typical Bolognese dish* is tagliatelle, invented in 1487 by a cook named Zafirano for the occasion of the marriage of the Duke of Ferrara to what historically infamous daughter of the Spanish Pope, Alexander VI? In all fairness, it should be noted that many of the stories of her crimes and vices are unfounded. ***Who was this woman?**

56) *This innovative rock group* of the 1960's and 70's went by the name *The Mothers of Invention*.
*Identify its Italian-American founder and leader.

57) *Verdi's seventeenth opera* was composed in what has been termed his "second period," during which he also wrote *Rigoletto* and *La Traviata*. These operas firmly established his position as perhaps the greatest operatic composer ever. This particular opera has enjoyed uninterrupted success from the day of its premier, and its melodies are possibly more widely known than those of any other opera. ***Name this work.**

58) *Born Nicolas Coppola* in 1964, he is the nephew of legendary film director, Francis Ford Coppola. This versatile actor won an Oscar for his portrayal of an alcoholic screenwriter in the 1995 hit, *Leaving Las Vegas*. Besides the Oscar, he received a Golden Globe award and was named Best Actor by the New York and Los Angeles Film Critics Associations. Recent hit movies include, *The Rock, Con Air*, and *Face Off*. ***Who is he?**

59) *What is the Italian word* meaning the rate of speed of a musical piece or passage indicated by one of a series of directions and often by an exact metronome marking?

60) *To go with tagliatelle* and other pasta dishes like tortellini, the Bolognese invented a rich sauce made with beef, ham, vegetables, butter and cream. ***Name the sauce.**

61) *What opera tenor* was the first singer ever to sell a million records?

62) **What motion picture** and its sequel won the Academy Award for best picture?

63) **The song**, *Some Enchanted Evening*, was a hit in the musical, South Pacific. ***What singer introduced it?**

64) His mother's family emigrated from Calabria to Detroit, where he was born at the turn of the century. A martial arts expert, he has starred in a string of action-packed thrillers, including *Under Siege, Hard to Kill*, and *Fire Down Below.* ***Who is he?**

65) **In his first year out of college,** he landed the part of the Italian-American boxer and driver on the hit TV series, *Taxi*. He has since starred in and produced a number of television shows including *Who's the Boss*, and *Before They were Stars*. His movie credits include *Angels in the Outfield* and *She's Out of Control.*
*Who is this popular Italian-American actor?

66) **Invented in Livorno** (Leghorn), this famous dish, called *Cacciucco*, is meant to be served as a main course. ***What is it?**

67) **His collaborations with Mozart** in the 1780's produced such masterpieces as *The Marriage of Figaro, Don Giovanni,* and *Cosi Fan Tutte*. In America, in 1825, he promoted the Italian language and culture, was appointed the first professor of Italian at Columbia College, and began importing Italian opera companies to the United States. (Hint: Knowing about bridges would help.) ***Name this Italian.**

68) **Pulitzer Prize winner** for music in 1950 and 1954, his *Amahl and the Night Visitors* has become an American Christmas tradition.
*Identify this Pulitzer Prize winner.

69) **The son** of an Austrian father and Florentine mother, this versatile actor was one of Italy's top leading men during the 1950's. He was married at one time to actress Shelly Winters. ***Who is he?**

70) **Handsome**, athletic, blue eyed leading man of Hollywood films, he is recognized by his portrayal of Mafia mobster Henry Hill in Martin Scorsese's *GoodFellas* (1990). (Hint: Other films include *Copland, No Escape,* and *Field of Dreams* - as Shoeless Joe Jackson.) ***Who is he?**

71) **A successful Hollywood actor,** director, and producer, this Italian-American started out at the age of 18 as a hair stylist in his sister's New Jersey beauty salon. Determined to get into acting, he attended the

American Academy of Dramatic Arts. His major break came when he repeated his stage performance in the screen version of *One Flew Over the Cuckoo's Nest* (1975). He gradually evolved into a popular comic screen personality and won an Emmy as Best Supporting Actor for his memorable role as Louie De Palma in the hit TV series, *Taxi*, which ran from 1978 to 1983. His recent movies include: *L.A. Confidential, Mars Attacks,* and *Get Shorty.* (Hint: Married to Rhea Perlman, better known as Carla, of *Cheers.*)　　　　　　　　　　　　　***Who is he?**

72) *In 1964,* Yesterday, Today and Tomorrow won an Oscar for Best Foreign Language Film starring Marcello Mastroianni.
　　　　　　　　　　　　　*Name his costarring leading lady.

73) *Brian De Palma* directed what chilling, horror motion picture classic starring Sissy Spacek? (Hint: Adapted from a Stephen King novel.)

74) *The golden city* of Umbria is Perugia.
　　　　　　　　　　　　　*For what is this city famous?

75) *Michael Cimino* directed what Vietnam era movie starring Robert de Niro? (Hint: Hailed as a masterpiece, it was nominated for nine Academy Awards, and won five Oscars, including Best Picture and Best Director for Cimino. One critic called it the greatest anti-war picture since *The Grand Illusion.*)

76) *Name the Tuscan wine* that has become a legend. (Hint: Named after the region where it is produced.)

77) *Beyond a doubt*, he is an artist in the realm of motion picture improvisation, and was considered one of the world's great directors. (Hint: He won Oscars for *La Strada, Nights of Cabiria, 8 1/2,* and *Amarcord.*)　　　　　　　　　　　　　***Who was he?**

78) *The western look* in fashion became all the more popular after the motion picture *Urban Cowboy* was released.
　　*Name the Italian-American actor who started this fashion craze.

79) *Salvatore Guaragna* wrote, among other hits, *Chattanooga Choo-choo, Lullaby of Broadway,* and *An Affair to Remember.*
　　　　　　　　　　　　　*His professional name is:
　　　　　　a) Blake Harding　b) Harry Warren　c) Sal Garrett

80) *Eaten as a vegetable*, it is used most typically in Roman dishes such as *carciofi alla romana,* where it is stuffed with bread crumbs, parsley, anchovies, salt and pepper.　　　　　　***What is it?**

81) *The Garden of the Fenzi Continis* won the Academy Award for Best Foreign Language Film in 1971.
*Identify the internationally known director.

82) *Gennaro Lombardi* is believed to have opened the first parlor of this type 1905 on Spring street in Manhattan. ***What did he open?**

83) *Anna Magnani*, with her ability to move an audience from tears of anguish to gales of laughter, won the Best Actress award for her virtuoso performance in what Tennessee Williams work?

84) *After Rudolph Valentino's* tragic death, another Italian-American in the early 1930's appeared to be headed toward replacing Valentino as America's heartthrob. However, his career tragically ended when he was accidentally killed in a firearm mishap. ***Who was he?**

85) *One of the most famous* dishes of the Abruzzo region is *maccheroni alla chitarra.* ***How did this dish come by its name?**

86) *One of the first* variety shows on television was *The All Star Revue* on NBC. What Italian-American comedian starred and hosted this show?

87) *Golden Boy* was a 1939 motion picture about a violin playing boxer who had a conflict in regard to what path to follow. William Holden starred as a young Italian-American who fights his way to the championship. (Hint: We think of him as a Frenchman.)
*What was the name of the character he play in the movie?

88) *What are the names* of Francis Ford Coppola's motion picture company, located in San Francisco, and his winery, located in the Napa wine region of California?

89) *His opera* about a prima donna is set in Rome in 1800, and was first performed there in 1900. ***Name the composer and the opera.**

90) *This Italian dramatic tenor* enjoyed worldwide popularity. Because of his tremendous power and brilliance, he was especially known for his lead roles in *Pagliacci, Tosca, La Boheme*, and *Aida.*
*Who was this famous tenor?

91) *Centerbe* is the most powerful of any produced in Italy. It is recognized by its distinctive emerald green color. ***What is it?**

92) *Verdi composed this opera* at the invitation of the Turkish viceroy of Egypt, who asked him to write an opera on an Egyptian subject for the 1869 opening of the Italian Opera House in Cairo as part of the celebration in honor of the dedication of the Suez Canal.

Identify this still popular opera.

93) *Rossini's* delightful opera *La Cenerentola* (1817), is based on a considerably modified version of what story?

94) *Set in a Sicilian village,* this opera by Pietro Mascagni has held its place over the years as one of the most popular works on the operatic stage.

What is the name of this opera?

95) *Created by* Raffaele Esposito Brandi in Naples as a special culinary treat in honor of Queen Margherita of Savoy, wife of Italy's king, Umberto I, this dish still bears the queen's name, and its composition echoes the colors of the Italian flag.

What is it?

96) *What Italian word,* meaning a musical work marked by extreme freedom of style and structure, or spectacular show or event, is now used in English?

97) *Considered one of the greatest* sopranos of her time, she received great acclaim on her tours before she debuted at the Metropolitan Opera Company as Desdemona in 1955.

Who was she?

98) *Born Penny Marscharelli* in Brooklyn, New York in 1942, she is the first female to direct a motion picture that grossed over $100 million. The movie, *Big*, also earned Tom Hanks his first Best Actor Academy Award nomination. Her third movie, *Awakenings,* starring Robert De Niro and Robin Williams, was nominated for Best Picture in 1990. Her 1992 hit, *A League of Their Own*, grossed over $100 million. (Hint: Laverne ring a bell?)

Who is this talented director?

99) *What do we call* the leading female singer in an opera?

100) *When eating* spaghetti, any true Italian prefers it cooked al dente.

What does al dente mean?

101) *Italian-American producer*, Albert Broccoli, was most successful in producing what extremely popular and lucrative motion picture spy series?

102) *This Italian-American politician* was colorful enough to inspire a Broadway musical in 1959.

28

103) This comedienne and singer started in vaudeville and later made her screen debut in *In Caliente* in 1935. Her hillbilly humor and ear-bursting yodel were her trademarks. ***Who was she?**

104) *A former school teacher,* Tony Musante was born in Bridgeport, CT in 1936. After appearing in a number of Hollywood films, he had a successful career in leading roles in Italian movies. In 1973 - 1974 he played the role of a real-life Italian-American policeman in New Jersey in a popular television show that was a precursor of Baretta.
*What was the show?

105)) *What is the* internationally famous and highly regarded Lacrima Christi?

106) *Piero Gherardi* won an Oscar for his costume design in 1961 for an Italian motion picture that translates to *The Sweet Life.*
*What is the Italian title?

107) *During World War II,* he directed a much heralded Army documentary series, *Why We Fight.* The first of the series, *Prelude To War,* won the Best Documentary Oscar in 1942.
*Who was the Italian-American director?

108) *1961 was the first time* in the history of the Academy Awards that an actress appearing in a non-English speaking role was chosen as Best Actress.
*Identify the actress or the motion picture in which she appeared.

109) *Born in 1915,* this Italian-American has been in films since the early 1940's, usually as a mobster or in other unpleasant parts. (Hint: First movie was Johnny Apollo.)
*Who was this actor with a famous tenor's name?

110) *In this region,* they still make huge loaves of bread, some weighing more than twenty pounds, which will last an entire family a week. (Hint: North of Sicily.) ***Identify the region.**

111) *One of the leading* directors of the so-called Golden Age of Italian movie making, Mario Caserini, specialized in what type of subject matter for his films? a) Westerns b) Mysteries c) Historical pageants

112) *Italian-American* motion picture star Al Pacino has been nominated

for four Best Actor awards since 1973.
*Identify two of the four movies for which he received nominations.

113) *Character player* of American stage, TV, and films, Richard Castellano was nominated for an Academy Award for his role in *Lovers and Other Strangers* in 1970, a role he had earlier played on Broadway. ***He is best remembered for his role in what 1972 blockbuster motion picture?**

114) *Three Italians* were nominated for Best Actor Oscars in 1976. They were: Robert DeNiro for *Taxi Driver*, Giancarlo Giannini for *Seven Beauties*, and an actor who, though he did not win Best Actor, won a Best Picture Oscar for a movie he wrote.
*Name the actor and the movie.

115) *The people* of this region are considered the champion pasta eaters of Italy. ***Can you name the region?**
a) Apulia b) Abruzzo c) Campagna

116) *Joe Renzetti* won an Oscar in Music (adapted score) for what 1971 movie about an early rock'in'roll star killed in an air crash?

117) *What is the* Centro Sperimentale di Cinematografia (C.S.C) located in Rome?

118) *Robert DeNiro* won his second Academy Award in 1980 for his portrayal of an Italian-American boxer in *Raging Bull*.
*Who was the boxer he portrayed?

119) *Craggy faced,* suave mannered, and evil-eyed, he typically played criminal masterminds and gang bosses, though he occasionally could be seen in benevolent roles. His career spanned four decades, in both the U.S. and Italy. His last American film was *The Secret of Santa Vittoria*.
*This distinguished character actor is:
a) Eduardo Ciannelli b) Giuseppe Furia c) Lido Cantarutti

120) *According to historians,* the origins of this dish go back to the Neolithic Age. With the arrival of tomatoes in the sixteenth century, and other ingredients in the eighteenth century, the dish became fit for a king. It was offered by the Bourbons at their receptions in the Palace of Casterta, and Ferdinand IV had them cooked in the ovens of the famous porcelain factory at Capodimonte. This dish also has an infinite number of recipes and is very popular in many nations around the world. In northern Italy they call it focaccia and in Tuscany schiacciata. ***What is it?**

121) *A Brash,* diminutive, character actor with a penchant for portraying tough gangsters, he received an Oscar nomination for Best Supporting Actor in *Raging Bull*, and won an Oscar in the same category for his role in Martin Scorsese's *GoodFellas* (1990). Turning to comedy roles, he starred in the box office hits, *Home Alone* and *My Cousin Vinny*.
*Who is this talented Italian-American actor?

122) *The son* of an Italian immigrant fireman, he was undoubtedly one of the best-known Italian Americans in the world. He has been described as an American pop-culture icon, the ultimate definition and epitome of style and technique. He was a true superstar of films, TV, recordings, and nightclubs. In 1971, he received the *Jean Hersholt Humanitarian Award* at that year's Academy Award ceremony. In 1983, he was the recipient of Kennedy Center honors for life achievement, and in 1985 he was awarded the *Medal of Freedom*, America's highest civilian honor, from President Ronald Reagan at the White House.
*Who was this superstar recording artist and Academy Award winning actor known as the "Chairman of the Board of Show Business?"

123) *She won* the Academy Award as best actress in 1996 for her portrayal of Sister Helen Prejean in *Dead Man Walking*. Early in her career, she became a cult favorite after appearing in The *Rocky Horror Picture Show*. Other hits include *Bull Durham* and *Thelma and Louise*.
*Who is she?

124) *This magnificent* motion picture ushered in a new world of film-making -- a world populated by real people, trying to solve real problems -- according to the description given by the Academy of Motion Picture Arts and Sciences when, for the first time in, 1947, it made a special award to a foreign language film. Many believe that *Shoe Shine*, which told the tragic effect of war's aftermath, was one of the finest films ever made. ***Who was its renowned Italian director?**

125) *Wild suckling pig,* skewered and roasted beside an open fire of juniper mastic and olive wood (whose aromatic properties impart a unique flavor to the meat), is a specialty of the shepherds of what Italian region?

126) *Sergio Leone* is credited with inventing a type of American western cowboy movie that was directed and produced in Italy.
*What is the name given to these types of westerns?

127) *He was nominated* for an Oscar for his portrayal of a shell-shocked G.I. in the 1964 movie, *Captain Newman, M.D.* (Hint: His first wife was Sandra Dee.)   ***Who was this 1960 Grammy winner?**

128) *The success* of these brothers in comedy (vaudeville and movies) was based partly upon a crude and, by today's standards, tasteless caricature of the early Italian immigrants in the United States.

*Can you name this comedy team of brothers?

129) *Born James Ercolani* in Philadelphia in 1936, he became a popular teen actor for his roles in *Gidget* and other youth oriented movies. He has done several TV series; including *Time Tunnel* and *T. J. Hooker.*

*Who is he?

130) *The trifolau* of Piedmont hunt for what buried treasure?

131) *Virtually* a small lute, it was intended as a melodic instrument. Its four strings are tuned like a violin and it is played with a plectrum.

*Identify the instrument.

132) *Joseph Barbera and Bill Hanna* created cartoons that won seven Oscars and were known world wide for their ingenious gags, hair trigger timing, and expressive animation.

*What cartoons did Barbera and Hanna create?

a) Tom and Jerry b) Mighty Mouse c) Wily Coyote

133) *This Italian vegetable,* long a favorite among Italian-Americans, is now found on the menus of elegant restaurants and is appreciated by the general population.   ***Name this green squash.**

134) *A piano prodigy* as a child, this well known and popular composer won an Oscar for the score of *The Right Stuff* in 1983. (Hint: He is Sylvester Stallone's favorite composer.)   ***Who is he?**

135) *The pride of* Milanese pastry cooks, it was originally hardly more than a spiced bread. Over the centuries, however, it has been transformed into a light cake, rich with butter and eggs, candied citron and raisins.

*What is it?

136) *With his wife* Keely Smith, he and his band set nightclub records all over the country throughout the 1950's. One of their memorable recording hits was *That Old Black Magic.*   ***Who was this jazz great?**

137) *Born Walter Lanza* in New Rochelle, New York in 1900, he received an honorary Oscar at the 1979 Academy Award ceremony ". . .

in recognition of his unique animated motion pictures and especially his creation of Woody Woodpecker."
*Identify his better known professional name.

138) *The French aside,* identify the two delicious Milanese dishes, *Lumache alla Milanese* and *Rane in Guazzetto.*

139) *A Motion picture tough guy* with the foghorn voice, he started his movie career in 1951. He co-starred with Humphrey Bogart in *We're No Angels* and John Wayne in *The Green Berets.* He starred in over 40 films spanning four decades, including, *Miss Sadie Thompson, God's Little Acre,* and *The Naked and the Dead.*
*Who was this Italian-American actor, born in Crockett, California?

140) *The ambition* and grandeur of the costume epic reached its peak with the Italian motion picture *Cabiria* in 1914. Nothing like it had been produced anywhere before. The picture took two years to complete and its budget exceeded one million dollars. The script was written in part by the famous poet-novelist Gabriele D'Annunzio. The picture was an enormous international box-office success and, in the U.S., it influenced the work of two famous American film makers. ***Name one of them.**

141) *Robert Loggia* was raised in Manhatten's Little Italy and has had a career as a leading man and character player of American stage, TV, and films. His portrayal as a seedy detective in this suspense film earned him a nomination for Best Supporting Actor in 1985.
*Identify this movie.
a) Relentless b) Jagged Edge c) Prizzi's Honor

142) *He was born* Alphonso Giuseppe Giovanni Roberto D'Abruzzo in 1914 in New York, the son of a barber. His Hollywood film debut came in 1945 when he portrayed George Gershwin in Warner Brothers' *Rhapsody in Blue.* He went on to make other pictures, but his major successes came on the Broadway stage in productions such as *Guys and Dolls.* His son is a leading man of screen, stage, and television. He starred in one of the most popular television series' ever, which began in 1972 and ran through 1983. For this series he won Emmys for Best Actor, Best Director, and Best Writer. He was also awarded the prestigious "Actor of the Year" Emmy in 1974. (Hint: *M*A*S*H*)
*Identify this very talented father and son.

143) *In 1962 Gualtiero Jacopetti,* a documentary director, turned out the first, and commercially most successful, of several sensational, feature length documentaries that focused on lurid and cruel aspects of life. ***Identify this classic documentary film.**

144) ***Bernardo Bertolucci***, born in Parma, Italy in 1940, is one of the most accomplished directors of the young generation of Italian cinema. He is best known for his highly controversial 1972 film starring Marlon Brando. (Hint: Arthur Murray would have loved it!) (Note: His film *The Last Emperor*, won nine Academy Awards in 1987, including Best Movie, Best Director, and Best Adapted Screen Play.)
*Give the title of this movie.

145) ***What is the most*** important ingredient of Venetian cooking?

146) ***Born Concetta Ann Ingolia*** in Brooklyn, New York, this vivacious actress starred in many teen-oriented movies during the 1960's. She also made a number of popular recordings and starred in several popular TV series'. ***Name this multi-talented performer.**

147) ***He is*** the first film maker in fifty years to direct his own Oscar winning performance, and only the fourth to receive Oscar nominations for Best Actor, Best Director, and Best Screenwriter for a single film. (Hint: He would certainly say that life is truly beautiful. ***Who is he?**

148) ***This Italian-American*** actor made his motion picture debut in *What Ever Happened to Baby Jane*, for which he received an Oscar nomination. Weighing in at close to 300 pounds, he is often cast as a villain in a variety of Hollywood and Italian productions and television spots. ***Identify him.**

149) ***He reached his peak*** in *The Great Caruso* (1951), in which he portrayed the legendary tenor. ***Who was he?**

150) ***This Italian city*** is celebrated for having invented ravioli at a time when it had not yet been discovered that pasta could be made with soft-grain flour by binding the dough with eggs (a problem not posed by hard-grain flour). ***Identify the city.**

151) ***Sophia Loren*** starred with Gary Grant and Frank Sinatra in this epic 1956 adventure motion picture. ***What is the title?**

152) ***This beautiful Italian*** actress with a sensual voice debuted in Hollywood in the 1964 movie, *The Pink Panther*. She has attained international stardom and has appeared in Italiàn, French, British, and American films. ***Who is she?**

153) *In 1946,* her enormous dramatic talent was displayed in Roberto Rossellini's monumental, neo-realistic masterpiece, *Open City.* De Sica called her Italy's finest actress and one of the most interesting actresses in the world. In 1955, she won an Oscar for her magnificent performance in *The Rose Tattoo.* (Hint: Other films include *Wild Is the Wind* (Oscar nominated) and *The Secret of Santa Vittoria.*)
*Identify this Italian actress.

154) *Nearly broke* and with his wife pregnant, this Italian-American was determined to create his own opportunity to become a star by writing his own screenplay. In three days he completed the first draft and went on to sell it to two Hollywood producers with the stipulation that he be assigned the starring role in the film. He has been a leading screen personality not only in the United States, but around the world.
*Name this outstanding Italian-American who never gave up.

155) *A child prodigy,* this composer wrote four symphonies, eight operas, several concertos, ballet scores, and many other orchestral works, in addition to numerous scores for the Italian stage and screen. He won an Oscar for the music in *The Godfather, Part II* (1974), but his most notable film work was with Federico Fellini, an association that lasted a quarter of a century. ***Who was this composer?**

156) *Michael Cimino* wrote and directed for Clint Eastwood before embarking on his own first important production in 1978. This work garnered him the New York Film Critics Award for Best Picture and Best Director and nine Academy Award nominations. ***Identify his movie.**

157) *He was among* the wealthiest men in show business and had a reputation for kindness and generosity which had expressed itself in magnanimous acts of philanthropy for individuals and organizations.
*Who was this great Italian-American?

158) *Popularly dubbed* "Hollywood on the Tiber," what is Cinecitta?

159) *Raised in Dallas,* Texas, she began her career in the early 1960's and has appeared in many stage productions, numerous television programs, and motion pictures. In 1975, she was nominated for an Oscar as Best Supporting Actress for her role in the movie, *Once Is Not Enough* by Jacquelline Susann. (Hint: Other movie roles include: *Midnight Cowboy, Airport '77,* and *Supergirl.*) ***Who is she?**

160) *Siena* is the home of a delicious Christmas cake made of flour, almonds, hazelnuts, cocoa, spices and fruit. ***Identify this delicious cake.**

161) *His marriage* to actress Jean Acker was never consummated after she locked him out of a hotel bridal suite on their wedding night.
*Identify this unfortunate bridegroom.

162) *This Italian actor* starred in Italian cinema in the late 1940's and 50's. He is also known for his television work and various roles in Hollywood films. Many will recognize him from his last role in the popular National Lampoon's *Animal House* in 1978. (Hint: Other movies include *Viva Las Vegas,* with Evis Presley, and *Cleopatra* with Burton and Taylor.) ***Who was he?**

163) *Lovable and chubby,* this comic character player has appeared on stage, TV, and movies. He first gained popularity on TV as *Dominick the Great,* a bumbling magician. (Hint: Has appeared in a number of Mel Brooks movies.) ***Who is he?**

164) *Newsweek* magazine wrote in 1964, "A literary triumph . . . In all the centuries that writers have sought to explain the Italian people, none up to now really had succeeded." And the Chicago Tribune reported, "Altogether wonderfully readable. Luigi Barzini paints a full-length portrait of his countrymen that is at once grave and witty, cynical and compassionate, somber and glittering, scholarly and stimulating."
*Identify the title of this international best seller.
a) An Italian's Perspective b) The Italians c) My People

165) *Three classics* of the cuisine found in this region include *saltimbocca, fettuccine,* and *sweet peppers in oil.* ***Identify the region.**

166) *He first attracted attention* in 1973 when he portrayed a dying baseball player in *Bang the Drum Slowly.* ***Identify this actor.**

167) *Farinelli* (Carlo Broschi) was the most famous and celebrated singer of the 18th century. ***Identify his type of voice.**
a) Castrato Soprano b) Tenor c) Baritone

168) *The son* of an orthopedic surgeon, this Italian American film director is known for his bold, often dazzling, visual flair. During the 1970's he was dubbed the "poor man's Hitchcock". (Hint: More recent films include *Raising Cain, Carlito's Way,* and *Mission Impossible* (1996) and, of course, *Carrie,* in 1976.) ***Who is he?**

169) *Born in Scotland* in 1941, he won a Tony for his portrayal of a sculptor paralyzed from the neck down in *Whose Life Is It Anyway?*, and was nominated in 1983 for an Academy Award for his performance in *Reuben, Reuben.*

*Name this leading man of British and American stage, TV, and films.

170) ***What is*** the legendary Abruzzese *panarda*?

171) ***Lorenzo Da Ponte*** composed the libretto for Mozart's opera about the adventures of the Spanish libertine, Don Juan.

*Identify the opera.

a) Don Giovanni b) Don Pasquale c) Don Leone

172) ***This noted Italian*** cinematographer, Pasqalino De Santis, won an Oscar for what 1969 Franco Zeffirelli film?

a) Endless Love b) The Champ c) Romeo and Juliet

173) ***What is the term*** used to describe the text of an opera or other dramatic musical work as distinct from the musical score?

174) ***Born Mary Grace Messina***, this versatile operatic and jazz singer played Mamma Corleone in *The Godfather* and its sequel.

*Who is she?

175) ***Masterpieces of opera buffa*** (comic opera) during the nineteenth century are Rossini's *The Barber of Seville* and Verdi's *Falstaff*; the third is *Don Pasquale*, composed by what renowned nineteenth century Italian composer? (Hint: His other works include: *Anna Bolena, Lucrezia Borgia* and, what many believe to be his best opera, *Lucia di Lammermoor.*)

176) ***Musical experts*** and opera fans from around the world considered this tenor equal to the great Enrico Caruso. Upon Caruso's death at the age of 47, this tenor was pronounced his successor, and subsequently expressed the following sentiments in a letter to the New York Times: "I believe to speak of a successor to Caruso is a sacrilege and a profanity to his memory; it means violating a tomb which is sacred to Italy and the entire world. The efforts of every artist today aim to gather and to conserve the artistic heritage received from the great singer, and everyone must strive to do this, not with vain self-advertisement, but with tenacious study for the triumph of the pure and beautiful. He struggled for this, and we for the glory of his art must follow his example with dignity."

*What great tenor was responsible for this statement?

177) ***What internationally acclaimed*** Italian motion picture director

37

and actor made his screen debut in 1932 in *What Rascals Men Are*, and directed his first motion picture, *Red Roses*, in 1939?

178) *Mario Gallo* is known as the father of cinema for what South American country?   a) Argentina b) Brazil c) Venezuela

179) *Teen idol* Ralph Macchio, born in 1961 in Huntington, New York, has starred in three popular movies involving the martial arts.
*Identify the movies.

180) *Fill in the blank.* Capocollo, a type of _____, is made of meat from the pig's neck and shoulder, packed into a bladder and then smoked.

181) *Marion Copretti* was the character played by Sylvester Stallone in what action packed movie?   a) Paradise Alley b) Cobra c) Victory

182) *As a composer alone*, his twenty-four musical caprices (an instrumental piece in free form usually lively in tempo and brilliant in style) inspired and influenced such great composers as Liszt, Schumann, Brahms, and Rachmaninoff. However, the world remembers this Italian, born in Genoa in 1782, as perhaps the greatest violin virtuoso ever to have lived. Who was this legendary figure who established the definitive standard for violin-playing excellence?

183) *Born in the city* of Pesaro on the Adriatic coast in 1792, this Italian composer is regarded as the most important composer of Italian opera during the first half of the 19th century. He made major contributions towards the development of a new form of opera called *opera buffa* which was a developing form of comic opera about everyday life, common people, and romantic liaisons. His masterpiece, *The Barber of Seville,* was written in 1816. For twenty brillant years he composed works that entertained his fans, influenced his contemporaries, and inspired generations of future composers. (Hint: Other works include, *Otello, Cinderella*, and *William Tell,* whose overture eventually became the best-known operatic music of all time in America when it was used as the theme music for the popular radio and TV series, *The Lone Ranger.*)
*Who was he?

184) *Alberto Grimaldi*, made a quick fortune in the late 1960's when he produced several very popular spaghetti westerns before turning to serious production with films by such directors as Fellini, Pasolini, and Bertolucci. ***What American actor starred in Grimaldi's westerns?**

185) *Because of their body* and high alcohol content, the wines of this rich wine growing region are widely used for blending and improving many other Italian wines. ***What is the region?**
a) Lazio b) Liguria c) Apulia

186) *The first Italian* newsreel footage was shot in Turin in 1904 by:
a) Roberto Omegna b) Leroy Chedda c) Mario Ghilotti

187) *Born in 1942* in Utica New York, she was a cheerleader of the Mouseketeers on Disney's *Mickey Mouse Club'* TV show. She is best remembered wearing a bathing suit in a string of popular beach-party movies co-starring fellow Italian-American, Frankie Avalon.
*Who is she?

188) *Filoteo Alberini and Dante Santoni* built Italy's first movie studio in Rome in 1905 and turned out the country's first ambitious story film, which would become a traditional genre of the Italian cinema: the historical spectacle. ***What is the title of this historic film?**
a) Il Sacco di Roma b) La Presa di Roma
c) La Bella di Roma

189) *What Italian word,* now used in English, means the highest singing voice of women, boys, or castrati; the highest part in 4-part harmony?

190) *Rice,* which plays such an important role in much of Italy's regional cooking, is practically unknown here, although it was introduced into Italy by the Arabs through this area. ***Identify this Italian region.**

191) *Considered to be Italy's* most outstanding literary figure of the post-World War II era and one of the most important Italian writers of the twentieth century, he possessed a unique narrative style and brillant mind that critics feel redefined the writing of fiction. ***Who was he?**
a) Giorgio Silvestri b) Bartolomeo Ingargiola
c) Italo Calvino

192) *What was unique* about Gennaro Rigbelli's 1930 motion picture, *La Canzone dell'Amore*?

193) *Regarded as one* of the founders of modern Italian opera, Amilcare Ponchielli was a gifted musician and the teacher of Puccini. In Italy, he became almost as famous as Verdi. His masterpiece, which takes place in Venice, was the only one of his operas to bring him universal renown. *What was his opera?

194) *Whose was the singing voice* of actor Edmund Purdum in the movie, *The Student Prince?*

195) *The magnificent lobsters* of this region find their way to many of the great restaurants of Europe. *Name the region.
a) Liguria b) Sicily c) Sardinia

196) *This gifted and brilliant composer*, designated as the heir to Giuseppe Verdi, was born in the city of Lucca in 1858. His opera, *Manon Lescaut*, which premiered in Turin in 1893, transformed him into a worldwide success literally overnight. (Hint: Following *Manon Lescaut*, he produced three of his most popular operas: *La Boheme, Tosca*, and *Madama Butterfly.*) *Who was he?

197) *What is the Italian word,* now common in English, that means an elaborate embellishment in vocal music; music with ornate figuration?

198) *Grammy award winner* Chuck Mangione is famous for playing what instrument? a) Guitar b) Saxophone c) Trumpet

199) *This Italian composer* is the dominant figure in the history of early baroque music. His works are noted for their dramatic expressivity, adventurous harmonies, and careful orchestration. The four violin concertos, known collectively as *The Four Seasons*, may be the most recognizable music in the world. This prolific composer wrote at least 825 authenticated musical works, including 78 sonatas, 21 sinfonias, 457 concertos and other works, 48 stage works and opera, 100 separate arias, 59 secular cantatas, 2 oratorios, and 60 sacred vocal works. Experts believe there is still more to be found in private collections, archives, and libraries. (Hint: His music was essentially forgotten until it was rediscovered in the mid 19th century.)
*Identify this Italian who was born in Venice in 1678.

200) *One of the most famous* Piedmontese dishes is made with fontina cheese and white truffles. *What is it?

201) *The movie*, *Yes, Giorgio*, starred what opera superstar?

202) *What is an Italian word,* now used in English, that means a musical composition or movement in a moderately slow tempo; used as a direction in music?

203) *Two operas* called Otello were written by two great Italian

40

composers. Rossini wrote the first in 1815.
*Who wrote the second in 1887?

204) *At nineteen years of age,* this cellist with a traveling Italian opera company performing in Rio de Janeiro, Brazil stepped in after the orchastra's conductor abruptly resigned to conduct that evening's performance of Verdi's *Aida*, without using a score. At 31, he became the chief conductor of La Scala Opera House in Milan and conducted the first performances of a number of famous operas, including Leoncavallo's *Pagliacci* and Puccini's, *La Boheme.* (Hint: Born in Parma, Italy in 1867, he died in Riverdale, New York on January 16, 1957. For seventeen years he was the conductor of the NBC Symphony Orchestra.)
*Name this legendary figure, whose name has become synonymous with musical conducting.

205) *Name the classical Italian soup* containing a variety of vegetables in a broth base.

206) *Giuseppe Verdi* wrote his last opera at the age of eighty. Based on Shakespeare's *Merry Wives of Windsor* and *King Henry IV*, it is considered a great comic masterpiece. ***Name the opera.**

207) *What is the Italian* (and now English) word that means a singer with a bass voice?

208) *She was born Sofia Scicolone* and her mother instilled starring aspirations in the skinny little girl who was nicknamed, *Stechetto,* (the stick). Her first Hollywood part was as an extra in *Quo Vadis* in 1949 at the age of sixteen. Since then, she has appeared in over 70 films. She won an Academy Award in 1961 for her role in De Sica's *Two Women* (based on Alberto Moravio's novel). Regarded as the most beloved and popular Italian film star of the 20th century, she is the prototype of the sexy, sulty, voluptuous Italian woman.
*Who is this international icon of beauty and sophistication?

209) *Identify the Italian word,* now used in English, that means a choral work usually on a scriptural subject consisting chiefly of recitatives, arias, and choruses without action or scenery.

210) *A great dish* that has given Milanese cooking its world wide reputation, is stewed shin of veal.
*What is its better known Italian name?

211) *She received* a Tony for her 1961 performance in the Broadway production of *Carnival*. She began singing at age six and debuted at Carnegie Hall in 1950 at age thirteen. ***Who is she?**

a) Anna Maria Alberghetti b) Pier Angeli
c) Laura Antonelli

212) *Born in New York* in 1942, he is one of America's most respected film directors. Under his direction, actors seem to do some of their best work, evidenced by the awards they garner. His most memorable motion pictures include: *Alice Doesn't Live Here Anymore* (1975), for which Ellen Burstyn won an Oscar for Best Actress; *Taxi Driver* (1976), with Robert De Niro and Jodi Foster; *Raging Bull* (1980), with Robert De Niro, who won a Best Actor Oscar for his portrayal of boxer Jake LaMotta; and *The Color of Money* (1986), giving Paul Newman an Academy Award for Best Actor. *GoodFellas* (1990), one of this director's most powerful achievements, gave Joe Pesci an Oscar for Best Supporting Actor, and Sharon Stone received an Oscar nomination for Best Actress in his 1995 movie, *Casino*. ***Who is this well-known director?**

213) *One of his most memorable* roles was as Alexander Graham Bell in the motion picture, *The Story of Alexander Graham Bell,* in 1939. In 1985, he won an Academy Award for Best Supporting Actor for his role in *Coccoon*. (Hint: His brother was a star in the NFL.)
*Who was this Italian-American actor?

214) *In 1949,* she gained world wide popularity as the voluptuous star of the Giuseppe De Santis drama, *Bitter Rice*. She married producer Dino De Laurentiis that same year and went on to star in many other Italian films. She is most known to American audiences for her dual role in the movie *Ulysses* with Kirk Douglas in 1955, where she played both Penelope and Circe.(Hint: Her last U.S. role was in Dune in 1984.)
*Who was she?

215) *It is a staple* food of a large area of Northern Italy, but nowhere is it more popular than in the region of Veneto. (Hint: Brought back from the New World.) ***What is it?**

216) *The composer of the opera,* Turandot, died before completing its last act. At the request of Arturo Toscanini, Italian composer Franco Alfano completed the opera. ***Who was the original composer?**

217) *A trumpet prodigy* at the age of nine, he turned to singing as a

teen. At seventeen, his hit single *Venus*, a million seller twice-over, was number one on the top forty charts for five weeks. In the early sixties, he teamed up with Annette Funicello to appear in a series of California beach movies. (Hint: In 1987 he was reunited with Annette Funicello in *Back to the Beach,* a nostalgic tribute to the "beach party" series of movies that highlighted their careers in the 1960's.)   ***Who is he?**

218) *What is the Italian word* that means a musical composition for an individual voice or instrument, with or without accompaniment; or any performance accomplished by a singing individual?

219) *She won* the Golden Globe award in 1968 for her performance as Mrs. Robinson in *The Graduate.*   ***Who is she?**

220) *In Venice* it is called bisi, and is one of the main ingredients of a classical dish that now belongs to international cookery, *risi e bisi.*
   *What is it?

221) *This singer* is regarded as one of the all-time top nightclub performers in the country. Born Anthony Benedetto he was discovered by Bob Hope in 1949.   ***Who is he?**

222) *She was nominated* for an Academy Award and won the New York Film Critics Award for her performance in the movie *The Godfather, Part II* (1974). Another memorable performance was given in *Rocky* (1976) as the plain and very shy girlfriend of the movie's hero. (Hint: Younger sister of one of the leading directors in American cinema.)
   *Who is she?

223) *This singing* and comedy team was extremely popular in the 1960's and 70's. Their popular TV variety series, which began in 1971, added a new dimension to their success as recording and concert artists. In later years, the male counterpart of this husband and wife team entered politics and was elected to Congress from California. He was tragically killed in a skiing accident in 1998. ***Name both members of the team.**

224) *This tenor* was an international phenomenon, earning record amounts for singing appearances. On April 11, 1902, he recorded ten arias in Milan which would make him very wealthy and preserve his singing for future generations to enjoy.   ***Who was he?**

225) *This version of pizza* is made with black olives, garlic, and large quantities of anchovies, which distinguish it from the more familiar Neapolitan version.   ***Where is this type of pizza produced?**

43

226) *Born* Rodolfo Alfonzo Raffaele Pierre Philibert Guglielmi, he starred in such films as, *The Conquering Power, Blood and Sand, A Sainted Devil,* and *Cobra.* ***Who was this actor?**

227) *He played* the sadistic sergeant, Fatso Judson in, *From Here to Eternity.* ***Who is he?**

228) *In 1974,* he played one of the leads in the movie, *The Lords of Flatbush.* The following year he had supporting roles in such films as *Farewell My Lovely, Capone,* and *Death Race 2000.*
*Who is this Italian-American superstar?

229) *The first production* of this opera by Giacomo Puccini was a complete failure. Revised and presented again four months later, the opera was a brilliant success. The heroine of this opera is Cio-cio-san.
*What is the name this popular opera?

230) *Tagliatelle,* tortellini, and pappardelle are Emilian specialties.
*What are they?

231) *After seven Academy Award* nominations without an Oscar, this intense and complex actor finally was rewarded with an Oscar after an eighth nomination in 1992 for his performance in the movie, *Scent of a Woman.* Despite his tremendous success and popularity in motion pictures, he remains committed to his first love, the stage. Here he has garnered two Tonys and an Obie.
*Who is this Italian-American actor, born in the Bronx (1940) of Sicilian parents?

232) *This versatile actress* was born in Columbus, Ohio in 1953. After studying art in Italy, she worked as a cartoonist for the Hanna-Barbera studios. She soon switched careers and began touring as a coffeehouse singer and later as a vocalist with a rock band named *Elephant.* She appeared on Broadway in the rock musical, *Rockabye Hamlet.* She made her motion picture debut in 1977 and proved a capable actress in both dramatic (as Patsy Cline in *Coal Miner's Daughter*) and comic (National Lampoon's *Vacation*) roles. ***Who is she?**

233) *What Italian city* is the birth place of Enrico Caruso?

234) *Bartolomeo Pagano* was the screen's first strongman when he starred in Giuseppe Pastrone's landmark epic motion picture *Cabiria* and numerous other silent action movies. He enjoyed worldwide popularity several years before the advent of Hollywood's *Tarzan.*

*What year did this former Genoese longshoreman appear in *Cabiria*? a) 1909 b) 1914 c) 1920

235) *The art of cooking* the celebrated *Bistecca alla Fiorentina* is handed down from generation to generation in Italy. ***What is it?**

236) *What is the Italian word* that means an artificially produced singing voice that overlaps and extends above the range of a full voice, especially of a tenor?

237) *Who was* affectionately known in show business as The Schnozzola?

238) *What is the Italian word* that describes the last section of an instrumental musical composition, or the closing part, scene or number in a public performance?

239) *He was a regular* on the *Jackie Gleason Show*, doing his characterization of *Crazy Guggenheim*.
*Who was this talented comedian and singer?

240) *The finest fish soup* of Marche (a region on the Adriatic above Rome) is called *brodetto* and is comparable with the best fish soups of Italy and what well known soup of southern France?

241) *His voice* was heard publicly for the first time at the Christmas service of St. Mary Magdalene de Pazzi, one of the oldest Catholic churches in Philadelphia. The congregation listened in awed disbelief to a 19 year-old tenor's rendition of Gounod's, *Ave Maria*.
*Who was this young gifted tenor with the glorious and powerful voice?

242) *What is the Italian word,* now commonly used in English, that means the text of a work (as an opera) for the musical theater?

243) *John H. Secondari* was responsible for much of the finest historical biographies and documentaries yet seen in television. His notable productions for this television network, before forming his own company were: *The Vatican: The Saga of Western Man; I, Leonardo da Vinci; Beethoven; The Pilgrim Adventure*; and *The Birth of Christ*. A novelist, he also wrote *Three Coins In The Fountain*, which was made into a motion picture.
*What television network had he been associated?
a) ABC b) NBC c) Public Television

244) *Few substances* have had so many powers attributed to it as this

bulb, and the Italians have mastered its culinary uses. (Hint: The stinking rose, allium sativum.) *What is it?

245) *In Rome*, you will find Falerno and the equally famous *Est! Est!! Est!!!* from Montefiascone and Bolsena. *What is it?

246) *He was born* in Cremona in 1567, less than a hundred years before Antonio Stradivari. His large-scale dramatic works became the models for future operas and he is universally credited to be the father of modern opera. *Identify opera's first true musical genius.
a) Claudio Monteverdi b) Martin Bramante
c) Roberto Valentino

247) *How many* music lovers are aware that this Italian is credited with the introduction of a completely new vocal singing style? His innovative compositions were an enormous step forward in the development of opera, oratorio, and cantata, as well as allowing the consummate realization of the musical style known as baroque. He changed the way songs were written and sung, and ushered in an era replete with marvelous musical forms still being performed today.

*Identify this innovative musical genius.
a) Leone Ceccotti b) Giulio Caccini
c) Tomaso Cinquini

248) *It was a big year* for Italian-Americans at the Academy of Motion Picture Arts and Sciences. *The Godfather* was selected Best Picture. Liza Minnelli won Best Actress for her performance in *Cabaret*. Mario Puzo with Francis Ford Coppola won an Oscar for *The Godfather* screenplay.

*Identify the year this occurred.
a) 1970 b) 1972 c) 1974

249) *Who played* Rick on the popular *Magnum P.I.* television series?

250) *What is* the Mostaccioli of Calabria?

251) *Considered the most famous* interpreter of Mozart in his vocal range, he has been a star at the Metropolitan Opera Company since his debut as King Philip in *Don Carlos* in 1949. *This opera star is:
a) Cesare Siepi b) Roberto Saccuzzo
c) Eugenio Boscacci

252) *After winning two Obies* on the New York stage, he came to

prominence with his role as Fredo Corleone in *The Godfather* in 1972. He died of cancer after appearing in five of the most acclaimed motion pictures of the 1970's: *The Godfather* (1972), *The Conversation, The Godfather, Part II* (1974), *Dog Day Afternoon* (1975), and *The Deer Hunter* (1978).   ***Who was he?**

253) *This Italian-American* was elected president of the Motion Picture Association of America in 1966. He left his position as President Johnson's special adviser to take this position. During his long-term office, which was extended into the 1990's, he has been responsible for instituting the current film rating system which protects and informs the public on the content of films.
*Name this Italian-American and former WW II fighterpilot who hails from the state of Texas.

254) *In 1977*, the Best Foreign Language Film award went to *Madame Rosa*, an Italian film starring what well known French actress?

255) *Torta di Frutta Secca* is better known in the United States as what?

256) *One of the last* operas written by Gaetano Donizetti has the double advantage of a sparkling score and a witty, interesting libretto. It has outlived many of its contemporaries because of its wealth of charming, vivacious melody and its rich vein of comedy.   ***Identify this opera.**

257) *A Bold and controversial* superstar, this singer and actress was born in Bay City Michigan in 1958. Immediately recognized by her single first name, the rest of her name is Louise Veronica Ciccone. Described as a true feminist, she has changed and influenced popular culture with her recordings, concerts, videos, and fashion statements. This influence can be felt in many aspects of contemporary life in music, dance, and video. (Hint: Movie roles include *Dick Tracy, A League of Their Own*, and *Evita*. Her hit albums include, *Like A Virgin, Vogue*, and *Truth or Dare*.)   ***Who is she?**

258) *The title* of this play was the name given to the mimes and comedians who were the trademark of the strolling players of sixteenth century Italy. The composer of this opera was Ruggiero Leoncavallo.
                                              *Identify this famous opera.

259) *This Italian-American* comedian, world famous for his popular movies of the 1940's and 50's, is instantly recognized when his *Whose*

on First routine is mentioned.
*Who was this popular radio, stage, motion picture, and television comedian?

260) *His movies include* Paradise Alley, The Mambo Kings, 1492, Hoffa, Fatal Instinct, and Striptease.
*Who is this handsome leading man and supporting player of the New York stage, Hollywood films, and television?

261) *After being given the lead role in* The Four Horsemen of the Apocalypse in 1921, he was catapulted into instant stardom and became a national phenomenon of unprecedented sensual appeal to women. His funeral was attended by more than 100,000 in New York City in 1926.
*Who was this early motion picture super star?

262) *The story* of this opera takes place at a time when Rome was torn by fierce political strife between the Bonapartists and the monarchists. In this drama, Puccini is brilliant in infusing his natural lyricism with dramatic expression.
*Name this opera of intrigue, violence and passion.

263) *This highly regarded* writer and film director brought Shakepeare and grand opera to the masses of the twentieth century through the medium of film. Since the 1950's, he has directed numerous plays and operas, and has the reputation of producing lavish and opulent productions. His 1968 film version of *Romeo and Juliet* received an Oscar nomination and was a huge financial success. His 1977 TV drama *Jesus of Nazareth* has been aired for years during the Easter season.
*Identify this director who apprenticed under the direction of the great Luchino Visconti.

264) *What is the Italian word* for a female ballet dancer?

265) *Marsala is a wine* of international reputation.
*From what region of Italy does it come?

266) *This successful* Italian film producer married actress Sophia Loren in Mexico in 1957. His notable film productions include *La Strada* (1954), *Two Women* (1960), *Boccaccio '70* (1962), and *Yesterday, Today, and Tomorrow* (1963). ***Who is he?**

267) *Identify* the former Ivy League star and professional football player who played Officer Joe Coffe on the popular television series, *Hill Street Blues*.

268) *The first film to win* an Oscar for Best Foreign Language Film was a 1956 Federico Fellini classic starring Anthony Quinn and Giulietta Masina. ***Identify the film.**

269) *Corzetti stampati,* named after the old Genoese money pieces, are stamped on both sides like a coin. Traditionally, the stamps were highly personal, using a family coat of arms on one side, and perhaps a ship or some other image of Genoa's maritime glory on the other.
*Identify the substance being stamped.

270) *It is in this region,* with records dating as far back as 1250, that references to maccaruni are made. Maccaruni is the name given to the original pasta. ***Identify the region.**
a) Emilia-Romagna b) Umbria c) Sicily

271) *Arturo Barone,* the author of the excellent reference book *Italians First*, notes that, in his opinion, Italians probably are the only people in the world who take their food seriously. Not only have they created a culture of food, but they are exceptionally concerned and vigilant about its purity and integrity. This has been perfectly illustrated in the fact that, in February of 1998, the Italian government decided that it was time to stop the abuse by the rest of the world of the concept of this particular and extremely popular Italian dish. The government proceeded to codify into law the essential requirements (ingredients and cooking technique) to create this authentic recipe. The Italian government has officially re-stated that the fundamental ingredients of this dish are: tomatoes, mozzarella cheese and olive oil. It has been made quite clear that the tomatoes must be plum tomatoes in 8mm dice. The mozzarella cheese must be made from buffalo milk, and the olive oil must be extra virgin. If salt is to be used, it must be sea salt. Furthermore, the pastry must be tossed by hand and the end result must be cooked in a wood oven at between 420° F and 480° F. The crust must be thin and the pastry not overcooked. ***Identify this Italian dish which has been reproduced in many variations throughout the world.**

272) *What is the popular* Neapolitan song composed by the Abruzzese, Francesco Paolo Tosti, that has become a favorite of Luciano Pavarotti and Andrea Bocelli? a) Marechiare b) Torna a Sorrento
c) O Sole Mio

273) *Celebrate the Century* stamp series is a program sponsored by the US Postal Service to select subject matter for postage stamps. Over

800,000 Americans participated in the process to choose subjects to be depicted on US stamps illustrating the most important events, persons, or trends, in each decade.

*What Italian-American sports figure was chosen for the 1950's?

274) *Italian-American* Patricia Fili-Krushel, the new president of this network, is the first woman ever to direct a major US television network.
*Identify the network.
a) ABC b) NBC c) CBS

275) *Boiled candies* (sweets) were invented in Turin, and a certain beverage from a roasted, powdered seed was introduced into Italy by King Emanuele Filiberto. ***What had the king introduced?**

276) *What was* the first television show to portray an Italian-American woman as a crime fighter? (Hint: This series was a spinoff series from a TV show in which her husband was a master detective.)

277) *Louis Bellson,* born Louis Balassoni, is considered, along with Gene Krupa, Art Blakey, and Max Roach, to be one of the greatest big-band and jazz performers in music history. He recorded or appeared on more than two hundred albums, and played with Ella Fitzgerald, Stan Getz, Dizzy Gillespie, and Louis Armstrong, to name a few.
*Identify the musical instument he played.
a) Piano b) Drums c) Bass

278) *Until recently,* every Venetian home had a bigolo permanently attached to the kitchen table. ***What is a bigolo?**

279) Who played the likable Al in the TV series, *Happy Days*?

280) *What is the name* of the cake that can be found on the table of almost every Italian family around the world at Christmas?

281) *Based on a true story* of an Italian-American police officer, Al Pacino played a narcotics officer in a story that revealed police corruption in New York City.
*What was the name of the powerful 1973 movie that earned Al Pacino an Oscar nomination?

282) *Of these* four TV heros from the 70's, *Toma, Delvecchio, Petrocelli* and *Baretta,* who was the Harvard educated lawyer?

283) *On the* hit TV series, *Hill Street Blues*, name the character played by Italian-American actor, Daniel Travanti.

284) *Many credit* Dominic "Nick" La Rocca with the invention of this form of jazz. His band was the first to bill itself with that name, first to cut a record in that musical style, first to sell over one million records using that style of jazz, and first to play in Chicago, New York, and Europe with that form of jazz. (Hint: La Rocca composed the classic song *Tiger Rag*, now known as *Hold That Tiger*)
*Identify the form of jazz or the name of the band he founded with fellow Italian Anthony Sbarbaro in New Orleans in 1913.

285) *Lombardy* is known for cheeses and is the home of one of the finest cheeses in the world. A blue cheese usually made from cow's milk that begins with the letter G.   ***What is it?**

286) *William Ferrari* won an Oscar for Art Direction (black & white) for a movie in which Ingrid Bergman won the Oscar as Best Actress. The year was 1944.   ***Identify this chilling mystery motion picture.**
              a) Gaslight b) Notorious c) Spellbound

287) *Who sang the* hit song, *That's Amore?*

288) *Lamar Trotti* won an Oscar for his original screenplay of the 20th Century Fox release, *Wilson,* which received six Oscars in all. His other notable credits include *Young Mr. Lincoln* (1939), and *The Ox-Bow Incidents* (1943). ***What year did he receive his Academy Award Oscar?**   a) 1939 b) 1944 a) 1951

289) *The song*, *When You Wish Upon A Star*, was introduced in what film? (Hint: About an Italian little boy made of wood.)

290) *It blends well* with meat, game, and fish. It can be eaten with or without sauce, roasted, toasted, fried, or boiled and served straight from a copper pan.   ***What is it?**

291) *What Italian-American* singer appeared with the *Hoboken Four?*

292) *Behind a naive facade,* there lived the deductive brilliance of a master sleuth. In his scuffed shoes and battered raincoat, he was the Sherlock Holmes of the working class.
              *Who was this popular TV detective?

293) *Popular comedian*, Jay Leno, is the host of what late night TV show?

294) *As an opera composer*, Vincenzo Bellini's works were characterized by elegance and lyrical charm. His principal opera and

51

masterpiece was *Norma*. He was a close friend of one of the most outstanding pianists and composers of the Romantic era, and it is said that Bellini's music had some influence on this composer.

*Identify this half-French, half-Polish composer.

295) *Curly endive,* a form of chicory, is one of the most popular salad plants in northern Italy.

*Name the Italian salad that is becoming popular in the U.S.

296) *Who starred* in the television series', *Happy Days* and *Charles in Charge*?

297) *What accomplished* pianist always wanted you to meet his brother, George, on his popular television shows of the 1950's and 60's?

298) *As an actor*, Joey D'Auria has the credentials to play *Hamlet* or *King Lear*. However, he chose and was accepted to fill the shoes of Bob Bell, who, after twenty-three years, retired from his legendary clown role on WGN-TV in Chicago.

*What character is Mr. D'Auria clowning around with?

299) *What is* the name of Judy Garland's eldest daughter?

300) *One of the finest* of all Emilian delicacies is *Culatelli*. It is similar to ham, but is more spicy and has a penetrating, aggressive aroma. It is very recognizable because its shape resembles what fruit?

a) Pear b) Banana c) Melon

301) *The son of Sicilian immigrants,* Ben Gazzara was born in New York City in 1930. He has had a successful career on Broadway, motion pictures, and television. Memorable roles include *Anatomy of a Murder* in film and the television series, *Run For Yor Life*. (Hint: Facial scars were in.)

*What gangster did he portray in the 1975 movie of the same title?

302) *This actor director* was born in Katonah, New York in 1960. He is described as a dependable and versatile actor with an often imposing screen presence. For years he had been active in films and television without much notoriety until the 1990's when more substantial roles came his way. He astounded critics with his writing and directing debut in the movie *Big Night* in 1996. His other movies have included, *Prizzi's Honor, Billy Bathgate, Beethoven, The Pelican Brief,* and *It Could Happen To You*. ***Who is this multi-talented Italian-American?**

303) *What is* the name of the hand gun carried by James Bond?

304) *This Italian-American production company* has dominated Saturday morning children's entertainment for thirty years, with 250 series', specials, and films.
*Name the leading production company so familiar to baby boomers.

305) *This Tuscan city* is famous the world over for its olive oil trade and its imposing walls that surround the city.   ***Identify this city.**

306) *Charlton Heston* played what Renaissance genius in the motion picture, *The Agony and the Ecstasy*? (Hint: He did not paint lying on his back as depicted in the movie.)

307) *Comedian Pasquale Caputo* is better known by what name?

308) *This Italian actor* starred in many of film director Lina Wertmuller's movies over the years. In 1973 he won Best Actor award at the Cannes film festival for *Love and Anarchy*. In 1976, he received much critical praise and an Oscar nomination for his performance in *Seven Beauties*.
*Identify this accomplished Italian motion picture star.

309) *Born in Los Angeles* in 1974, this handsome young actor got his start in television sitcoms and then made the jump to major motion pictures, where he consistently takes on challenging roles with great self-confidence. He reached stardom at an early age, he has impressed audiences and critics alike with his versatility, specifically with his Academy Award-nominated role as the mentally challenged young boy in *What's Eating Gilbert Grape*? However, he has attained super stardom with his role in the mega block buster, *Titanic*. (Hint: Other roles include *The Quick and the Dead*, with Sharon Stone, and *Romeo and Juliet*.)
*Who is he?

311) *Born in 1923* in Fontana Liri, Italy, this handsome, suave, and debonair leading man enjoyed, since the mid 1950's, a universal popularity as the prototype of the modern-day urban European male. During his career, he appeared in over forty films, including such classics as *La Dolce Vita*; *Divorce Italian Style*; *8-1/2*; *Yesterday, Today and Tomorrow*; *City of Women*; *Ginger and Fred*; *Intervista*; and *Henry IV*.
*Who was this internationally acclaimed dramatic and comic actor who died in Paris on December 19, 1996?

312) *This Italian region* has a variety of pastas that are its own. Trenette, the pasta made without eggs, is the classic recipient of their unique pesto sauce. It is also traditionally paired with another sauce made from artichokes. ***Identify the Italian region.**

313) *What Italian-American* football coach's career was portrayed in the television movie, *Run to Daylight*?

314) *Angelina,* *Zuma, Zuma,* and *C'e la Luna* were hit songs made popular by what Italian jazz great in the 1950's?

315) *White Capri* is considered by experts to be one of the best in Italy. ***What is it?**

316) *This opera* by Pietro Mascagni was based on a novella by Giovanni Verga. Its English translation means *Rustic Chivalry*.
*What is its better known Italian title?

317) *Born in* Oak Park Illinois in 1958, this attractive and feisty leading lady of the American stage and screen is the daughter of a first-generation Italian-American bronze foundry operator. A music major, she left college to pursue an acting career in New York. She made her screen debut in 1983 as Al Pacino's sister in the motion picture, *Scarface*. She went on to garner an Academy Award nomination for Best Supporting Actress in *The Color of Money* in 1986. Other movie roles include: *The Abyss, Class Action, Robin Hood: Prince of Thieves* (as Maid Marian), and *Two Bits*.
*Who is she?

318) *The Italian* card game, briscola, is considered to be a traditional Italian card game, but, in fact, it arrived in Italy from another country in the late 16th century. ***Where did the game originate?**
a) Holland b) France c) Spain

319) *What Italian-American* singer was known as Mr. "C"?

320) *Tome,* robiole, and the world famous fontina come from Piedmont.
*What are they?

321) *Whose hit song* was titled *Spanish Eyes*? (Hint: Played the role of Johnny Fontaine in *The Godfather*.)

322) *Italian composer* and musician Philip Traetta opened two of these in the United States in the early part of the nineteeth century.
*What were they?

323) *Who played* "the sweetest music this side of heaven"? (Hint: Famous for conducting his orchestra on New Year's Eve.)

324) *Its modern form*, in which the bar lines are scored vertically throughout the parts, first appeared in the 16th century in the madrigals of *Cipriano de Rore* and the orchestral music of Giovanni Gabrieli. It is the name given to the copy of a work of music containing the notation for one or many performers.   ***Identify this musical term.**

325) *Unlike the majority* of Italians, the Piedmontese are inclined to prefer broth or soup to rice or pasta.   ***Is this statement true or false?**

326) *What is* the name of the barber in *The Barber of Seville*? (Hint: His name is often repeated in one of its well-known arias.)

327) *He is considered* one the greatest Italian composers of the high Renaissance. He is best known for his more than one hundred masses and 250 motets, which have long been considered a yardstick of judgment for polyphonic music used in the Roman Catholic Church. (Hint: Born in the town of Palestrina, near Rome, circa 1525.)   ***Who was he?**

328) *A kind of voice* popular in rock and soul music is literally Italian for "unreal voice."   ***Identify the musical term.**

329) *Born in Chicago* in 1947, this smooth leading man of stage and screen won a Tony in 1984 for his role in the Pulitzer Prize winning Broadway play, *Glengary Glen Ross*. A rabid Chicago Cubs fan, he won an Emmy for co-writing the TV baseball play, *Bleacher Bums*, in which he also starred. (Hint: His other memorable movies include, *The Money Pit*, *Three Amigos!*, *House of Games*, *The Godfather Part III*, and *Searching for Bobby Fisher.*)
***Who is he?**

330) *A fine wine* that is produced in Lombardy is called *Sangue di Giuda*.
***What is the English translation?**

331) *Historians say* that this composer completed the opera, *The Barber of Seville*, in thirteen days.   ***Who was he?**

332) *Arturo Ambrosia* is considered the founder of the Italian film industry. He established the first Italian film studio in 1905 and started turning out documentary films, then feature films like the classic spectacle *The Last Days of Pompeii*. It can be said that Ambrosio won the first prize in the world's first film competition held during the International Exposition in Turin.   ***What year did this occur?**   a) 1911 b) 1914 c) 1919

333) *Mario Lanza* made eight movies between 1949 and 1959, the year he died. ***Identify two of the films.**

334) *Born in Cagliari*, Sardinia, this actress enjoyed a modest career in Hollywood as a leading lady, usually playing frail, innocent heroines. She co-starred with Paul Newman in the movie about Rocky Graziano, *Somebody Up There Likes Me*. She was married to singer Vic Damone from 1954 to 1958. ***Who was she?**

335) *Italian cooking* relies heavily on the use of what type of oil?

336) *Born* Maria Grazia Rosa Dominica D'Amato in New York City, her unique Louisiana blues style still appeals to packed clubs across the country. (Hint: Remembered instantly by her major hit single, *Midnight at the Oasis*.) ***Who is she?**

337) *Daniela Bianchi* played a beautiful Russian agent and the love interest of Sean Connolly in what 1966 James Bond classic?

338) *Who asked* the musical question, *Who's Sorry Now*?

339) *Born Michael Gubitosi* in 1933, he started his acting career in *Our Gang* shorts in the late 1930's and early 40's. Among his notable motion pictures are *The Treasure of the Sierra Madre, In Cold Blood,* and *Tell Them Willie Boy Is Here*. He also starred in the popular television series, *Baretta*, where he won an Emmy for Best Actor in 1975.
*Who is this versatile and talented actor?

340) *Panettone* was the best kept culinary secret of this Italian city until the turn of the 19th century. This feathery light bread is as representative of Christmas in Italy as mistletoe is in America.
*What Italian city is associated with panettone?
a) Palermo b) Milan c) Genoa

341) *His big break came* with his TV role as Vinnie Barbarino in *Welcome Back Kotter*. His portrayal of Tony Manero, in the motion picture, *Saturday Night Fever,* gave rise to the disco craze in dance and the disco look in fashion in the late 1970's. His role in *Urban Cowboy* helped popularize western wear in the 80's. His critical and box office success in the movie, *Pulp Fiction,* catapulted him back as one of Hollywood's most popular and highest paid actors. (Hint: Other memorable movies include: *Grease, Look Who's Talking, Staying Alive,* and *Face/Off* with Nicolas Cage.) ***Who is he?**

342) *She is the first* female vocalist ever to achieve four top hit songs from a single album.   ***Who is she?***

a) Connie Francis b) Cindy Lauper c) Madonna

343) *Rudolph Valentino's* good looks and torrid love scenes in what memorable movie revolutionized the film industry and had a dramatic effect on American culture?

a) Uncharted Seas b) Blood and Sand c) The Sheik

344) *From Emilia* comes the finest zamponi of Italy and the world.

What is zamponi?

345) *Already known* to have been produced in Bologna in the early Middle Ages, *mortadella* is the father of seasoned sausages known collectively as what?

346) *This comic actor* was known for his wild rolling eyes, walrus mustache, and bellowing voice. He was very popular in radio, and made comic appearances in a number of Bob Hope movies.
What was the first name of this Italian-American born Geraldo Luigi Colonna?

347) *Imogene Coca* was a star on what early television comedy show which began on NBC in 1950? (Hint: Her comedy partner on the show was Sid Caesar.)

348) *Victor Hugo's* drama of intrigue, treachery, and revenge at the court of Francis I of France greatly impressed this composer as material for an operatic plot. The result was *Rigoletto*.

Who was the great composer?

349) *Forceful and intense,* this talented character actor found stardom and critical success on television in the dramtic police detective series, *N.Y.P.D. Blue.* (Hint: Recognized by his red hair.)   ***Who is he?***

350) *Ovieto and verdicchio* are wines that are considered to be among the best in Italy. From what region or regions in Italy are they produced?

a) Umbria - Marche b) Tuscany c) Lazio

351) *Identify the early television show* which portrayed Italian-Americans in a situation comedy. (Hint: Its title began, *Life with* _____.)

352) *A favorite* of opera lovers, Verdi completed this opera in four weeks rather than his customary four months. The opera is based on a

story of the tragic romance of Violetta Valery, a beautiful courtesan of Paris, and Alfredo Germony, a sincere and poetic young man of a respectable provincial family.   ***Identify this popular opera.**

353) *Born in Los Angeles* in 1954, this stunning beauty began her career as a model-cover girl. She turned her interest in acting toward television which led to a part in the motion picture *Major League* in 1989. She has since proven herself a capable, compelling actress in sensitive drama as well as romantic comedies such as *Tin Cup* with Kevin Costner. Her most recent movie, *The Thomas Crown Affair*, (1999) has propelled her to super-star status.

*Who is this beautiful and talented Italian-American?

354) *As conservative* an authority as Grove's Dictionary states, "...the type of singer he represents is not to be expected in his perfection more than once in a generation."

*To what great Italian tenor does this statement refer?

355) *How* would you describe rigatoni?

356) *His third book*, *The Fall of the Roman Umpire*, was written by what retired former baseball umpire? (Hint: He also played football for the Detroit Lions.)

357) *In what television* comedy series was the character, Arthur Fonzarelli featured?

358) *This talented screenwriter*, director, producer, and actor, was born in Knoxville, Tennessee in 1963. After making his debut in the 1992 film, *Reservoir Dogs,* as director-screenwriter-actor, he quickly established himself as a filmmaker to be reckoned with. His movie, *Pulp Fiction*, only two years later, won him an Oscar for his screenplay and a nomination for Best Director.   ***Who is he?**

359) *Beautiful, talented, and Harvard educated,* this leading lady is the daughter of a versatile character lead and supporting player of the American stage and screen. Her unique approach to developing distinctive characters earned her the Best Supporting Actress Oscar for her comedic role in Woody Allen's *Mighty Aphrodite* in 1995.

*Who is this gifted actress?

360) *This Italian* opera composer was portrayed by Philip Holmes in the 1935 movie, *The Divine Spark*.   ***Who was the composer?**

a) Vincenzo Bellini b) Giuseppe Verdi c) Antonio Vivaldi

361) *This 1967 television special* was a tribute to one of the most popular singers ever. Fill in the blank. _____: *A Man and His Music.*

362) *This magnetic,* versatile, lead and character actor of American stage, screen, and TV, was born in Bayonne, New Jersey in 1940. Winner of three consecutive Obies and a Tony for his performance as the slithering lizard in Edward Albee's *Seascape.* He portrayed the sexiest Count Dracula ever to stalk the stage or screen.
*Who is this accomplished and good-looking Broadway actor?

363) *"The House I Live In"* was recorded by what Italian-American singing idol in 1942 to demonstrate America's ethnic unity?

364) *This assertive, handsome* leading man of the American stage, screen, television, and motion pictures was born in Brooklyn, New York in 1938. His career took off after his debut in the Broadway play, *The Night of the Iguana,* in 1961. On TV he was featured in *The Lawyers, Cool Million, Dynasty, Blue Thunder,* and *Mary,* among other productions. His movies include *The War Lord, Me, Natalie* (Al Pacino's film debut), *The final Countdown,* and *Bulletproof.* ***Who is he?**

365) *Carlo Rambaldi* created the 3'6" tall model for what record breaking 1982 Steven Spielberg movie?

366) *Name* the hip Catholic priest played by actor Don Novella, who was featured on *Saturday Night Live.*

367) *This San Francisco nightclub* has the reputation of having the world's greatest female impersonators. (Hint: Translates to the Italian word for the anise plant.) ***Name the night club.**

368) *Joseph Gramaldi* (1778-1821) was the first theater clown to wear a clown suit and to paint his face. He played a character whose name is synonymous with the word clown even today.
*Identify the name.

369) *In the early 1900's,* the great Luisa Tetrazzini was internationally known for what musical talent?

370) *In 1977, Lew Ferigno* was featured with Arnold Schwarzenegger in George Butler's documentary, *Pumping Iron.* In 1983, he starred in *Hercules,* a movie tailored to fit his impressive physique. His best known television role was opposite Bill Bixby. ***What was the role.**

371) *Italian film director* Michelangelo Antonioni has been described as one of the most remarkable creative artist of post-war cinema. His first major international triumph came in 1960 and starred the beautiful Monica Vitti (born Maria Louisa Ceciarelli.)   ***Identify the film.**
a) L'Avventura b) La Signora senza Camelie c) Le Amiche

372) *Romano Mussolini,* the son of Benito Mussolini, is the brother-in-law of what Italian film actress?

373) *What singer,* along with his band, shot to the top of the charts during the 1980's with the songs *You Give Me a Bad Name* and *Wanted, Dead or Alive*?

374) *Born* in the seaport resort of Viareggio off the Tuscan coast near Lucca in 1915, this Italian film director scored his first international hit with *Big Deal on Madonna Street*, which was a delightful satire about a gang of fumbling would-be robbers. Other award winning films include *The Great War*, a biting satire about WWI and *The Organizer*, an incisive study of Italian labor unions.***Identify this highly regarded Italian film director.**
a) Mario Monicelli b) Gari Polizziani c) Antonio Nicco

375) *Bob Guccioni* is the publisher of what popular men's magazine?

376) *John Moschitta* is the fast-talking businessman in a popular TV commercial where he speaks at a rate of 530 words per minute. (Hint: A major air freight company.)
*Identify the commercials he appeared in.

377) *What 1962 Italian film* won an Oscar for Best Story and Screenplay? (Hint: Marcello Mastroianni received an Oscar nomination for best actor.)

378) *What annual salary* was paid to Frank Sinatra in 1980 for advertising Lee Iacocca's Chrysler products?

379) *What Italian-American* composer won an Academy Award for his music, *Days of Wine and Roses*?

380) *Allan Silvestri* wrote the music for two box office smash hits of the 1980's. One starred Michael Douglas and the other, Michael J. Fox.
*Identify one of the movies.

381) *Director, producer, and screen writer* Garry Marscharelli was born in New York city in 1934. A graduate of the School of Journalism of Northwestern University, he began show business as a stand-up comedian and drummer in his own jazz band. He began writing comedy material for Joey Bishop, Phil Foster and others in the 1950s and early 60's. By the mid 60's he started to contribute material to such hit shows as *Jack Parr Show, The Danny Thomas Hour, The Lucy Show*, and *The Dick Van Dyke Show*. His career skyrocked when he became executive producer in 1970 of the hit series, *The Odd Couple*. After this, came a string of television hit series' that include *Happy Days, Laverne and Shirley*, and *Mork and Mindy*. If this was not enough, he directed his energies to film directing and turned out the following hits: *Beaches, Pretty Woman*, and *A League of Their Own*, among others. (Hint: You know his sister.) ***Who is this multi-talented Italian-American?**

382) *In Italian cuisine,* what is known as Pulpo?

383) *Francis Ford Coppola* won an Oscar in 1970 for original story and screenplay about a World War II general. The film was also selected as Best Picture for that year. (Hint: George C. Scott starred.)
*What was the movie?

384) *In 1958, this musical* score was the first TV soundtrack album to sell a million copies. (Hint: Popular detective show starring Craig Stevens.) ***Name the television show or the composer.**

385) *Can you name* Italy's homespun brandy? (Hint: It really grabs you.)

386) *Caesar Cardini* is responsible for inventing what type of culinary delight? (Hint: It's all in the name.)

387) *What are* Sardo, Caciocavallo, Grana, and Scamorze?

388) *What* Italian liqueur is made from bitter almonds?

389) *What is* the type of pasta that translates into *Little Muffs?*

390) *Beautiful and talented* actress, Susan Lucci, finally won what award after countless nominations?

391) *A frustrated opera singer,* after eighteen years of vocal lessons, finally decided his future was in acting. His roles include *Dick Tracy, GoodFellas, The Rocketeer, Nixon, Romeo and Juliet,* and *Money Talks.* (Hint: Daughter is an Oscar winner.)
*Who is this tall, heavyset, and versatile character actor?

392) *The three provinces* of Parma, Reggia and Piacenza have claimed to have invented it. ***What is it?**

393) **Born Armando Catalano,** this handsome leading man is best known as the dashing character of Walt Disney's television series, *Zorro*, and as John Robinson of the popular television series of the mid-1960's, *Lost In Space*.   ***Who is he?**

394) **The pizzelle iron** is used for what purpose?

395) **David Chase,** born David De Cesare, wrote, produced, and directed the popular and successful television series', *I'll Fly Away* and *Northern Exposure*. His current hit, which airs on HBO, is controversial in the Italian-American community in that its subject matter and characters are violent, criminal, and of Italian descent.
    *Identify this popular television series.

396) **Ficco d' India** is a cactus that grows in Sicily. In America, it is cultivated in Florida, Arizona, and California for its fruit.
    *What is the more common American name?

397) **What yellow** Italian liqueur goes into a Harvey Wallbanger?

398) **Born Bernadette Lazzara** in 1944 in Ozone Park, New York, this leading lady of the American stage, nightclubs, TV, and films made her stage debut in 1955 in *The Most Happy Fella*. She later won a Tony for Andrew Lloyd Weber's *Song and Dance* in 1985. Many know her from her movie roles which include *The Jerk, Pennies From Heaven, Annie* and *Pink Cadillac*.
*Who is this beautiful and vivacious actress and singer known for her bubbly personality?

399) **Who said,** "Everything you see, I owe to spaghetti"?

400) **His ancestors, Italian protestants,** fled Italy and settled in Holland in the 17th century, then immigrated to New York state. This descendant of Italian/Dutch settlers was born in Grand Island, Nebraska in 1905. His engaging sincerity, natural style of delivery, and characteristically "American" personality proved ideal for the movies. His first motion picture role came in 1935 with *The Farmer Takes a Wife*. Four years and seventeen movies later, came three memorable movie roles still enjoyed today: *Young Mr. Lincoln, Drums Along the Mohawk,* and *The Grapes of Wrath*. During World War II, he was awarded the Bronze Star and a Presidential Citation. After the war, he enjoyed a very successful career and appeared in a long list of American film classics. In 1980, he received an honorary Oscar for "the consummate actor, in recognition of his brilliant accomplishments and enduring contribution to the art of motion pictures." Several months before

his death in 1982, he won the Academy Award as Best Actor for his glowing performance in the 1981 movie *On Golden Pond.*
*Who is this film legend?**

401) *His contributions* to the science of instrument making and the art of music making greatly influenced the future of two disciplines and elevated performing to its highest level. Of the 1500 musical instruments it is believed he made, 600 survive today and are considered close to priceless.
Identify this renowned instrument maker, born in Cremona, Italy in 1644.

402) *Is the* following statement correct? Spaghetti and meatballs is an entirely unknown dish in Italy.

403) *Massimo Troisi,* Italian actor and director, tragically died at the completion of this movie, set in the beautiful Lipari islands off the north coast of Sicily. **Identify his beautifully filmed and acted movie.**

404) *This once working-class American* is now a musical superstar on both sides of the Atlantic. His music is about his girlfriend, his home town, and his car/bike. His album *Born To Run,* in 1975, propelled him and his band to rock stardom. *Born in the USA* arrived in 1984 and sold over 12 million copies. **Who is this rock-n-roll superstar?**

405) *Cruising and celebrating* the joys of life as only the Italians can, is the credo of this company. Headquardered in Genoa, all ship's officers and most of the crew are Italian. **Identify this popular cruise line that sails the Mediterranean, Caribbean, and Alaska's Inside Passage.**

406) *It was in 1846 that this Italian* started the brewery that would become the leader of the Italian beer market. Today, one hundred and fifty years later, his family still oversees the company's four breweries, making it possible to maintain an extremely high standard of excellence.
Identify its founder or his beer company from the following choices.
a) Peroni b) Moretti c) Rossi

407) *What region,* established by Cosimo de Medici, is the world's oldest officially defined wine-growing region of Italy?

408) *Jerry Vale* and the late Sergio Franchi are two extremely popular Italian-American entertainers in the TV and nightclub venue.
Give the stage name of one of these singers:
a) Roberto Ridarelli b) Joan Babbo
c) Frank Castelluccio

ART, SCIENCE, & LITERATURE

Art, Science, and Literature

409) ***Born in Pisa*** on February 15, 1564, this man is considered by many to be the most influential of all Italians throughout history because of his major ground breaking contributions in the areas of *astronomy, cartography, entomology, hydrodynamics, mathematics, mechanics, physics, and timekeeping.* (Hint: He conducted an important experiment from the Leaning Tower of Pisa.)   ***Who was this intellectual giant?**

410) ***In the course of*** their trading expeditions to the Orient, the Venetians are credited with introducing to Europe what instrument essential to navigation?

411) ***What is the Italian word,*** now a part of the English language, that means enthusiastic, vigorous enjoyment or appreciation?

412) ***This noted Italian American*** archaeologist headed the Metropolitan Museum of Art in New York City. Under his skillful guidance, the institution became our country's outstanding art museum and the third largest in the world during his lifetime. (Hint: Congressional Medal of Honor recipient during the American Civil War.)

*Who was he?

413) ***The gifted Italian artist,*** Constantino Brumidi, spent nearly twenty five years painting frescoes and murals in what nation's capital buildings?

414) *This sculptor* was born in Florence in 1386 and is considered one of the founders of Renaissance art. He favored a more vigorous style than the serenity of idealized beauty in vogue during the 15th century, and stressed dramatic action and power of expression. His masterpieces include *David*, which was the first life-size bronze freestanding nude since classical times, and the bronze life-size equestrian statue of *Gattamelata*, the first of its kind since antiquity. Also, his bronze plaque of *St. George Slaying the Dragon* was the first time a carved relief utilized the use of perspective. ***Who was this sculptor?**

a) Ghiberti b) Brunelleschi c) Donatell

415) *Leonardo da Vinci* is credited with an invention that enabled vessels to get from one level of water to another, and which simplified the dangerous job of lowering and lifting of boats.

*What was this invention?

416) *In the Italian language,* this word means foundry. Its modern English meaning came out of Venice and is used to describe a section of a city to which an ethnic or economically depressed minority group is restricted. ***Identify the term.**

417) *Giulio Romano,* one of the founders of *Mannerism*, and an eminent painter and architect in his own right, was the principal heir to one of the greatest artists of Italy. It is clear that he finished a number of works left incomplete at this master's death. ***Name this artist.**

a) Raphael b) Titian c) Bramante

418) *Born in Pisa* around 1180, he has been described as the greatest Western mathematician of the Middle Ages. He is responsible for bringing to Europe a system of mathematical notation called Arabic, an innovation that changed mathematics and made a monumental contribution to the progress of science and technology. Prior to this, Western Europe used Roman numerals for all mathematical calculations. (Hint: Also known as Leonardo Pisano and was famous for his numerical "*sequence*".) ***Name him.**

419) *Name the adventurer* who dictated *Travels* to a Pisan writer while a captive of the Genoese in 1298.

420) *What Italian American artist* created the statue, *St. Francis of the Guns*, which was made from turned-in guns after the assassination of Martin Luther King Jr. and Robert Kennedy? (Hint: First name was Benny.)

421) *What 18th century Italian* instrument maker brought the art of violin making to its apex? (Hint: His name is synonymous with the violin.)

422) *Cicero's secretary,* Tiro, invented what system of rapid handwriting employing symbols to represent words, phrases, and letters?

423) *What is the Italian word,* now a part of the English language, that means a proportional part or share? (Hint: Starts with the letter Q and was synonymous with Russian economics.)

424) *Rafael Sabatini,* an Italian-born English novelist, wrote best selling historical and adventure romances. Among his many works are two of particular note. The first, about a gentleman pirate, was later made into a motion picture starring Errol Flynn. The second is about a strolling actor during the French Revolution.
        *Give one of the two titles of these popular novels.

425) *What Latin poet* was Dante's guide through the *Inferno*?

426) *Brother Cipolla* was a character who specialized in duping villagers with fake religious relics. In what literary work did this fictional character appear? (Hint: Written by Giovanni Boccaccio, it remains one of the masterpieces of world literature.)

427) *Tradition holds* that this Florentine painter, born Bencivieni di Pepo, was the father of Italian painting and the teacher of Giotto. He is considered to be directly responsible for the style of painting that we associate with Western Renaissance art. (Hint: Known by a single name, it has come to mean "bullheaded" in Italian)   ***Name him.**

428) *This Italian poet,* novelist, dramatist, and soldier was an ardent Italian nationalist who, in 1919, led an expedition into the city of Fiume and held it for fifteen months in defiance of Italy's obligations under the *Treaty of Versailles.*   ***Name this famous Abruzzese poet.**

429) *What is the Italian word,* now a part of the English language, that means a sentence, phrase, or word appropriate to its character; an appropriate inscription?

430) *Giovanni Della Casa* was a 16th century author of the popular courtesy book, *Il Galateo*. In 1576, it was translated into English by Sir Robert Peterson, and greatly influenced what well-known English period?

431) *The sister of* Americo Vespucci, one of the four great Italian explorers, possessed such beauty that she was immortalized by Sandro Botticelli in what has become one of the world's most famous nudes. Botticelli's artistic visions contributed immeasurably to a change in the 15th century's philosophical approach to art. (Hint: Title of painting taken from a planet.)

*Name this famous painting that has the central figure rising from the sea in the cradle of a huge white seashell.

432) *In 1847,* the Italian chemist, Ascanio Sobrero, produced a new, powerful, and dangerous explosive. He produced it by slowly pouring half a measure of glycerin into a mixture composed of one part nitric acid and two parts sulfuric acid. (Hint: Also adapted for use as a cardiac-anginal agent.)   ***What did his experiment produce?**

433) *Luigi Da Porto,* an Italian soldier and courtier, published a story by Masuccio in 1530. The story, with its definitive plot and characters, reached Shakespeare through English translators. What was Shakespeare's title of Da Porto's story? (Hint: World's most famous lovers.)

434) *Born in 1250,* this Italian painter was the founder of the Sienese school of painting, and is noted for the refinement and delicacy of his style. His masterpiece is the Virgin in Majesty (1311).

*Name this painter.

a) Giotto b) Simone Martini c) Duccio Di Buoninsegna

435) *What is the Italian word,* now a part of the English language, that means a public declaration of intentions, motives or views?

436) *In 1808,* the Italian inventor Pellegrini Turri developed a writing machine for a friend, the Countess Franconi, who was blind.

*What is this machine called today?

437) *The renowned Italian poet,* Torguato Tasso, was born in 1544 at Sorrento and educated by Jesuits at Naples. His works have strongly influenced English poets, from Spencer to Byron. His most celebrated romantic epic was based upon the historic events of the First Crusade.

*Name this famous Renaissance romance.

438) *Luigi Alamanni,* a Florentine poet and playwright during the Renaissance, was one of the first to write an extensive guide on what type of outdoor activity?

439) *Passionately in love,* Petrarch wrote a magnificent series of poems, the Canzoniere (Songbook) in honor of a woman he loved. The

book elevated him to a select group of Italian literary geniuses.
*What was the woman's name?

440) ***Born in 1474 at Reggio Emilia,*** he is regarded as the greatest poet of the Renaissance (Rinascimento), and is the author of the *Orlando Furioso*, the most famous chivalric poem in Italian literature and the most perfect expression of Renaissance classicism.   ***Identify him.**
a) Ludovico Ariosto b) Lorenzo Caretti c) Gaetano Cipolla

441) ***The set of lines*** on which music is written is credited to the Italian monk Guido d'Arezzo. In the 11th century, this innovator advocated the use of four lines on which different keys and colors served as points of reference.   ***What is his innovation called?**

442) ***Give the Italian word,*** commonly used in English, that means a sheet of paper used to cast a secret vote.

443) ***This Italian painter's name*** at birth, in 1387, was Guido di Pietro. A Dominican friar, his religious painting combined simplicity and grace with a sense of purity and a delicacy of color. Among his famous works is a series of frescoes at the monastery of San Marco, and several scenes from the life of St. Lawrence. (Hint: Known by his angelic name.)   ***Name the painter, who died in 1455.**

444) ***In 1910,*** the first radio-retransmission in the United States took place from the Metropolitan Opera House involving what opera star singing an aria from *Cavalleria Rusticana*?

445) ***Can you name*** the well known Italian playwright responsible for the work, *Six Characters in Search of an Author*?

446) ***What is the Italian word,*** now a part of the English language, that means smuggled goods or merchandise illegally imported or possessed?

447) ***Evangelista Torricelli*** was born in the Romangna region of Italy in 1608. Torricelli was greatly influenced by Galileo's work and subsequently became his secretary and assistant. A great scientist in his own right, his discoveries and inventions made a major contribution to *meteorology, hydrodymanics, and optics.* ***He is best remembered for what invention having to do with meteorology?**

448) ***The invention*** of crystalline glass is attributed to a master glass maker named Beroverio, who perfected the very transparent glass in 1463.

*What is the better known name for this glass?

449) *The famous opening sentence* of Caesar's *Gallic War* states that all Gaul is divided into how many parts?   a) 3 b) 5 c) 7

450) *This term refers* to an exuberant style which started in architecture and was later applied to similar tendencies in painting, music, sculpture, and literature. The style was dramatic, grandiose and ornate. It originated in Italy in the latter 16th century and soon spread throughout Europe.

*Identify the term.

451) *Though his style* was strongly influenced by Leonardo da Vinci, his work is characterized by the use of noble types and gestures. His masterpieces include *Last Judgment* and *Virgin and Child with Saints*.

*Name this Florentine painter.

452) *Giorgio Bassani,* an Italian novelist and writer of short stories, saw his most famous novel turned into a motion picture and received an Oscar for Best Foreign Language Film. It narrates the plight of an aristocratic Jewish family of Ferrarra during the Fascist racial persecutions. (Hint: A work that should be read outdoors, especially in a garden.)   *What is the name of this novel?

453) *When this Italian* scientist died in Rome on July 20, 1937 at the age of sixty-seven, every radio station in the world went silent for two minutes in honor of the great contributions he pioneered and discovered in the technology of wireless communication.

*Who was this Nobel Prize winner?

454) *What is the Italian word,* now a part of the English language, that means small bits of brightly colored paper, usually thrown on special occasions?

455) *His work* on nuclear fission marked the beginning of the atomic age. *Who was this brilliant Italian scientist who was awarded the Nobel Prize in Physics in 1938 for his work on the atomic particles known as neutrons?

456) *In 1602*, this celebrated Italian scientist discovered the laws and properties of the pendulum and applied the knowledge to regulating fixed timekeeping instruments. In 1641, his son constructed the first pendulum clock, using his father's writings.   *Identify this Italian scientist.

457) *This Italian is credited* with the discovery that chemical energy could be converted into electrical energy. For this great discovery, he is considered the founder of electrochemistry. ***Who was this early 19th century Italian who also is credited with the invention of the battery?**

458) *Italian author,* Alberto Maravia, wrote the best sellers *Conjugal Love* and *Two Women*, which was later made into a motion picture starring what Italian actress?

459) *Giovanni Bellini* was an innovative force in art in 14th century Italy. Among his masterpieces are *Agony in the Garden, Pieta,* and *Christ's Blessing.* Bellini's interest in light and color, when contrasted with the Florentine emphasis on line and modeling, was to become in the hands of Giorgione and Titian, his two greatest pupils, the glory of what school of painting?

460) *Girolamo Benivieni* was a highly regarded Florentine poet and the author of the famous Renaissance poem, *Canzone dell'Amor Divino.*
*Translate this title into English.

461) *In this best selling* novel, Umberto Eco wrote of murder in a 14th century monastery. (Hint: Sean Connery starred in the motion picture.) ***Give the title of this book.**

462) *Gabriele Fallopius,* a 16th century professor of anatomy at the University of Padua, is credited with developing a device for males made from a certain type of woven material that would inhibit conception and disease. ***What was this invention?**

463) *What is the Italian word,* now a part of the English language, that means an acute, highly contagious viral disease that includes fever, aches, pains, and respiratory inflammation?

464) *Lorenzo Bernini* was the dominant influence of European sculpture for more than a century. He was a typical 17th century baroque artist who did not shy away from whirling movement and illusionistic representation in stone. (Hint: Fed by the Acqua Vergine, an ancient aqueduct of Rome.) ***He is known for his consummate portrait busts and for what world famous fountain?**

465) *The first model* of this weapon was produced by the Italian Villa-Perosa in 1915. It is a lightweight automatic or semiautomatic gun, fired from the shoulder or the hip. ***What is this weapon called?**

466) *His book sold* more than 21 million copies worldwide, and spawned movies that became American cinematic classics. The son of

illiterate Italian immigrants, he won two Oscars for his screen adaptations of his novel. (Hint: It's an offer you can't refuse.)
*Name him or his best-selling novel.

467) *His many works* of prose and poetry were the first of their kind in Italian or European literature entitled him a place beside Petrarch as a founder of the Italian Renaissance. ***Name this great scholar and writer whose great classic still influences writers today.**

468) *The first history* written on the American Revolution was by an Italian in 1819. It was translated into English in 1834 under the title, *A History of the War of Independence.* Identify the author.

a) Charles Botta b) Luigi Mazzei c) Giovanni Duccio

469) *What is the Italian word,* now a part of the English language, that describes one appearing in the state of disguise?

470) *This Florentine painter* depicted both religious and mythological subjects in a style dependent on the graceful elongation of idealized figures, and on the swaying beauty of linear design. His masterpieces in this style include *The Adoration of the Magi, The Madonna of the Magnificent,* and *The Primavera,* which were painted for the Medici family, and now hang in the Uffizi Gallery in Florence. (Hint: Provided illustrations for Dante's *Divine Comedy.*)
*Name the artist.

471) *Brabantio* was a character in which of the following plays?

a) Otello b) Taming of the Shrew c) Merchant of Venice

472) *Give the Italian word,* now a part of the English language, that means a confused heap; a tangle, or a difficult situation.

473) *This Florentine architect,* engineer, and sculptor reintroduced the technique of linear perspective, which had been abandoned during the Middle Ages. Through study and experimentation, he identified the phenomenon of the "vanishing point," the point at which parallel lines appear to meet on the horizon. His greatest accomplishment was designing and constructing the huge, double-shell dome for the uncompleted Santa Maria del Fiore cathedral of Florence.
*Who was this Renaissance architect?

474) *What is the Italian word,* now a part of the English language, that means a material made of portland cement, sand, and lime, used as a covering for exterior walls?

475) *What Italian city boasts* of having established the first anatomy hall?   a) Pisa b) Florence c) Padua

476) *The true innovation* in the art of coffee making belongs to the Italian, Gaggia.   ***What did he invent in 1946?**

477) *In 1895,* an Italian physicist, with a Russian colleague, invented a signal-strengthening radio antenna, and produced the first working radio device to send the first wireless transmission to travel a distance of 2400 meters.   ***Name the physicist.**

478) *What is the Italian word,* now a part of the English language, that means a fluid rock that issues from a volcano or from a fissure in the earth's surface?

479) *Apprenticed to the workshop* of artist Andrea del Verrocchio, he learned the fundamentals of sculpture, painting, and mechanical arts. He was a vegetarian and animal rights activist. He has been described as *"the fullest man"* of the Renaissance.   ***Who was this Italian they call genius?**

480) *This Italian-American created* the first money pyramid in 1920. Conservative estimates indicate that he took in $20 million before his scheme was detected.   ***Name him.**

481) *For 25 years,* Tony Di Preta was the alter ego of this famous comic strip hero. The major character of the strip was boxing's heavyweight champion of the world, who exemplified the All American spirit.   ***Identify this comic strip hero.**

482) *Baldassare Castiglione,* an Italian diplomat, writer, and courtier, was one of the most influential authors in Europe during the Renaissance. His chief work was titled *The Courtier,* and establishes the author's concept of the ideal courtier and the norms of courtesy in a cultured society. A friend of Castiglione's painted his portrait, which today is one of the most treasured masterpieces of the Louvre museum.
                *Name the painter.
        a) Raphael b) Filippo Lippi c) Gentile da Fabriano

483) *James Oppenheim* wrote what famous poem about the Italian-American inspired Lawrence textile mill strike? (Hint: An organization that helps the elderly shares this name.)   ***What is the title?**

484) *A Florentine monk* of the Carmelite order, he painted religious

easel paintings and frescoes in a style stressing charm, imaginative detail, and sinuous outline. He was influenced primarily by Masaccio, Fra Angelico, and Donatello, and, in turn, was the teacher of Botticelli.
*Name this artist, who was one of the best-known and most influential Tuscan painters of the 15th century.

485) *This Italian writer* is especially noted for his book, *Christ Stopped At Eboli.* *Name this author.*
a) Carlo Levi b) Stefano Porcu c) Michael Geraldi

486) *Identify part I* of Dante's *Divine Comedy*. (Hint: Intense heat.)

487) *The most famous work* of art depicting this scene is a fresco by Leonardo da Vinci, housed in the refectory of Santa Maria delle Grazie, Milan. It shows the consternation of the disciples when Jesus told them that he would be betrayed that night. *Name this masterpiece.*

488) *In 1895,* A. Sclavo and several international colleagues developed a serum against an infectious, usually fatal disease of animals—especially in cattle and sheep. *What is the name of this serum?*

489) *The first of these procedures* took place in Bologna, Italy in 1281. The Italian anatomist, Mondino di Luzzi, published his work *Anatomy* in 1316, in which he discussed his work in this field.
On what topic did his work focus?

490) *What is the Italian word,* now a part of the English language, that means art work applied to a wall or ceiling?

491) *Born in 1628,* this Italian physician and biologist is regarded as the father of histology, the microscopic study of plant and animal tissue. He is also credited for discovering capillary circulation after observing capillaries in frogs' legs, and he was the first to describe red corpuscles in the blood. *Who was he?*
a) Carlo Ubaldini b) Marcello Malpighi c) Girolamo Fabrizio

492) *What Shakespearian play* featured the character Shylock?

493) *Identify the term* that means an attitude of the mind that accompanied the flowering of the Renaissance. The term is derived from the Italian word umanista. The Tuscan poet Petrarch is regarded as the first proponent of this philosophy which, in essence, refers to several varied literary and scholarly activities inspired by the study of antiquity.

494) *This Florentine* is regarded as the greatest painter of the pre-

Renaissance. He was a pupil of Cimabue and a friend of Dante. His work brought a new force and strength to art. The quality of his genius is best seen in a series of 38 frescoes in the Scrovegni Chapel in Padua, depicting the life of Christ and other biblical subjects. He is also responsible for designing and beginning construction of the famous Campanile of the Duomo of Florence. ***Name him.**

495) *Modern air conditioning* can be traced to what innovation made in 1155 by the Italian, Agricolo, who described his system and its use in mines?

496) *In 1626,* Dr. Santoria, an Italian physician, developed the first instrument to gauge a patient's temperature. ***What was it?**

497) *Give the Italian word,* now a part of the English language, that means the spread of ideas, information or rumor that either helps or injures a cause or a person.

498) *Fifteenth century Italy* witnessed a revival of the creative spirit. A flowering of arts, sciences, and philosophy began in Italy, and for two centuries swept the cobwebs of the Dark Ages out of Europe and ushered in the modern western world. ***What is this period called?**

499) *What Italian word* is known as a universal exclamation for excellence?

500) *A Venetian printer* gave us a standing printing type style. (Hint: A type style with characters that slant upward to the right.) ***Name it?**

501) *This definition states:* friendly to or favoring what is Italian.
*Identify the word.

502) *The translucent impression* found on a sheet of paper first appeared in 1282 at Fabriano, Italy. This innovation arose due to the need to mark paper indelibly without taking space from its writing surface. ***Identify the innovation.**

503) *What is the Italian word,* now a part of the English language, that means a mosaic flooring made by embedding small pieces of marble or granite into mortar.

504) *Who, almost single-handedly,* made the Florentine dialect the literary standard language of Italy?

505) *Lazzaro Spallanzani* was the first scientist to theorize and prove that spermatoza was necessary for the fertilization of a mammal. He applied his finding to an experiment that was essentially the blueprint for a procedure that has now become common—he artificially inseminated a dog.

*This ground breaking experiment occurred in what year?
a) 1780 b) 1809 c) 1824

506) *Name the Abruzzi birthplace* of the great Italian poet, Gabriele d'Annunzio.　　　　　　　a) Villalfonsina b) Pescara c) Ortona a Mare

507) **His ideas,** found in his writings, included the rudimentary designs for the airplane, air conditioner, oil lamp, alarm clock, printing press, odometer, pedometer, magnetic compass, eyeglasses, telescope, differential transmission, water turbine, machine gun, tank, under water diving suit, life preserver, and parachute.
*Who was this Italian visionary?

508) *Born in Pisa* on February 15, 1564, this man, who developed the scientific method, is considered by many to be the most influential of all Italians because of his major contributions to the sciences of astronomy, cartography, entomology, hydrodynamics, mathematics, mechanics, physics, and timekeeping.　　　*Identify this Renaissance man.

509) *What is the Italian word,* now a part of the English language, that means a long-necked, straw-covered bottle of wine; a complete failure?

510) *Credited to this Italian* automotive genius are: one piece cylinder block and crankcase, replacement of the erratic chain drive with the universal jointed drive shaft-to-axle system, the first steel wheels (when everyone was using wood), the first integral electrical system, the first V engine, and the first V 12 engine. If this were not enough, in 1921, two historic innovations were developed by this Italian genius: unit body construction and independent front suspension.
*Name the man responsible for these incredible innovations.

511) *What famous Italian scientist* proved, through a series of biological experiments, that life among lower life forms was not a result of spontaneous generation? To prove his theory, he performed some of the first biological experiments ever to employ the use of proper scientific controls.　　　　　　　　　　　　　　*Name him.
a) Francesco Redi b) Lazzaro Spallanzani c) Marcello Malpighi

512) *As NASA's* Apollo Program director, Rocco Petrone was among the most responsible for getting what astronaut safely to and from the moon?

513) *An internationally recognized* biochemist and nutritional researcher, he is renowned as the inventor of the time-release concept and was the pioneer developer of the mineral chelation process. This major breakthrough in nutritional science made inorganic minerals much more absorbable for the first time.

**Name this distinguished researcher.*
a) Paul Ferrari b) Roberto Dores c) Anthony Pescetti

514) *Where is* Michelangelo's Pieta?

515) *What well known* Italian-American poet was arrested for publishing Allen Ginsberg's poem, *Howl*? (Hint: Occurred in San Francisco.)

516) *Quintus Ennius* is considered one of the greatest epic poets of Rome and regarded as one of the founders of Latin literature. Because of his style, he is regarded as the forerunner to what man, known as Rome's greatest poet? (Hint: Acted as a guide in a great literary work.)

517) *In 1956,* Italian-American researcher, Joseph Mazzitello, along with a colleague at 3M, developed an essential product for the video industry. **What was it?*

518) *Vannoccio Biringucci,* Italian metallurgist and armament maker of the 16th century, is chiefly remembered for his descriptions of processes for the extraction of medals and the preparation of chemical substances in his book *The Pirotechnia.*
**He is credited with initiating what subject as a serious science?*

519) *Among his many works,* sculptor Attilio Piccirilli is known for his design of what monument in Washington D.C.?
a) Marconi Monument b) Lincoln Memorial c) Statue of Constantino Brumidi

520) *Gasparo Tagliocozzi* was born in Bologna and was a professor of anatomy and surgery at the University of Bologna. The most common use of the skills he pioneered is in the field of cosmetic surgery. His repair techniques centered around nasal reconstruction, and he developed procedures to avoid the rejection of transplanted tissue. He was successful in replacing noses, ears, and lips that had been removed for disease or

punishment. *Identify the year he was born.

521) *Taken from the Italian language,* this word literally means "one who takes delight in a thing," especially in reference to the fine arts; a person having a superficial interest in an art or a branch of knowledge. *Identify the word.

522) *This 18th century Italian* physician, anatomist, and pathologist discovered and described so many structures and internal organs of the human body that if his discoveries were named after him, over a third of the human anatomy would bear his name.
*Identify this man, who essentially founded the science of pathological anatomy, and defined the art and science of modern diagnosis.
a) Guido Alfonso b) Giovanni Morgagni c) Camillo Cassotto

523) *These three notable Romans:* Plautus, Terence, and Seneca, were associated with which of the following areas of literature:
a) military historians b) playwrights c) pastoral poets

524) *What 19th century Italian* chemist, born in Palermo in 1826, is famous for his discovery of cyanamide and his method of synthesizing alcohols? He was also responsible for explaining how atomic weights could be determined and distinguished from molecular weights. Together with Amedeo Avogadro, he was responsible for defining the modern science of chemistry. *Name this scientist.
a) Giovanni Costa b) Stanislao Cannizzaro c) Rudolfo Spinola

525) *Give the Italian word,* now a part of the English language, that means a close reproduction or facsimile of something, especially by the maker of the original.

526) *This twenty-two volume* work titled, *The City of God,* was a defense for Christianity against the accusation that the Church was responsible for the decline of the Roman Empire. (Hint: A saint in the Catholic Church.) *Name the author.

527) *Italian-American historian* and critic, he first gained attention with his work, *Mark Twain in America* (1932). However, his most important writing was devoted to the area of history. His principle works were *The Year of Decision: 1846* (1943), *The Course of Empire* (1952), and *Across the Wide Missouri* (1947) for which he won a Pulitzer Prize.
*Name this Italian-American writer.
a) Bernard DeVoto b) Bob Valentino c) Steven Compagno

528) *In 1545,* Girolamo Cardano, a famous mathematician and physician of his period, described a joint he had invented in a treatise on physics entitled *De-subtilitate Rerum.* This invention allows for the relative angular movement of two shafts whose geometric axes converge at a single point. Today it is utilized in automobiles to couple two turning shafts whose positions can vary in relation to each other.
*What is the name of this important invention?

529) *What is the Italian word,* now a part of the English language, that means the art of painting on freshly spread, moist lime plaster with pigments suspended in a water vehicle?

530) *Giosue Carducci* was a 19th century poet and literary critic. He was professor of Italian literature at the University of Bologna from 1860 to 1904 and is considered the national poet of modern Italy.
*In 1906, a year before his death, he received what prestigious award?

531) *In 1583,* Andrea Cesalpino published a sixteen volume series entitled *The Book of Plants, Volumes 1-16.*
*This tremendous work is believed to be the first comprehensive textbook devoted to what science?

532) *Legend has it* that the first wind rose was made by an Amalfi craftsman named Flavia Giova. ***What is a wind rose?**

533) *What is the Italian word,* now commonly used in English, that means an outline or synopsis of a play, or an account of a possible course of action?

534) *Bernardo Accolti,* an Italian poet and dramatist was born in Arezzo in 1458. His best known work, entitled *Virginia*, is drawn from what famous work of Boccaccio's?

535) *Among his masterpieces* are *St. Jerome in His Study*, and the *Virgin Annunciate*. Influenced by the Flemish style of painting, particularly the use of oils, he became the chief sponsor of this new technique. ***Who was he?**
a) Paolo Uccello b) Rosso Fiorentino c) Antonello Da Messina

536) *Name the eleven-volume,* prose romance by the Roman writer Lucius Apuleius, which is the only Latin novel that still survives in its entirety. (Hint: Title relates to a change of physical form, structure, or substance especially by supernatural means.)

537) *Matteo Bandello,* an Italian author of the 15th and 16th century, wrote and compiled a collection of over 200 short tales which were later translated into English and French. These short stories provided the basic plots for another author's work which include, *Much Ado About Nothing, Twelfth Night,* and *Romeo and Juliet.* ***Name the other author.**

538) *This well known* and gifted author was born at West Point and has written twenty novels, including *Burr, 1876, Washington D.C.,* and *Lincoln.* He also has written five plays and five collections of essays. He proudly traces his family to the Jewel of the Adriatic, Venice. (Hint: Known for his liberal stance in American politics.)
*Name this controversial and truly talented author.

539) *Guido d'Arezzo* (Guido Aretinus) is responsible for conceptualizing and then charting the musical staff, one of the most important developments in musicology. His staff and system of music notation allowed music to be systematically written, read, played, and preserved. His system of solmization assigned syllables to notes, which greatly simplified the sight-reading of music. Everyone is familiar with his mnemonic device which renders the scale as *do, re, mi, fa, sol, la, ti, do.* In addition to this note-naming technique of solmization, d'Arezzo devised a four-line musical stave of different colors to chart melodies.
*Identify the century in which these innovations took place.
a) 11th century b) 12th century c) 13th century

540) *Give the Italian word,* now a part of the English language, that means a rounded vault resting on a circular base and forming a roof or ceiling.

541) *Bassanio* is the penniless but quick witted friend of Antonio in what Shakespearean play?

542) *The President's Room,* located directly off the Senate floor of the Capitol building, has been described as "the most exquisite room in America." The Italian artist who created its elaborate designs was known as the Michelangelo of the United States Capitol.
*Identify this artist who also painted *The Apotheosis* of Washington, the vast allegorical fresco in the dome of the U.S. Capitol.

543) *The development* of the atomic bomb was the work of scientists from around the world. The four major researchers involved in the project were two Americans, a Hungarian, and ***what Nobel Prize winning Italian scientist?**

544) *Whose name* is printed on almost every electrical device in the world?

545) *What is the Italian word,* now a part of the English language, that means a freestanding bell tower?

546) *Girolamo Fracastoro* was a 16th century physician and poet who developed epidemiology, a branch of medical science that deals with control of disease. He wrote an epic poem detailing the specifics of a venereal disease. The disease and the poem have the same name.
What is it?

547) *Among his lesser known works* were illustrations of Dante's *Divine Comedy* and two frescos entitled, *Punishment of Korah,* and *Nathan and Abraham,* done for the Sistine Chapel. His real name was Alessandro di Mariano dei Filipepio.
*What was this well known painter's more familiar name?

548) *Originally a sculptor,* this artist gave up sculpture in favor of architecture when he lost the competion (to Lorenzo Ghiberti) to create bronze panels for the doors of the Florence Baptistry. As an architect and engineer, he used his knowledge of Romanesque and Gothic architecture to construct a huge, double-shelled dome for the Florence catheral of Santa Maria del Fiore, considered impossible due to the building's immense size. He invented and built innovative cranes and derricks to assist in the construction of the revolutionary dome, which was completed in 1436.
*Who was this gifted Renaissance architect?

549) *Born Giorgio Barbarelli* in the Republic of Venice in 1477, he is credited as the forefather of the High Renaissance style of painting. The style defined by its utilization of a soft technique with a subtle, mysterious atmosphere or quality. (Hint: Known by a large first name.)
*Identify this artist whose masterpieces include *The Tempest, The Three Philosophers, Sleeping Venus, Boy with an Arrow*, and *Shepherd with a Flute.*

550) **In 1280,** the Florentine physicist Salvino Armati found a way to enlarge objects by using two pieces of glass having specific thicknesses and curves.   ***With what invention is he credited for?**

551) *The principle for this invention,* which is used to inject fluids into the body or draw them from it, was developed by the Italian Gattinara in the 15th century.   ***Name this medical instrument.**

552) *The Florentine jeweler,* Masa Finiguerra, discovered a new intaglio process when he got an inspiration to ink an engraved silver plate and then apply a sheet of paper to it to obtain a printed impression.

*Name this innovative process.

553) *This Italian* and his grandson are remembered for their innovations in the fields of printing, publishing, and orthography. Their innovations include the creation and distribution of the first inexpensive, pocket-size book; the design and implementation of the first italic typeface; and the definitive cataloging of what is now considered to be modern punctuation, including the comma, semicolon, colon, and period.

*Identify this Italian born in 1449 in the Papal state of Bassinia.
a) Giorgio Aldine b) Aldo Giovaniello c) Enrico Compodonico

554) *What is the Italian word,* now a part of the English language, that means a colonnade or covered ambulatory especially in classical architecture, often at the entrance of a building?

555) *His* **Commentaries on the Gallic War** and *Commentaries on the Civil War* show him to have been a clear and vigorous prose stylist.

*Who was he?

556) *This work by* Pietro Di Donato attempted to describe and understand the plight of the Italian immigrant in regard to family and neighborhood life. Published in 1939, the book was a best seller that later became a motion picture. ***What is the title?**

557) *What is the alternate title* of the masterpiece, *La Gioconda* , painted by Leonardo da Vinci?

558) *Ghiberti and Ghirlandaio* were renowned artists from Florence; one a sculptor, the other a painter. Match the artist with his discipline.

559) *After arriving in the United States* in 1945, Count Alessandro Dandini patented more than 22 inventions, including the rigid, retractable automobile top, and the spherical system which concentrates and extracts solar energy.

*He is also responsible for what type of light bulb found today in most American homes?

560) *On March 28, 1899* he made the first wireless telegraphic transmission between England and the continent, a distance of over 50 kilometers. ***Who was this Italian?**

561) ***Born in the Campania*** region of Italy in 1225, this saint and doctor of the Catholic church strove to prove in his publications, *Summa Theologica* and *Five Proofs for the Existence of God,* the existence of God through logic and reason rather than faith or revelation.

*Who was he?

562) ***What is the Italian word,*** now commonly used in the English language, that means a small piece of sculpture on a stone or shell, cut in relief in one layer, with another contrasting layer serving as a background?

563) ***What famous Italian author*** wrote "The first method for estimating the intelligence of a ruler is to look at the men he has round him" and "One who deceives will always find those who allow themselves to be deceived"?

564) ***16th century Florentine wool merchant***, by the name of Giovanni Cecchi wrote some fifty comedies, farces, and religious plays.

*He was one of the first professionals in what field?

565) ***What city*** is graced by Michelangelo's David?

566) ***What abbreviation*** comes from libra, meaning pound in Latin?

567) ***The list of this family's inventions*** are impressive. They include the toothpick propeller, used by the Allies in World War I, the world's first enclosed cabin style monoplane (honored in the Smithsonian's National Air and Space Museum), and a jet injector pump for deep wells. Later developments by this company include jet propulsion units for boats, propeller fans for keeping frost out of orchards, and a variety of jet and submersible pumps. But their most famous invention involved bathing and became synonymous with their family name.

*Identify this world famous product.

568) ***The Metamorphoses,*** a series of tales in Latin verse dealing with mythological, legendary, and historical figures beginning with the creation of the world and ending with the deification of Caesar and the reign of Augustus, was written by which of the following Roman poets? a) Calullus b) Virgil c) Ovid (Note: Not to be confused with the satire of the same title written by Apuleius more commonly known as *The Golden Ass.*)

569) ***Who made*** the following statement in 1924? "I affirm that the doctrine of Machiavelli is more alive today than it was four centuries

ago." a) Benito Mussolini b) Adolf Hitler c) Joseph Stalin

570) *The Farina family,* Italians living in Cologne, France in 1709, are credited with what invention? (Hint: Look to their city.)

571) *Give the Italian word,* now a part of the English language, that means a vent in the planetary crust from which molten or hot rock and steam issue.

572) *Because this culture's* ancient language has yet to be deciphered, archaeologists have been able to piece together a picture of everyday life in Etruscan times only by studying what?

573) *From a design* by sculptor Daniel C. French, the Piccirilli brothers hewed from marble a gigantic statue of this great president.
*Name this president and the Washington monument where it is on display.

574) *Name two* of the six major Italian dialects.

575) *This Italian-American* is considered the inventor of a new style of writing called "new journalism", in which the techniques of fiction are applied to the craft of nonfiction. He gained fame for his work, *Honor Thy Father,* which sold over 300,000 copies in a four-month time span.
*Name this well-known Italian-American author.

576) **The Prince,** often called the shrewdest, most audacious and infamous book ever given to the world, was written by whom and for whom?

577) *The 13th century Capulet palace,* with its balcony made famous by Shakespeare's immortal Romeo and Juliet, stands at 23 Via Capello. A mailbox there receives letters from all over the world addressed to the unfortunate lovers. *In what Italian city is it located?

578) *This English poet* and painter of Italian parentage was the driving force of the Pre-Raphaelite Brotherhood. When his wife died in 1870, he put a collection of poems in her casket, only to have her exhumed later when he found he had no copies. *Name this well known poet.

579) *What is the Italian word,* now a part of the English language, that means the trunk of a human body.

580) *This Italian mathematician* is considered the father of ballistics: the science of projectiles and weaponry. In 1537 his treatise, A New

Science, essentially invented and defined the science then referred to as gunnery. ***This mathematician was:**

 a) Niccolo Tartaglia b) Girolamo Cirutti c) Giovanni Martinelli

581) *What is the Italian word,* now a part of the English language, that means a soldier trained, armed, and equipped to fight on foot?

582) *Many regard him* as the greatest genius ever to have worked with marble. ***Who is he?**

583) *What Italian city* is home to Leonardo Da Vinci's *The Last Supper?*

584) *An Italian architect and painter* remodeled Florence's Palazzo Vecchio and built the world famous Uffizi Gallery—but his fame comes from his work as a biographer. In 1568, he published the second edition of *Lives of the Most Eminent Painters, Sculptors, and Architects,* which comprised 161 precise and meticulous biographies and a great deal of other valuable historical data of the period. This man of many talents is credited with inventing the discipline that is known today as art history.

*Identify this Tuscan who lived from 1511 to 1574.

 a) Luca Signorelli b) Giorgio Vasari c) Giovanni Lisanti

585) *D'Ancona Ciriaco,* a 15th century scholar, was an expert and enthusiast for antiquity during the Italian Renaissance. He is reported to have said of his journeys, "I go to awake the dead!"

 *This scholar was an early proponent of what academic discipline?

586) *Vince Marotta* invented the coffee filter and developed a better way to extract oil from coffee beans. He also invented the world's best-selling coffee maker. (Hint: Synonymous with Joe DiMaggio.)

*What is it?

587) *It was not until* the 16th century that third and fourth degree equations were solved by Italian mathematicians, Girolamo Cardano, Ludovico Ferrari, and Niccolo Fontana.

*These men contributed greatly to the advance of what mathematical discipline?

588) *What is the Italian word,* now a part of the Italian language, that means the working place of a painter, sculptor, or photographer?

589) *Leone Battista Alberti* invented the cipher wheel which was a device that encrypted text into an undecipherable code.

*By his work in this field, he established himself as a pioneer in what science?

590) *In the early 1970's,* her smile was unofficially valued at forty million dollars during a two month visit to Tokyo. *Who is she?

591) *This father and his two sons* defined the Venetian school of Renaissance painting and directly influenced the great artists Giorgione and Titian. The family that was responsible for the distinctly Venetian heritage of the High Renaissance of the late 15th to early 16th centuries. (Hint: Their first names were Jacopo, Gentile, and Giovanni.)
*Name this famous Italian family.

592) *Capulet and Montague* are the English names for two mythical families that resided in 14th century Verona. The feud between the two families has been immortalized in Shakespeare's *Romeo and Juliet.*
*Give the Italian names for these two families.

593) *Give the Italian word that means* fired clay, brownish orange in color, used for statuettes, vases, and roofing.

594) *Giovanni Schiaparelli,* an Italian astronomer and senator of the Kingdom of Italy, made extensive studies of Mercury, Venus, and Mars. In 1877, he observed peculiar markings on Mars.
*What were they?

595) *In the late 15th century,* he designed a system of canals around the city of Milan. *Who was he?

596) *Because of his discoveries,* it is now possible to study and evaluate the nerves and the nervous system. He received the Nobel Prize for Medicine in 1906. He also developed a method of staining cells with silver nitrate, which allowed the researcher to see clearly all the varied features of nerve elements. *Who was this medical scientist?
a) Antonio Scarpa b) Bruno Zanobio c) Camillo Golgi

597) *Give the literal translation* for the term carbonari.

598) *Born Michelangelo Amerighi* in 1573, he revolutionized Italian painting with his conception of light, color, and iconography, and infused the objects in his paintings with a degree of reality which was almost tangible. His naturalistic method earned him much opposition in his day, but his influence was important to such later painters as Rubens, Valazquez, Rembrandt, and George de la Tour. Typical of his best work

is the masterpiece, *Christ at Emmaus.* (Hint: Known by the name of his birthplace, a small town near Brescia in Lombardy.)
*Name this 16th century Italian artist.

599) *Who* discovered Saturn's rings?

600) *Although William Harvey* is credited with the demonstration of blood circulation, this Italian anatomist completed the scheme of blood circulation by demonstrating something Harvey never saw: capillary action. ***Name this famous scientist.**
a) Marcello Malpighi b) Lucien Sabella c) Nunzio Alioto

601) *What is the Italian word,* now a part of the English language, that means to organize rigidly, especially for the sake of regulation or control?

602) **The Aeneid,** an epic work by Virgil, glorified the legendary Trojan origin of the Roman people and endorsed the newly formed principate established by Octavius Caesar (later Augustus). It thus was greeted with enthusiasm by all educated Romans because of its nationalistic purpose.
*Name the hero of Virgil's poem.

603) *Cinzio Giraldi,* was a Ferrarese scholar and teacher who wrote plays, literary criticism, and a collection of 100 novelle called *Gli Ecatomiti,* which was later used by another author as a plot source for two of his plays, *Othello* and *Measure for Measure.*
*Who was the second author?

604) *This Italian-American sculptor* designed the John F. Kennedy Memorial Medal as well as 300 medallion portraits, including those of fourteen presidents. ***Name this Italian-American sculptor.**
a) Angelo Turrini b) Mario Pieri c) Ralph J. Menconi

605) *This Florentine humanist* wrote poetry, plays, moral and philosophical essays, and dabbled in the arts. He is particularly known for his treatise on painting, *Della Pittura* written in 1436. This three-volume work explained for the first time how to use the vanishing point and other techniques of the science of perspective developed by Filippo Brunelleschi. In his commentary on architecture, *De Re Aedificatoria,* he popularized Brunelleschi's innovations concerning the scientific study of vision and the use of ancient monuments as sources. This work, published in 1485, became known as the bible of Renaissance architecture and was the first printed book on the subject.

*Who was this individual often mentioned as the prototype of the Renaissance man? a) Leone Battista Alberti b) Domenico Attilio Alberti c) Luigi Marco Alberti

606) *Along with two colleagues,* this Italian-American won the Noble Prize in 1969 for discoveries concerning the replication mechanism and the genetic structure of viruses that set the solid foundation on which modern molecular biology rests.
*Who was this well known Italian-American scientist who was the former director of the Center for Cancer research at MIT?
a) Salvador Luria b) Claudio Manzzo c) Francesco Alberti

607) *Leonardo da Vinci* was the first to sketch a design for a parachute and a wing, a device that would allow man to realize the age old dream of flight. In 1948, an Italian-American by the name of Francis Rogallo devised a supple and flexible wing made of woven metal covered by a silicon base. ***What had he invented?**

608) *Filoteo Alberini* was an inventor and film pioneer who invented and developed the Cinetografo (Kinetograph), an apparatus capable of recording, developing, and projecting animated motion pictures. He also invented the Autostereoscopio, a 70 mm stereoscopic process and one of the first efforts to create a wide screen technique. ***What was the time frame in which these important innovations took place?**
a) 1885-1905 b) 1895-1915 c) 1905-1925

609) *What is the Italian word,* now commonly used in English, that means a commissioned officer in military service who ranks above a lieutenant general, and whose insignia is four stars?

610) *Rita Levi-Montalcini* has done research in tumor and nerve-cell growth which will lead someday to new techniques for battling cancer and regenerating damaged nerves. With a colleague, she discovered a protein from a tumor that could spur new nerve growth.
*For this discovery, she and her colleague were awarded the Nobel Prize in medicine in what year? a) 1961 b) 1978 c) 1986

611) *Ugo Cerletti and Lucio Bini* developed this medical technique in 1937. This psychiatric procedure is used to treat severe depression, manic depression, schizophrenia, and schizophrenic catatonia. It is recommended today by the American Psychiatric Association for patients who do not respond to drug therapy. Its effectiveness is indisputable.
*Identify the procedure.

612) *What is the Italian word,* now a part of the English language, that means a collapsible shade consisting of fabric stretched over hinged ribs?

613) *Name the Italian poet* and native of Ferrara, who wrote the first Renaissance pastoral drama, *Sacrificio* in 1554.

614) *Bernabo of Genoa* is a character in what classic work of Boccaccio?

615) *Antonio Scarpa* was the first physician to correctly determine that arteriosclerosis consisted of thickened lesions lining the walls of arteries. Because of this, another Italian was able to greatly advance the foundational knowledge of arterial flow, ligation, and torsion and move forward to make the enormous contribution he is credited for: the development of modern vascular surgery. ***Identify this medical pioneer who was born in 1800 in Pavia, Italy.** a) Luigi Porta b) Benedetto Castelli c)Franco Cesare

616) *Who carved* the famed Medici tombs in Florence?

617) *The daughter of an Italian poet* and political exile, this English born woman was one of the outstanding poets of the Victorian era. Her works include, *The Prince's Progress* and *Monna Innominata*.
                              *Can you name this poet?

618) *The wheel lock,* by producing its own sparks, enabled the early firearm user the freedom of not having to keep a wick or match constantly lit. It is also the direct ancestor of the present day bicycle chain, and its operating principle was applied to lock and watch making.
                     *Who was the inventor of the wheel lock?

619) *How many major dialects* are there in the Italian Language?
                                        a) 4 b) 6 c) 8

620) *What is the Italian word* that means a process of painting with an albuminous or colloidal medium (such as egg yolk), instead of oil?

621) *It was Leonardo Da Vinci* who first envisioned this flying machine. In 1877, Enrico Forlanini, another Italian inventor, constructed the first of its type, which rose to an altitude of 42-1/2 ft. and hovered in the air for approximately twenty seconds.
               *What early version of this machine had he created?

622) *A ray of light,* reflected off any object and passing through a small hole in a dark box, projects onto the opposite wall of the box the inverted image of the object. Using this phenomenon, the Neapolitan Giambattista della Porta, in 1593, constructed the necessary equipment to reproduce engravings. He would simply trace the outlines produced onto white paper. ***What was his invention called?**

623) *What beverage was first drunk* in Italy in 1640? It probably was introduced to Italy, and thereby the rest of Europe, by Italian merchants.

624) *This Italian physicist demonstrated* that a solid body will fall at a velocity that is independent of its mass, if the resistance of the air is discounted. In his work, *In Discourses* and *Mathematical Demonstrations Concerning Two New Sciences*, published in 1638, he formulated the principle of inertia. ***Who was he?**

625) *Born in the region of Calabria* in 1914, he emigrated to the United States in 1947. This virologist, through his pioneering research, has shown that the key to understanding and eliminating cancer lies in DNA research. The recipient of many academic honors and awards, he received the Nobel Prize in Medicine in 1975 for his research into cancer replication. ***Who is this distinguished scientist?**
a) Romano Buoncristiani b) Antonio Castellucci c) Renato Dulbecco

626) *The Milanese chemist* Manfredo was one of several to discover the secret process for making a hard, white, translucent ceramic.
*What had he discovered?

627) *Plavio Biondo,* a 15th century Italian historian, was the author of *Historiarum ab Inclinatione Romanorum Decades.*
*This was the first attempt by a historian to treat what subject?

628) *He was the first to think* of the concept for contact lenses. In his *Code On the Eye,* he described an optical method which would correct poor eyesight with small lenses in the eye. ***Name the Italian inventor.**
a) Leonardo Da Vinci b) Romano Della Santina c) Antonio Cocco

629) *In 1896,* the Italian A. Salimbeni developed, in concert with several foreign colleagues, a serum to neutralize an acute, infectious, often fatal epidemic disease characterized by diarrhea, vomiting, cramps, suppression of urine, and collapse.
*Name the disease for which this serum was made.
a) Cholera b) Yellow fever c) Maleria

630) *The first wireless* telegraph connection across the Atlantic was

accomplished on December 12, 1901 by an Italian inventor who, eight years later, received the Nobel Prize in Physics.   ***Who was he?**

631) *Francesco Bonaventura Cavalieri* was an Italian mathematician whose development of the geometry of indivisibles paved the way for the development of two mathematical inventions: integral calculus and differential calculus. These two branches of mathematics were to become critical to the many advances in science that followed their widespread dissemination and use.
*The time period during which this mathematician lived and worked was: a) 1425 - 1474 b) 1598 - 1647 c) 1700 - 1749

632) *Professor Dal Monte,* an international expert and specialist in aerodynamics, designed what vehicle that broke the speed record of 49.48 km/h in 1984?

633) *In 1811*, Amedeo Avogadro, professor of physics at the University of Turin, established a law that was subsequently named in his honor. In essence, his hypothesis was the first to make a clear distinction between atoms and molecules, one of the basic concepts in modern chemistry. (Hint: The hypothesis was not generally accepted until after Stanislao Cannizzaro, in 1858, constructed a logical system of chemistry based on it.)   ***What law is named after him?**

634) *Published in 1634,* his work—a collection of fifty stories written in the Neapolitan dialect—was one of the first European books of folk tales. Included in his book were such favorites as *Cinderella, Puss and Boots,* and *Beauty and the Beast.*   ***Name this famous Italian writer.**

635) *In 1786,* this anatomist noted in his laboratory in Bologna that, upon contact with two different metals, the muscles of a frog reacted convulsively. He understood that this contraction was due to the passage of an electric current. He concluded that animal tissue contained a previously unknown force which he called animal electricity. His discovery is deemed to be extremely important because it led to Alessandro Volta's invention of the electric battery, and is credited as being the genesis of all future developments in the science of electricity generation.   ***Who was he?**
a) Tomaso Barzoni b) Luigi Galvani c) Eduardo Massa

636) *This 13th century Italian theologian,* mystic, and scholastic philosopher placed more emphasis on faith than on reason, and is best known for his *Journey of the Mind to God.* (Hint: An American university

91

and city in New York are both named after him.   ***Who was he?**

637) *He is the author of* The Devils Own, and *The Kiss of Judas*. His novels are known for their hard-hitting action and intricate character development.   ***Name this popular Italian-American author.**

638) *According to legend,* the first to practice human body transplants were the Italian brothers, St. Como and St. Damian. It is perhaps due to this operation that the brothers were canonized and are the patron saints of surgeons.   ***What did they transplant?**

639) *In the year his work,* Algebra,was published (1572), this Italian mathematician invented complex numbers of imaginary roots.
          *Who was he?

640) *This small Italian town,* which lies southeast of Florence, was the birthplace of five monumental Italian historical, cultural, and scientific figures: the writers, Petrarch and Giorgio Vaspari; the physician, Francesco Redi; the botanist, Andrea Cesalpino; and the music theorist, Guido Aretinus.   ***Identify the Tuscan town.**
          a) Montepulciano b) Cortona c) Arezzo

641) *Born in Bologna Italy* in 1618, this Italian mathematician worked in the fields of astronomy and physics. He is credited with the discovery and definition of light diffraction as a specific, quantifiable result when light rays bend or are deflected as they pass some obstacle. This proved to be an important basic development in the sciences of astronomy, physics, and medicine, and it served to advance improvements in telescopes, microscopes, and other optical devices that use lenses and light.   ***Who was this Italian?**
          a) Francesco Grimaldi b) Antonio Cattani c) Stefano Scarpa

642) *The Roman gourmet, Apicius,* compiled and wrote a type of book that is probably found in almost every home.
          *What type of book is it?

643) *Who is credited with establishing* the custom of the Christmas nativity scene?
          a) Pope Julius II b) St. Francis of Assisi c) St. Thomas Aquinas

644) *Guglielmo Marconi* was born in what Italian province?
          a) Bologna b) Lombardy c) Tuscany

645) *Born in Padua in 1655,* Bartolommeo Cristofori would

revolutionize music with an invention that would change how people played and listened to music from that period forward. (Hint: The most versatile instrument in the realm of music.)

*What had Cristofori built in 1709?

646) *In 1855, before Pasteur,* an Italian zoologist demonstrated that microorganisms can act as infectious agents in disease.

*Name this famous scientist.

647) *Who was the first* to use Italian rather than Latin in scientific works?

648) *In 1928,* Louis Giliasso filed a patent for a submersible barge. It was constructed in 1933 and named after its Italian-American inventor.

*How was this invention primarily utilized?

649) *The late Leo Buscaglia* wrote what best selling book that helped people live their lives better?　　a) Living, Loving and Learning
　　　　　　　　　　　　　　　　　b) The Art of Living
　　　　　　　　　　　　　　　　　c) My Life To Share

650) *Known in Rome for his epigrams,* which were terse, witty, and often paradoxical, he published his first book to celebrate the opening of the Coliseum. His epigrams have come down to us in fifteen books, and present a graphic picture of life and manners in first century Rome.

*Name him.
a) Martial b) Ovid c) Horace

651) *In 1862,* A. Giovanni Caselli, an Italian physicist, was the first to reproduce fixed images that had been transmitted over a distance.

*What is this invention called?

652) *Giuseppe Franzoni,* one of the founding fathers of American art, was the first carver of what famous American symbol?

653) *Emilio Segre received* a Nobel Prize in physics in 1959. He was a pupil, close friend, and collaborator of what internationally known Italian scientist who came to work and live in the United States during World War II?

654) *Derived from the Latin "I see,"* this term is part of television terminology.　　***What is the word?**

655) **The Fortunate Pilgrim,** beautifully written and insightful, is considered one of the finest novels about Italian-American colony life. The

author's first novel, *The Dark Arena*, was published in 1955.
*Identify this successful Italian-American author.

656) *A Greek born on the island of Sicily,* he is regarded as the greatest scientific mind of antiquity. He is credited with the invention of pi.　　　　　　　　　　　　　　　　　　　　***Name him.**

657) *Identify the Italian lyric form of verse,* whose subject matter could be political, satiric, or humorous, was popular during the Middle Ages and the Renaissance. It was employed by poets such as Dante, Petrarch, and Boccaccio.　　***What was the name of this verse form?**

658) *Italian poet,* librettist, and composer, he wrote the libretti for Verdi's *Otello* and *Falstaff.*　　　　　　　　　　　***Who was he?**

659) *A close friend of Chopin,* his principle operas are *I Puritani* and *La Sonnambula.*　　　　　　　　　　　　　　***Who was he?**

660) *Father Charles Pise* was the first Roman Catholic priest of Italian extraction to be born in America. The year was 1801. Twenty eight years later, he was responsible for accomplishing another first. (Hint: Father Pise was an author.)　　　　　　　　　***What was it?**

661) *Hailed at the time* as the greatest writer since the Renaissance, this Italian author is remembered for his masterpiece, *Il Promesso Sposi* (The Betrothed), written in 1827. The importance of this modern-style novel was that it defined the Italian language as we know it today, and helped to form a unified Italy. Such was his stature in Italian society that, at his death in 1873, Giuseppe Verdi wrote his brilliant *Requiem* in this author's honor.　　　　　　　　　　　***Identify this author.**
　　　　　　a) Italo Fellino b) Enrico Scatena c) Alessandro Monzoni

662) *Italian anatomist and student of* Gabriel Fallopius, he is remembered for his work concerning blood circulation and fetal development. As a professor at the University of Padua, he greatly influenced the English physician, William Harvey, who discovered the exact nature of blood circulation and the heart's role as a pump for circulating blood throughout the body.
*Identify this anatomist who was born in 1537.
　　　　　a) Girolamo Fabrizio b) Andreas Vanzetti c) Octavio Visconti

663) *Born* Tomasso di Giovanni di Simone Guidi in 1401, he is regarded by many as the greatest Florentine Renaissance painter of the 15th century. His most important work is the *Tribute Money* in the Brancacci chapel

of the Carmine church in Florence. Because of his occasional clumsiness, absentmindedness, and carelessness, he was given a nickname by which we know him today. (Hint: The name is an abbreviation of his first name Tomasso (Masa), which was combined with the pejorative suffix - acchio, meaning big clumsy, sloppy, or bad.) ***Who was he?**

664) *Such was his fame* as an artist that he was mentioned in glowing terms by his contemporaries, Dante, in *The Divine Comedy*, and Boccaccio in *The Decameron*. His impact was so great in the realm of art that he is credited indisputably for defining what we know as modern western art. For more than six centuries he has been revered as the father of modern art and the first of the great Italian painters. (Hint: Known by his first name, his surname was di Bondone.)
*Identify this great artist who was born near Florence in 1276.

665) *Benvenuto Cellini* was born in Florence in 1500. This Italian goldsmith and sculptor received high praise from contemporaries such as Michelangelo, who said, "I have known you all these years as the greatest goldsmith of whom the world has ever heard." However, it is from another area that he is celebrated and remembered. Because of it, we know Celini more intimately than any other figure of his time. ***What did he leave us?**

666) *Robert Gallo, M.D.,* a research scientist and virologist in Maryland, co-discovered what virus in 1984 and developed a blood test to screen for this disease?

HISTORY, GEOGRAPHY, & BUSINESS

History, Geography, and Business

667) *Name the Italian American* who gave the electrifying keynote address at the 1984 Democratic National Convention in San Francisco.
a) Geraldine Ferraro b) Mario Cuomo c) Joseph Alioto

668) *Identify the island,* off the coast of Tuscany, where Napoleon lived in exile from May 1814 to March 1815.

669) *Name the son* of Genoese immigrants who founded one of the largest and most successful financial institutions in the world. He is also credited with inventing branch banking. (Hint: His first two names are Amadeo Pietro.)

670) *Founded by successful businessman* Jeno Paulucci, what progressive Italian-American organization is involved in a multitude of cultural and educational programs, and is headquartered in Washington D.C.?

671) *What country,* located in northern Italy and covering approximately 24 square miles, dates from 885 AD and is considered the oldest republic in the world?

672) *Amerigo Vespucci* discovered this country, located on the northern coast of South America, and named it "Little Venice" in the Venetian dialect. ***Name this country.**

673) *From 1936 to 1943,* Italian-American mayors guided the affairs of three of the most important and largest cities in the United States.
*Name one of the cities and its mayor.

674) *What Italian statesman,* along with Giuseppe Mazzini and Giuseppe Garibaldi, was primarily responsible for creating the United Kingdom of Italy in 1861.   a) Camillo Cavour b) Stefano Spignesi c) Rudolfo Giovanniello

675) *Segments of Philip Mazzei's letter* to an American statesman were used in 1776 to write the Declaration of Independence. It was this Italian who first said, "All men are by nature equally free and independent . . . each equality is necessary in order to create a free government. All men must be equal to each other in natural law."
*Name the American statesman.

676) *The bishop of Milan,* in 374 AD, laid the foundation for medieval conceptual thinking on the relationship between church and state.
*He was: a) St. Aquinas b) St. Ambrose c) St. Damasus

677) *These Italian-American brothers* started a company that became the world's largest shipper of fresh fruit.
a) DelMonte b) Costa Brothers C) Di Giorgio

678) *What Italian explorer* is credited with the founding of Isabella, the first European city (now deserted) in the New World, located in the Dominican Republic?

679) *Filippo Toschi,* a merchant from Tuscany, settled in Northern California in the late 19th century. Among his many business enterprises, he arranged the importation of what popular olive oil from his native Tuscany to California?

680) *Regarded as the George Washington* of Italy, he led 1,000 volunteers, known as Red Shirts, in the conquest of Sicily, which led to the establishment of the Kingdom of Italy in 1861.   ***Who was he?**

681) *At the dawn of the 20th century,* the Italian government considered what U.S. city to be the "model colony" for Italians in America?   a) New Haven b) San Francisco c) Chicago

682) *From 568 to 774 AD,* what German tribe ruled most of northern Italy? An Italian region is named for them and the city of Milan lies

within its borders.   ***Identify the region.**

683) *Many experts estimate* that the number of Italian- Americans who served in the armed forces of America during World War II was:
a) 150,000 b) 375,000 c) 550,000

684) *What Florentine statesman,* historian, and political theorist, in response to the foreign invasions and the anarchic state of Italy in his time, wrote his most famous work, *Il Principe* (The Prince, in 1513), advocating the establishment and maintenance of authority by any effective means? (Hint: His name has become synonymous with political intrigue.)

685) *Marine gunnery sergeant* John Basilone was the first U.S. enlisted man during World War II to receive what commendation? (Hint: For his heroism at Guadalcanal where he single-handedly killed 38 Japanese soldiers.)

686) *At the time of Pearl Harbor,* Italians were the largest European-born immigrant group in the United States according to the 1940 U.S. Census.   ***That number was:**
a) 450,000 b) 985,000 c) 1.6 million

687) *What percentage of Italians,* during the great flood of immigration between 1875 and 1920 came from areas south and east of Rome known as the Mezzogiorno which emcompasses the regions of Abruzzo, Campania, Apulia, Basilicata, Calabria, and Sicily?
a) 60% b) 78% c) 90%

688) *Archaeological evidence* from the 4th century BC points to these people as the first to make pasta as we know it today.
a) Chinese b) Etruscans c) Romans

689) *Who was the first* modern European to actually reach the North American continent? (Hint: We know him by his English name.)

690) *School teacher and journalist,* he and his Blackshirts seized power in Italy with their "March on Rome," in 1922. (Hint: Parents named him after the Mexican revolutionary, Juarez.)

691) *Name the second largest island* in the Mediterranean, whose capital, Cagliari, was founded 3,000 years ago.

692) *Campi Flegrei* and the Bay of Pozzuoli lie to the west, Mount Vesuvius and the towns of Pompeii and Herculaneum to the east.

*Name this ancient Italian city.

693) *Name the key figure* in the Italian Risorgimento, who founded the patriotic group, Giovane Italia.

694) *This company,* based in Modesto California, is responsible for a high percentage of the total U.S. wine production.
*Identify this well-known company.

695) *The patriot, Pasquale Paoli,* was elected president of this island during its struggle against Genoa, and forced to resign after Genoa sold the island to France in 1768.   *Identify the island.
a) Corsica b) Sardinia c) Sicily

696) *Many are familiar* with the great air disaster of 1937 when the dirigible, Hindenburg, burst into flames as it was about to land at Lakehurst, New Jersey. Fifteen years earlier at Norfolk, Virginia, a giant dirigible, built by Italy for the U.S. Army, was involved in the greatest air disaster to befall American military aeronautics to that time. Hitting a high tension wire, the ship exploded into flames with the result of 34 dead.   *Name that airship.
a) Italia b) DaVinci c) Roma

697) *This medieval traveler* from Venice journeyed to Asia in 1271 as a merchant with his father and uncle. He stayed for almost seventeen years in China and neighboring lands in the service of the great Kublai Khan. He escorted a Chinese princess to Persia in 1292 and returned to Venice in 1295.   *Who was he?

698) *A variation of the Italian card game,* "primero," is what popular game played in the United States? a) Canasta b) Poker c) Hearts

699) *Revolt against the French conqueror* of Sicily, Charles I of Anjou, during the hours of vespers on Easter Sunday, 1282, resulted in the massacre of 2,000 French officials. (Hint: Name has a religious connotation.)   *Name the event.

700) *Identify the ancient Italian tribe* from which Italy derived its name.

701) *In the national U.S. census* taken in 1990, Italian-Americans ranked in population, at what number in comparison to other ethnic groups?   a) 5th b) 8th c) 11th

702) *In the 9th century* these invaders introduced cotton, sugar cane,

100

and citrus fruits (oranges and lemons) to Europe by way of Sicily. They were expelled by the Normans in the 11th century.

*Who were these people?

703) *Who was the first* European explorer to set foot on the mainland of South America?　　　a) Columbus b) Vespucci c) Cabot

704) *After the voyages of* Columbus, Cabot, and Vespucci, North America still remained unexplored and virtually unknown. (Hint: A bridge in the state of New York is named after him.) ***Can you name its true discoverer and the last of the four great Italian explorers?**

705) *This former congresswoman* from New York was nominated as the Democratic party's vice-presidential candidate in 1984.

*Who is she?

706) *Due to the discoveries* of John Cabot, King Henry VII of England named the discovery "New Isle."　　　***He later renamed it what?**
a) Nova Scotia b) Newfoundland c) Halifax

707) *In 1978,* A. Bartlett Giamatti, who later became commissioner of baseball, was appointed president of what prestigious Ivy League university. (Hint: President Bush's alma mater.)

708) *Name the major mountain range* located through most of central Italy.

709) *In 1908,* Charles J. Bonaparte founded what United States federal department?　　a) FBI b) IRS c) Department of Weights and Measures

710) *Italy invaded* Abyssinia in the 1930's.
*What is the modern name for this country?

711) *Name the four seas* that surround the Italian peninsula.

712) *The Capitoline Museum* in Rome is the oldest of its kind in the world.　　　***What is it?**

713) *In 1738,* after being lost for seventeen hundred years, these two ancient cities were rediscovered and unearthed near Naples. ***Name one.**

714) *In 1837,* John Phinizy (Finizzi) was the first known Italian-American to be elected as mayor of a major U.S. city.　***The city was:**
a) New Orleans b) Augusta c) Newark

715) *The only active volcano* on the European mainland is:

a)Mt. Etna b) Stromboli c) Mt. Vesuvius

716) **Peter Caesar Alberto** is regarded the first Italian to reside in Brooklyn. At the time of his residence, in 1639, the city was known by what name?

717) **What Italian island** has been called the "Jewel of the Mediterranean"?   a) Sicily b) Capri c) Sardinia

718) **Who offered Giuseppe Garibaldi** a commission of major general in the United States army?

719) **What judge's historic ruling** that executive privilege did not take precedence over constitutional requirements—forced President Nixon to hand over tapes and other material subpoenaed by the grand jury during the Watergate scandal?

720) **In 1588, Alexander Farnese,** the Duke of Parma, commanded an army that was to join an invincible fleet assembled by King Philip II of Spain for the invasion of England.   ***Name this ill fated fleet.**

721) **As acting head** of the Italian government, he accepted the "Conditions of Armistice" offered by General Dwight D. Eisenhower, commander of Allied Forces, on Sept. 3, 1943.
                              *Who was this Italian leader?
            a) Italo Balbo b) Benito Mussolini c) Pietro Badoglio

722) **Censure Beccaria** was an influential 16th century Italian penologist who opposed two forms of punishment common for his time.
                                              *Name one of them.

723) **The son of Sicilian immigrants,** he was born in Trenton, New Jersey in 1936. A graduate of Georgetown University and Harvard Law School, he taught law at both Stanford and the University of Chicago, and served as U.S. Assistant Attorney General and U.S. Court of Appeals. ***Name this first Italian-American to serve on the U.S. Supreme Court.**

724) **The infamous Borgia family** that rose to prominence during the Renaissance in Italy were not Italian. ***Name their country of origin.**

725) **Its leader once said,** "We wed thee, O sea, in token of perpetual domination." The year was 1177 and henceforth, this city was known as the "Bride of the Sea."   ***Name this Italian city.**

726) *This early Italian explorer* can be credited as the discoverer of the region now known as Illinois. ***Identify him.**
a) Enrico Tonti b) Amadeo Pucci c) Leone Ruggera

727) *As allies in the Holy League* organized by Pope Pius V, Venice and Spain defeated what invincible aggressor at the famous sea battle of Lepanto in 1571?

728) *Immigration statistics kept since 1820* show that Italy, in sending more than 5.3 million persons to America, was the second largest contributor of foreign-born U.S. citizens outside the western hemisphere. ***What European nation ranks first?**

729) *This symbol of the British empire* first appeared on a Roman coin around 161 AD. The figure reappeared on the English copper coin in the reign of Charles II in 1665. (Hint: She rules the waves.)

730) *Born Giovanni Bernardone,* his father changed his name to Francisco. He is known to the world by another name. ***Identify him and the U.S. city that was named after him.**

731) *What U.S. president* signed the Johnson-Reed Immigration Act that drastically limited Italian immigration to the U.S?

732) *Especially known* for its Blue Grotto and phosphorescent waters, this popular tourist resort island is off the coast of Italy not far from Naples. ***Name the island.**

733) *This 18th century Venetian* adventurer's name is synonymous with romance. He enjoyed his greatest success in Paris where he was appointed director of the state lottery and was in contact with such luminaries as Mme. Pompadour and King Louis XV. (Hint: New house.)

734) *After the American Civil War,* Italian immigrants comprised the largest foreign-born group in these two southern states. ***Identify one of these states.**

735) *Andrea Sbarbaro* founded what famous colony in California?

736) *As the wife of Henry II* of France, she was the Italian born queen of France and the great granddaughter of Lorenzo de Medici. Much of French cuisine owes its origin and refinements to her. ***Name her.**

737) *By 1930 he controlled 30%* of the banking business in California. By 1948 his bank had become the largest banking institution in the U.S. He also made major contribution to the growth of the American motion picture industry by authorizing loans to such filmmakers as Charles Chaplin, Mack Sennett and Darryl Zanuck.

*Name this banking icon.

738) *He single-handedly changed* the way business and government interact. In 1979, because of his lobbying, Congress passed the Loan Guarantee Act. This enabled the government to loan his company 1.2 billion dollars, thus saving the company and tens of thousands of jobs. The ten year loan was fully paid back to the government in three years.

*Name this Italian-American business giant.

739) *Milliners* were the hat makers of what Italian city?

740) *He started with a $4.50 peanut roaster* and a sign that said, "Obici, the Peanut Specialist." By 1930, 90% of all peanut production in the U.S. passed through his nut company.

*Identify this familiar company.

741) *We all know that venetian blinds* come from Venice, that roman candles are from Rome, and that neapolitan ice cream is from Naples. ***Off of what coast were sardines first caught commercially?**

742) *This organization was established* in 1905 in New York by Vincent Sellaro. It was initially founded as a fraternal insurance association. Today, it can boast of having over 2,500 lodges across the U.S. (Hint: Its logo is the lion which symbolizes the organizations strength and loyalty.)

743) *When this luxurious ocean liner* collided with the freighter Stockholm in 1956, 1,600 people were rescued and 52 were lost. (Hint: The ship was named after a famous Genoese admiral.)

744) *During the 1920's,* Italian-American women became the largest single group of workers in what U.S. industry?

745) *The Italians claim that in 1565,* Bernardo Buontalenti, at the request of Cosimo de' Medici, invented a concoction of cold cream, zabaione, and fruit.

*As we know it today, what had Buontalenti invented?

746) *His archaeological discoveries on Cyprus,* where he served as U.S. Consul, were the richest to that time and numbered in excess of 35,000 items. His book, *Cyprus, Its Ancient Cities, Tombs and Temples,* chronicled his tremendous discoveries ***Name him.**

a) Stefano Scarpa b) Joseph Marconi c) Luigi Palma Di Cesnola

747) *Her son debased the family name* by striking the first letter 'B' to form the word "orgy" in Italy.   ***Who was this woman?**

748) *She was the first U.S. citizen* to be canonized a saint in the Catholic church. Born in the region of Lombardy in 1850, she arrived in America in 1889 and was noted for her charitable work among neglected Italian immigrants. She was directly responsible for establishing 67 hospitals, schools, orphanages, and sanatoriums in the U.S.
*Who was she?

749) *Three luxurious cruise ships* of the Italian Line were named after three men who excelled in a particular field. Name the field and one of the men. (Hint: These famous men lived during the Renaissance period.)

750) *Felix Pedro,* born Felice Pedroni, was a prospector who discovered gold in 1902 in Alaska. The news of his discovery resulted in the founding of what major Alaskan city?   a) Fairbanks b) Nome c) Anchorage

751) *This son of Giovanni Caboto* (John Cabot) sailed on voyages of exploration for both Spain and England.   ***Name him.**

752) *Antonio Pigafetta* was one of twenty three Italians to accompany this Spanish explorer on man's first voyage around the world in 1522.
*Name the Spanish explorer.

753) *John Pastore* was the first Italian-American to serve in what U.S. governmental body?

754) *Naples* takes its name from the Greek "Neapolis."
*What is the English translation?

755) *The great flood of Italian emigration* to the United States began in what year? (Hint: This is the period from which most Americans of Italian heritage originate.)   a) 1850 b) 1870 c) 1880

756) *Name one of the two* great Italian cities located on the banks of the Arno river.

757) *What Italian American* was chairman of the House Investigating Committee during the Watergate crisis?

758) *One of the most famous flights* in early aviation history took place in July of 1933 and lasted 47 hours and 52 minutes. General Italo

Balbo, of the Italian air force, led 24 Savoia-Marchetti seaplanes in a mass transatlantic flight which covered 6,100 miles from Orbetello, Italy to what mid western U.S. city?

759) *In 1933,* he became the first Italian-American mayor of New York city.   ***Who was he?**

760) *Lottery games originated* in what northern Italian city with the concept being attributed to Benedetto Gentile?

a) Genoa b) Venice c) Trieste

761) *This language in its classical form* has survived and flourished in jurisprudence, literature and the Catholic church. It is the basis for Italian, French, Spanish, Portuguese, and Romanian. Though the English language is Germanic in origin, at least one-third of its words are derivatives of this language.   ***What is it?**

762) *Fifteenth century Italy* witnessed a revival of the creative spirit. This phenomenon, which sprung from central Italy, was primarily an attempt to recapture the greatness of the ancient Greeks and Romans. In Italy it is known as the Rinascimento. ***How is it pronounced in French?**

763) *Identify one of two* Italian Renaissance men considered by many to be the greatest intellects ever produced by mankind.

764) *George Delacorte* started this publishing house which eventually grew into one of America's largest. Twenty-five magazines list him as Chairman of the Board, and he is the largest comic book publisher in the country.   ***Identify his company.**

a) Random House b) Dell Publishing c) Ballantine Press

765) *Fileno Di Giorgio* formed his United Lens Company in 1916 and now it is the largest independent manufacturer of lens blanks for the optical industry in the world. His company was started with how much of a capital investment?   a) $500 b) $2,000 c) $5,000

766) *Ralph DeNunzio,* at the age of thirty-one, is the youngest man to ever have been elected to this position of president in its 192 year history.   ***Name this major U.S. business exchange.**

767) *The Italians were the first* to use this eating utensil 100 years before it appeared in England.   ***What was it?**

768) *Ross D. Siragusa* founded what major U.S. corporation that used a naval term as its company name. (Hint: Top naval officer.)

769) *In 1946,* a model named Micheline Bernardi introduced this type of bathing suit at a Paris fashion show.   ***What was she wearing?**

770) *Jeno Paulucci pioneered* the field of canned Chinese food when he formed the successful Chun King brand. He also started Jeno's, Inc., which made frozen pizzas and other Italian specialities.
*He was responsible for founding what influential Italian-American organization?   a) UNICO b) Italian Heritage Foundation
c) National Italian-American Foundation

771) *The earliest mention of the word* that describes this article of clothing dates from 1567 and appears to be a corrupt form of the word genoese. Pants of a twill cotton fabric were manufactured in Genoa and worn by seamen.   ***What is the common word used today to describe this article of clothing?**

772) *A leading "trust buster" lawyer,* this former and very popular two-term mayor of San Francisco made sports history with his suit against the NFL representing the Oakland Raiders.
*Name this son of Sicilian fishermen?

773) *What Italian-turned-Frenchman* made the city of Lucca in Tuscany a principality for his sister Elisa in the early part of the 19th century?

774) *Decimus et Ultimus Barziza,* a dashing Confederate officer in Hood's Texas Brigade during the American Civil War, became a brilliant criminal lawyer after the war and served two terms in the Texas legislature.
*What does his first name translate into from the Latin?

775) *The beautiful Lipari Islands,* to which the volcanic island of Stomboli belongs, is located off what coast of Italy?

776) *When this San Francisco restaurant opened* in 1937, the baseball playing owner was depicted on a neon sign.   ***Name him.**

777) *In 1849,* this Italian left a successful confectionery business in Peru to seek his fortune in the gold fields of California. Like many others, his luck in the gold fields proved unsuccessful, forcing him to return to what he knew best, chocolate. His San Francisco factory now houses many restaurants and exclusive boutiques and is a major tourist attraction located near San Francisco's Fishermen's Wharf.
*What major chocolate company did he establish in San Francisco?

778) **The birthplace** of this famous Italian admiral was Imperia, a popular winter resort on the Italian Riviera south of Genoa. (Hint: An ill faded luxury liner was named in his honor.) ***Who was he?**

779) **What city** is graced by the grand arch of Titus?

a) London b) Palermo c) Rome

780) **Can you name two** of the past three Italian-American mayors of San Francisco? (Hint: The most recent was felled by an assassin's bullet.)

781) **What is the largest** single-person residence in the world?

782) **Can you identify** the best known leader of the Free-Speech movement of the 1960's? (Hint: First name was Mario and he spoke from the steps of a Berkeley University building.)

783) **What terrorist group** kidnapped and murdered Italian Premier Aldo Moro?

784) **What Italian city** hosted the 1960 Summer Olympics?

785) **What famous Roman fountain** was featured in the motion picture, "*Three Coins In the Fountain?*"

786) **What volcanic peak** can be seen from Naples?

787) **In 1887,** Bishop Giovanni Scalabrini founded the Apostolic College of Priests to prepare the Italian clergy for work in America. However, the American Catholic Church was firmly controlled by what other ethnic group, which was very reluctant to see Italians tended by Italian clergy. They insisted that they were not qualified to "Americanize" the immigrants. ***Who was this other group?**

788) **Can you identify** the "*Island of Dreams?*"

789) **In the 1890's,** Salvatore Oteri, a native of Palermo, operated a company that was described as the largest importer in the world of tropical, foreign, and domestic fruit and nuts. He was one of several Italian-Americans responsible for developing the fruit trade from South America. ***What southern U.S. port city served as his company's headquarters?**

a) Miami b) New Orleans c) Galveston, Texas

790) **What famed strip of land** is a fifteen minute boat ride across the Venetian lagoon from Venice?

791) **Marco J. Fontana** was the founder of the Marca del Monte canning company. ***What is it known as today?**

792) *What are* Briscola and Scopa?

793) *Ferruccio Lamborghini,* known for his contributions to automotive design, has now turned his attention to one of Italy's oldest pursuits. ***What is he doing?**

794) *What is* the symbol of Venice?

795) *Major Anthony Martini,* in a 15-minute dog fight over the skies of this French city, shot down 22 Nazi aircraft. ***Identify the city.**
a) Calais b) Le Havre c) Paris

796) *Name either the city or the country* in which the Pope was residing when Dante wrote *"The Divine Comedy."*

797) *After thirteen terms in Congress,* this Italian-American became the House Judiciary Chairman. ***Who was he?**

798) *Identify the river* that flows through Rome on its way to the Mediterranean.

799) *U.S. Senator Patrick Leahy's* mother's family, (Zambons) is from northern Italy.
*What state does the honorable Senator Leahy represent?

800) *Name the system of government,* led by Benito Mussolini, that exercised a dictatorship of the extreme right— typically through the merging of state and business leadership— and featured a belligerent nationalism.

801) *On July 26, 1934,* the chancellor of this European nation was assassinated by Nazi agents. To insure this nation's independence, 75,000 Italian troops were mobilized and the Italian war fleet put to sea. This show of military power temporarily caused Germany to withdraw and cancel its plans. ***The country involved was:**
a) Czechoslovakia b) Belgium c) Austria

802) *What is* the English translation for the term, "Il Duce?"

803) *In America,* as well as in Italy, this room served as the focus for the family and its ritual gatherings for sharing food, wine, and talk.
*Identify the room.

804) *Television political correspondent* John Scali began reporting from Washington DC in 1961. A prestigious award created in his name is given to television reports which approach his degree of excellence.

*With what television network was he associated?

a) ABC b) CBS c) NBC

805) *Name the group of languages* derived from the spoken Latin of the Roman Empire.

806) *This color was created* in and takes its name from, an important northern Italian silk town. ***Identify this Italian city.**

a) Siena b) Magenta c) L'Aquila

807) *What is meant* by the Italian term "condadini?"

808) *The world's longest suspension bridge* was named after this Italian explorer. (Hint: New York State.) ***Who was he?**

809) *Vittorio Scialola,* a leading statesmen and jurist, collaborated in the drafting of the charter for what organization that became the forerunner of the United Nations?

810) *For their heroics* during the American Civil War, Luigi Palma di Cesnola, Joseph E. Sova, and Orlando E. Carunana received what military decoration?

811) *What is the city of Modena* famous for besides being Luciano Pavarotti birthplace?

812) *What percentage* of World War II veterans were Italian-Americans? a) 12% b) 19% c) 25%

813) *Eroded by wind and water,* these limestone mountains in the eastern section of the North Italian Alps, have assumed fantastic shapes and peaks.***What is the name of this famous Italian mountain range?**

814) *He stated unequivocally* that the Americas were indeed a "new world," and not part of Asia. In 1507, a German geographer and cartographer, Martin Waldseemuller, published a map that recommended that this "new world" discovery be named after him.

*Identify this Italian who was born in Florence in 1454?

815) *Handguns manufactured* in this Tuscan town in the 16th century gave us what word that is used to describe this type of weapon?

816) *The head of the Italian state* is referred to as the Prime Minister. **True or False?**

817) *During the early 1920's* this American automobile manufacturer

was quoted as saying, "Every time I see an Alfa Romeo pass by, I raise my hat."   ***Who was he?***

818) *What form of government* has Italy had since World War II?

819) *What was the last post held* by Umberto II of the House of Savoy?

820) *The late Joseph Bernadin* was elevated to the position of Cardinal in the Catholic Church while he was Bishop of what major U.S. city?   a) New York b) Chicago c) Los Angeles

821) *Menswear designer Angelo Litrico* supplied the shoe that was pounded on a desk during a United Nations assembly by what feared world leader? (Hint: "We will bury you!")

822) *Born Alfred Emanuele Ferrara,* he was the first Italian-American governor of New York (1919), and the first Italian-American presidential candidate. His paternal grandfather was born in Genoa in 1808. (Hint: This "happy warrior" and four term mayor of New York lost to Herbert Hoover in the 1928 U.S. presidential election.)
                                                          Who was he?

823) *In 1951 the term* "Grand Tourismo" or Grand Touring was first used to describe this company's new model. Today, "GT" still refers to a comfortable, luxurious, well-appointed automobile with sporting characteristics .   ***What Italian car company coined this term?***
                                        a) Lancia b) Fiat c) Alfa Romeo

824) **In 1946,** Michael Musmanno was appointed by President Harry S. Truman to be one of the presiding judges at the International War Crimes Trials in Nuremberg. In the 1920's, he also served for seven years on a team of lawyers that defended two men accused of murder. Though contrary evidence was presented that indicated the defendants were innocent, the pair was executed in 1927. Throughout the world, many felt that the trail was less than fair and that they were convicted for their radical, anarchist beliefs rather than for the crime for which they were tried. We know this trial by the men's two last names. ***Who were they?**

825) *This Italian American served* as Secretary of the Navy during the Theodore Roosevelt administration and in 1906 was appointed U.S. Attorney General. (Hint: Same surname as the leading figure in Corsican history.)   ***Who was he?***

826) *Enrico Berlinguer* had been a member of the Italian chamber of deputies since 1958, and became secretary general of this political party in 1972.
*Identify the political party he headed.
   a) Socialist Party b) Communist Party c) Christian Democratic

827) *In 1908,* Giulio Gatti-Casazza, previously of La Scala, became general manager of what internationally known U.S. opera company?

828) *In 1900,* Andrew Houston Longino was elected governor of what southern U.S. state?   a) Mississippi b) Georgia c) Arkansas

829) *They were promoted as* "The Greatest Human Phenomenon Ever Seen Alive." The Scientific American commented, ". . . probably the most remarkable human twins that ever approached maturity." The above comments refer to Giovanni and Giacomo Tocci, twins born in Turin, Italy on July 4th, 1875.   ***Why were they unique?**

830) *As the Arabs of today* have made a fortune in oil, a thousand years ago, the Venetians made their fortune in what substance?
        a) Salt b) Wine c) Marble

831) *What American president* was an acknowledged Italophile?
        a) James Monroe b) Thomas Jefferson c) Abraham Lincoln

832) *In the great wine producing region* of Napa, California, the vineyards of the historic Inglenook Wine Estate were divided in 1964. In 1975, this Italian-American purchased one half of the divided estate that included the original founder's home (Gustave Niebaum) and 1600 acres of vineyards. In 1995, he purchased the remaining front vineyard and restored the Inglenook Chateau, thus re-establishing the estate to its original historic dimensions. The wines produced at the estate have received much critical acclaim for their excellence.
   *Identify this well known and much admired Italian-American.
        a) Robert DiNiro b) Francis Ford Coppola c) Sylvester Stallone

833) *The Italian city of Trento* was the site of a council called by Pope Paul III in 1545. The "Council of Trent" met there for a period of eighteen years and launched what movement?

834) *Once a main route of invaders,* this lowest of the Alpine passes now channels throngs of visitors into Italy. ***Can you name this pass?**   a) Brenner Pass b) St. Bernard Pass c) St. Gotthard Pass

112

835) *What was the number* of passages made by Columbus to the New World?   a) One b) Three c) Four

836) *Luigi Antonini is considered* one of the most prominent Italian-American labor leaders in the history of American trade unionism.

*Identify the union he organized?
a) Ladies Garment Workers'
b) Steel & Mine Workers'
c) Transportation Workers'

837) *The world's best known opera house* was completed in 1778 and accommodates 2,800 persons. The adjoining museum contains mementos of the many famous composers, conductors, and artists who have performed there.

*Name either the opera house or the Italian city it is located in.

838) *At one point* in the 7.2 mile Mt. Blanc tunnel link with this country, motorists drive beneath a mile and a half of solid rock.

*Name the connecting country from Italy.
a) Austria b) Switzerland c) France

839) *The glacier-formed lakes* of this Italian district have attracted vacationers since Roman times.   ***Identify this Italian region.**
a) Piedmont b) Lombardy
c) Venetia

840) This jurist, during the Watergate scandal of 1973, was Time magazine's "Man of the Year."   ***Who was he?**

841) *She was the first woman* in Italy to receive a medical degree. However, she is better known for her innovations in the field of education. She developed methods of teaching children that emphasize a child's initiative and freedom of expression. Today, schools that use her methods are scattered throughout the western world.

*Name this Italian educator or the school she founded.

842) *On April 28, 1945,* Italian anti-fascist partisans captured this deposed leader and his mistress trying to escape into Switzerland. After a brief trial, they were executed.   ***Who was he?**

843) *The Immigration Act of 1924* was aimed at sharply reducing immigration from southern and eastern Europe. Italians who had poured into the United States by the hundreds of thousands each year were assigned what quota after 1924?   a) 3,845 b) 6,315 c) 15,000

844) *This city came under Austrian control* in 1382, and in 1719, began 235 years as a free port. A Yugoslav-Italian agreement in 1954 gave Italy administrative control over the city.
*Identify the city located in the Adriatic near Venice.

845) *Secchi de Casale* not only founded one of the most successful Italian-American agricultural communities, located in southern New Jersey and called Vineland, but also founded the first Italian-American newspaper, *L'Eco D'Italia*.. ***In what major U.S. city did this occur?**
a) New York b) Philadelphia c) Boston

846) *Galileo lectured* at its 13th century university. Dante, Petrarch, and Tasso studied there. Giotto decorated the Scrovegni Chapel with a series of 38 frescoes depicting the history of Christian redemption.
*Name the Italian city in which this all took place.

847) *This city was home* of the Stradivari, Amati, and Guarnieri families, makers of the world's most honored violins, violas, and cellos.
*Identify the Italian city in which they lived.
a) Cremona b) Piacenza c) Mantova

848) *Stately buildings* recall this city's past glories as an independent republic. In the 11th century, the city ranked with Genoa, Venice, and Amalfi as a maritime power.
*Name this Tuscan city, known for one of its towers.

849) *The last major eruption* of Mt. Vesuvius occurred in what year
a) 1932 b) 1944 c) 1959

850) *The birth of Petrarch* (Francesco Petrarca) in 1304, through the death of Titian (Tiziano Vecelli) in 1576, is generally regarded as the historical milestones that mark the beginning and the end of what unprecedented period of enlightenment and invention?

851) *This Italian is regarded* by many as the man who first developed the scientific method. He was born in the Italian city of Pisa in 1564 and is responsible for many ground breaking contributions to the sciences of physics, astronomy, mechanics, mathematics, timekeeping, entomology, hydrodynamics, and cartography. ***Who was he?**

852) *In 1941,* President Franklin D. Roosevelt praised this Italian for his contributions to the Declaration of Independence. In 1980, the U.S. Postal Service issued a stamp commemorating the 250th anniversary of his birth. His ideas influenced Thomas Jefferson and became the cornerstone for the most important document in the history of the United States. ***Who was he?**

853) *The Palio delle Contrade* is a medieval pageant that is staged in this Italian city every year. It begins with a colorful procession and culminates with a horse race around the paved square.
*In what Tuscan city does this take place?
a) Lucca b) Viareggio c) Siena

854) *He recognized—or perhaps discovered—*the fact that copper wire had the ability to transport sound. In 1849, he constructed a primitive telephone consisting of simple diaphragms placed at both ends of an eight foot length of copper wire hooked up to a battery. By the mid-1850's, an improved version of this telettrofono, ran through his home on Staten Island. This was twenty-six years before Alexander Graham Bell presented his invention at the Philadelphia Exposition in 1876.
*Name this Italian-American inventor.
a) Antonio Meucci b) Anthony Petruzzi c) Giovanni Lusardi

855) *It is a mountainous area* which stretches from the Adriatic to the highest peaks of the Apennines. Its central region contains the Italian National Park where the few bears, wolves, and other wild animals that remain in Italy are allowed to live peacefully under the protection of the law. ***Identify this region.**
a) Umbria b) Abruzzo c) Latium

856) *This Piedmontese city* serves as the center of Italy's automotive industry. ***Identify the city.**
a) Turin b) Saluzzo c) Milan

857) *Homer described sinister humor* as sardonic because, according to legend, a bitter herb grown here caused death by laughter.
*Where was this herb supposedly grown?

858) *This former Italian-American congressman* from New York's 24th district was the most decorated police officer in the United States. ***His name is:**
a) Mario Biaggi b) John Bizordi
c) Matteo Tarini

859) *Born in Palermo, Italy,* he was elected mayor of New York City in 1950 on the Experience Party Ticket. In defeating the nominees

of both the Democratic and Republican parties, it was the first such victory in the history of the New York mayority that goes back to 1665.

*Name him.

860) *Cagliari is the capital* of what Italian province that is surrounded by water?

861) *Four Italians were present* in the vicinity of this famous American battle that took place in 1876. John Martini, a trumpeter was the last man to see his commander alive. Also in the vicinity were Augusto DeVoto, Giovanni Casella, and Lieutenant Charles DeRudio. All four survived this infamous massacre. ***Identify the battle.**

862) *Founded in this Italian city* in the 11th century, it is the home of Europe's oldest university. ***Identify the city.**
a) Padua b) Bologna c) Verona

863) *Located in the state* of Massachusetts, this city was the largest textile manufacturing town in the world. On January 12, 1912, the textile mills of this town went on strike. The strike was organized and lead by Italians, and their victory for more humane working conditions and better wages marked a turning point in the history of American labor.

*Identify this famous strike.a) The Cambridge Strike b) The Lawrence Strike c) The Worcester Strike

864) *Capri, Ischia,* and the glorious coastline around Sant'Agata, Positano, Amalfi, and Ravello make this one of the most beautiful tourist areas in the world. ***What Italian region is being described?**

865) *Almost half the world's production* of bergamot comes from this region in Italy. The fruit of the bergamot tree furnishes an oil that is used as a perfume.***Identify the Italian region which cultivates this fruit.** a) Sicily b) Calabria c) Basilicata

866) *The Italian immigrant* responsible for America's leading brands of ready-to-eat spaghetti dinners, pizza, sauce and pasta, was Ettore Boiardi. During World War II, his company was the largest supplier of rations for the U.S. and Allied forces.

*Identify this familiar American company.

867) *Italian merchants* by the name of della Borsa are credited with establishing the first Stock Exchange in the Belgium city of Bruges, at the end of the 14th century. Before moving to Belgium and changing

116

their name to van der Bourse, they lived in what Italian city?

a) Genoa b) Venice c) Florence

868) *This Italian churchman* founded the Vatican museum, began the construction of St. Peter's, and employed the finest artists of the time, including Raphael, Bramonte, and Michelangelo. He died in 1513. (Hint: He is remembered as the "warrior" Pope.) ***What was his name?**

869) *This nationally known* attorney's client list has included such celebrities as Errol Flynn, Mae West, Tony Curtis, and Lee Harvey Oswald and his assassin, Jack Ruby. During the late 1960's, he even appeared in a Star Trek television episode. (Hint: This now deceased lawyer was known as the "King of Torts.") ***Who was he?**

870) *Giovanni Buitoni* brought his family's business to America after World War II. In 1952, he opened a state of the art manufacturing facility for his company in Hackensack, New Jersey. A plaque at the entrance of his plant reads, "In fond memory of my beloved and unforgettable parents, who taught me the religion of God and the religion of work."

*What type of business is the Buitoni family involved in?

a) Construction b) Food c) Furniture

871) *World renowned fashion designer* Oleg Cassini was born in Paris and graduated from the Academia Belle Arti in Florence. He moved to the United States in 1936 and became a noted designer for Paramount Pictures and Twentieth Century Fox.

*He gained both national and international prominence when he designed clothing for what First Lady?

872) *John Volpe* was named Federal Highway Administrator by President Eisenhower in 1957. He was elected governor of Massachusetts in 1961 and 1965. He was appointed to what cabinet post by President Nixon, where he is generally credited with turning the tide against air pollution?

873) *Italy's buttero* are a vanishing breed. From the wide open spaces of the midlands and parts to the south, their territories have dwindled to a corner of Tuscany's badlands. (Hint: Sergio Leone used them in his movies.) ***What is an Italian buttero?**

874) *On this island,* immigrants to the United States were subject to medical examinations and interrogations to determine if they had violated any of the strict immigration laws. Many early Italians referred to this island as Isola delle Largrine or Island of Tears.   *Name the island.

875) *The San Gennaro Festival* is a popular celebration for Italian-Americans in New York City.

*San Gennaro is the patron saint of what Italian city?
a) Rome b) Palermo c) Naples

876) *In 1972* the Justice Department, after years of protest from Italian-American groups, stopped using terms that defamed all Italian-Americans in their media descriptions of organized crime.

*Identify one of the two terms.

877) *An offer by a king* took Leonardo Da Vinci to this country in 1516 where he stayed until his death in 1519.   *Identify the country.

878) *The founders of both* Blimpie and Subway Sandwich chains are Italian-Americans. Blimpie has over 2,000 location and is in 13 foriegn countries. Subway has 13,136 locations and is in 64 countries.

*Match these successful companies with their founders'.
a) Anthony Conza b) Fred De Luca

879) *He served in the army* of the short-lived Roman Republic and, upon its defeat, escaped to the United States, where he became a naturalized citizen. He later returned to his homeland in order to help secure the eventual unification of Italy.

*Who was this great Italian military leader?

880) *Colonel Albert G. Albertazzie,* as the commander of U.S. Air Force One, was the first pilot in 20 years to land in this country when he flew Henry Kissinger there in 1971.   *Name the country.

881) *After 1890,* the heaviest concentrations of Italians were in the cities of the American Northeast. **In 1930, New York City had how many persons of Italian birth or parentage?**

a) 483,000 b) 768,000 c) 1,070,000

882) *Three Italian Americans were promoted* to the rank of brigadier general in the Union army during the American Civil War. They were Enrico Fardella, Eduardo Ferrero, and Francis Spinola.
Which of the three was a celebrated Union war hero, and elected to the U.S. Congress from New York after the war?

883) *Identify the famous* Florentine family that rose to prominence on the wings of economic power and widespread cultural activities during

the Italian Renaissance.

884) *On January 15, 1954,* this Italian-American sports legend and his famous movie star fiancee were married at San Francisco's City Hall.

*Who was he?

885) *Some authorities claim* that this term is an acronym for Morte alla Francia Italia anela (Italy desires France's death). It is linked historically to the Sicilian Vespers and their attempt to drive the French out of Sicily. ***Identify the term.**

886) *The first war in the 20th century* in which Italy participated was waged against what country? a) Tunisia b) Austria c) Turkey

887) *In his book,* The Twelve Caesars, written in the second century AD, what historian relates the fascinating, sordid, and juicy details that let us see these men as people rather than dry historical figures?

a) Plutarch b) Suetonius c) Josephus

888) *Philip Mazzei's* historic four-volume work, *"Studies of the Historical and Political Origins of the United States of North America,"* was the first accurate history written of America. What year was this work completed? a) 1779 b) 1788 c) 1799

889) *What treaty in 1929* recognized Roman Catholicism as the sole religion of the state of Italy? a) The Lateran Treaty b) The Religious Acts Treaty c) The Vatican Treaty

890) *Generoso Pope* came to the United States in 1904 from Benevento Italy. Starting out as a railroad laborer, he later worked for and eventually, in 1925, bought out a small construction company. He proceeded to turn this company into the largest supplier of building materials in the U.S. In 1929, he purchased *Il Progresso Italo Americano*, the long established Italian daily newspaper, with his son, Fortunato, becoming its editor. His other son, Generoso Pope Jr., became the publisher of what popular national newspaper that today can be found at every supermarket check out in the country?

891) *Antonio Monteleone* started the first shoe factory in this city at the turn of the century. He later diversified into real estate and the hotel business. His grand hotel still stands, and is one of the famous hostelries in this city's unique neighborhood quarters. ***Identify the city.**

a) Buffalo b) Philadelphia c) New Orleans

892) *As of 1997,* Italian-Americans held the two top positions in the Federal Bureau of Investigation (FBI). The Deputy Director of the FBI is William J. Esposito.   ***Identify the current head of the FBI, whose mother is an Italian-American.**

893) *His tally of 30 downed enemy aircraft* in 1944 made him the highest scoring fighter pilot in American history and earned him the title "Ace of Aces." Allied commander, General Dwight D. Eisenhower called him "a one-man air force." German Reichsmarshall Herman Goering remarked that he would gladly trade two Luftwaffe squadrons for "the Italian Gentile and his wingman, Godfrey." ***Identify this great Italian-American war hero who was born in Piqua, Ohio in 1920 to Italian immigrants.** (Note: Abruzzese father and Sicilian mother.)

894) *Peter F. Secchia* chaired a conference in 1998, featuring the following speakers: Thomas Foglietta, Marisa Lino, James Rosapepe and Peter Tufo.   ***What do Mr. Secchia and the people listed have in common?**

895) *Charles Albert,* king of Sardinia-Piedmont, vainly sought to lead the unification of Italy. After granting representative government in his kingdom, he declared war on what country to secure Italy's unification? After the defeats at Custozza in 1848 and Novara in 1849, he abdicated and died in exile in Portugal.

896) *St. Benedict founded* a monastic community here in 529 AD. The rules he composed for this community have served as the basics for Christian monastic organizations. (Hint: During World War II, the ancient monastery, located south of Rome, was totally destroyed by artillery and air bombardments.)   ***Identify the famous monastery he founded.**

897) *What was first distilled* in the year 1000 AD at the Salerno School of Medicine in the region of Campania, Italy?

898) *John Pastore* was the biggest vote-getter in the history of what state?   a) Rhode Island b) Vermont c) New Jersey

899) *Columbus* opened the New World on October 12, 1492, by sighting what island?

900) *His father, John Cabot (Giovanni Caboto),* is credited with the discovery of the North American continent. Cabot's son was an outstanding cartographer and explorer who attemped, in vain, as did his

father, to locate the Northwest Passage. ***Name the son.**

901) *He was defeated* and driven from his African kingdom by the Italian occupation of 1936-41. (Hint: His title was Emperor.)
*Identify this ruler.

902) *Former U.S. Senator Alfonse D'Amato* represented what state in the U.S. Senate?

903) *John Zaccaro* is the husband of this respected and nationally known politician from New York. To date, she is the only woman ever to be nominated for this national office.
*Identify the woman and the office for which she ran.

904) *In 1968,* Francis J. Mugavero was ordained Bishop of a New York diocese. He was the first ecclesiastic of Italian extraction to achieve the highest office of what may be one of the greatest dioceses in the world.
*Identify this diocese.
a) Manhattan b) Queens c) Brooklyn

905) *The puppet state* known as the Republic of Salo was headed by what Italian leader?

906) *In 1967,* this Italian-American congressman accomplished a goal that honored all Americans of Italian extraction by having Columbus Day established as a national holiday. (Hint: He represented the state of New Jersey.) ***Who was the congressman?**

907) *Il Progresso* was established in New York City in 1889 by Charles Barsotti. ***What was *Il Progresso*?**

908) *Colonel Leonetto Cipriani* headed the Italian Consulate established in San Francisco to care for Italians on the west coast.
*What year did this Consulate open? a) 1850 b) 1872 c) 1885

909) *Born on the island of Sicily,* he was the leading citizen of the ancient city of Syracuse and known as "the father of mechanics." (Hint: We associate him with Greece.) ***Who was he?**

910) *Senator Dennis De Concini* represented what state in the U.S. Senate? a) New Mexico b) Colorado c) Arizona

911) *Whose innovations in technique* and design gave Italy its early lead in European textile manufacturing and made textiles the chief export item of the Italian city-states during the Renaissance? (Hint: This

invader was expelled from southern Italy in the 11th century.)

912) *As a missionary and cartographer,* Eusebio Cino explored and charted much of the American southwest. His most significant work was to prove that California was not an island. Apart from his explorations, this priest founded twenty missions, of which the best known is located near Tucson, Arizona. ***Identify the religious order to which he belonged.** a) Dominican b) Jesuit c) Franciscan

913) *Who said,* "If we do not free and unite the whole of Italy, we shall never achieve liberty in any part of her?"
a) Giuseppe Verdi b) Filippo Mazzei c) Giuseppe Garibaldi

914) *This island takes its name* from the Siculi, whom the ancient Greeks identified as the native residents of the island.
*Name the island. a) Sardinia b) Stromboli c) Sicily

915) *In 1910,* The Society for Italian Immigrants, based in New York, was aiding new arrivals to America by protecting them from thieves and swindlers and giving them food and shelter for fifty cents a day until they could find work. ***Who subsidized this agency?**
a) The Catholic church
b) The Italian government
c) New York State government

916) *Giovanni Verrazanno* first named it Cape Pallavicini in honor of a famous Italian general.
*By what do we know this well known landmark today?
a) Cape Nantucket b) Cape Cod c) Cape Fear

917) *In 1890,* after a decade of struggle, this wine producing community, with Pietro Rossi as its chief wine maker, became an enormous success. Within the next decade, it acquired its own national marketing system and began receiving international acclaim. The company is still headquartered in Asti, California, the name given it by its founder.
*Identify the wine company.
a) Sabastiani b) Robert Mondavi c) Italian Swiss Colony

918) *Name the joint sovereigns* of Spain to whom Columbus first approached with his plan of a short-cut sea route to India.

919) *This city became the capital* of the Western Roman Empire in 404 AD. After the wars against the Goths, it was made the seat of the Byzantine government in Italy in 584. ***The city is:**

a) Ancona b) Pesaro c) Ravenna

920) *What mountain range* separates Italy from the rest of Europe?
*Name them.

922) *Benjamin Biaggini* was the president of what major U.S. Railroad?   a) Southern Pacific b) B & O Railroad c) Amtrak

923) *Sailors from this Italian city,* plying the highly profitable east-west trade routes, brought the plague from the Crimea to the Sicilian port of Messina in 1347. The plague would repeat in cycles all over Europe for the next 400 years. However, the first epidemic was by far the worst—killing at least a third of Italy's ten million people between 1347 and 1351. ***Sailors from what city brought the plague to Italy?**
a) Venice b) Pisa c) Genoa

924) *When the Italian Renaissance* was at its zenith in the late 15th century, what scion of Italy's most powerful banking family ruled Florence and nurtured its painters, sculptors, and architects to new heights?

925) *This Italian dialect* became more accepted as the standard of the land when Dante wrote Italy's first major literary work in the vernacular rather than in Latin.   ***Identify this Italian dialect.**

926) *He was threatened with torture* by the Vatican in 1633 for insisting that the planets revolved around the sun.
*Who was this Italian genius?

927) *In the first half* of the 7th century BC, a strange and mysterious people settled in the area now known as Tuscany. This eastern-flavored culture is responsible for planting the first seeds of civilization on the Italian peninsula, and for giving an early settlement called Rome its first hint of grandeur.   ***Identify these early settlers of Italy.**

928) *From Britain to Armenia,* this mighty empire counted at least 50 million subjects. Its capital numbered over one million citizens.
*Name this empire.

929) *Music lovers across Europe* welcomed a new art form popularized in Italy in 1607 by Claudio Monteverdi's, *Orfeo*.
*Identify this new art form.

930) *Italian fashion designers* lead the world in this field. From the following list, who was tragically shot and killed outside their home in

Beverly Hills in 1998? Gorgio Armani, Valentino, Renato Balestra, Gianni Versaci, Gianfranco Ferre, Daniela Zanetti, Maurizio Gucci, Carla Fendi, or Raffaello.

931) *Who did Niccolo Machiavelli have in mind* when he wrote that political leaders often must "operate against integrity, against charity, against humanity, against religion"?

932) *His music stirred nationalistic pride* to the point where patriots adopted as their unofficial anthem the soaring *"Chorus of Hebrew Slaves"* from his 1842 opera *Nabucco.*   ***Who was this Italian Composer?**

933) *Doctors and priests,* baffled by the fast moving plague racing through Italy in the 14th century, urged healthy citizens to eat garlic and leeks and pray to this patron saint of plague victims.   ***Identify him.**
                    a) St. Felix b) St. Stephen c) St. Rocco

934) *The Italian nation* is broken down into regions in the way the United States is broken down into states. There are nineteen regions with ninety-three provincial capitals.   ***Identify six Italian regions.**

935) *Marble from the Carrara quarries* in what Italian region is considered the best white marble for the sculptor's chisel?

936) *One of Italy's major industries* takes place in Genoa, Trieste, La Spezia and Castellamare, south of Naples.
    *What major construction takes place in these Italian port cities?

937) *What is the* "*Fratelli d' Italia,*" written by Goffredo Mameli?

938) *It was reported in 1997* that Italians drank an average of 17 gallons of wine per year in comparison to 1.7 gallons for their American counterparts.***Identify the number of gallons of wine produced in Italy every year.**   a) .95 billion b) 1.55 billion c) 2.1 billion

939) *Within ten million,* what is the current population of Italy?

940) *In what year did Mussolini* come to power in Italy?
                    a) 1919 b) 1922 c) 1925

941) *Only after WWI* was the final unification of Italy achieved. What treaty gave Italy the last two northeastern Italian regions under Austrian rule, Venezia Tridentina and Venezia Giulia?

942) *What former police chief* and mayor of Philadelphia was known for his "Law and Order" stance?

124

943) *Antonio Pasin* began making small red wagons in 1917 from wood. He named them the Liberty Coaster after the Statue of Liberty. Ten years later, he began using steel instead of wood and renamed the wagon. Today, the family-held company produces up to 8,000 wagons per day. ***Identify the wagon or the company that Antonio Pasin's grandson, Robert Pasin still heads today in Chicago.**

944) *In 1890, Giuseppe Airoldi* is credited with inventing a word game that is found in most newspapers across the world
*What did he invent?

945) *Cardinal Eugenio Pacelli* came to San Francisco on October 28, 1936 to bless the recently constructed Golden Gate Bridge.
*By what other title was he later known?

946) *Italian-American WW II hero* Anthony Damato was honored by the U.S. Navy when they named a ship after him. ***What was it?**
a) Destroyer b) Cruiser c) Aircraft Carrier

947) *Sardinia* lies nine miles south, across the Strait of Bonifacio, of what former possession of Genoa that was sold to France?

948) *It was known as* the League of Lodi and it established a twenty-five year non-aggression pact signed by the major city states of Italy. It was negotiated by Venice and is regarded as the first triumph of modern diplomacy. ***What year did this occur?** a) 1235 b) 1454 c) 1519

949) *What Italian city* serves as Italy's chief commercial and industrial center? a) Turin b) Milan c) Rome

950) *In 1381,* Venice won its Hundred Years War against what rival city-state? a) Genoa b) Pisa c) Amalfi

951) *What political machine* was defeated when Fiorello La Guardia was elected mayor of New York in 1933?

952) *What eastern European* country did Italy invade in 1939?

953) *The Allies opened* their campaign against Italy in World War II by capturing the island of Pantelleria off the coast of Sicily.
*The date when this occurred was:
a) August 1942 b) January 1943 c) June 1943

954) *What does the Latin* designation AD stand for in the Christian calendar?

955) *In 1414,* the de' Medici family became the bankers of what institution?

956) *The Elettra,* named after Guglielmo Marconi's youngest child, was the ship he used to test the best longitudes and latitudes for sending what type of signals?

957) *In what Italian region* is Lake Como located?

958) *What term is often used* to describe the area south of Rome that occupies the former Kingdom of Naples?

959) **La Dauphine and Matthew** were associated with the Italian explorers, Giovanni Verranzano and Giovanni Coboto (John Cabot)
*Who or what were they?

960) *Frank Carlucci* was named by President Reagan to head what important federal agency?
a) National Security Council b) The FAA c) The FBI

961) *What Italian city's* subway system is called the Metropolitana?

962) *Name the world's* largest Cathedral and its precise location.

963) *What city served* as Italy's capital for the newly founded Kingdom of Italy between 1865 and 1871?

964) *As Assistant Secretary of State,* Joseph Sisco served as chief American negotiator for this troubled part of the world during the mid-1970's. He was respected by all sides for his candor, impartiality, and knowledge.   ***What part of the world was this?**

965) *In ancient times,* the most important Greek colonies were located in southern Italy and Sicily.
*What was the name given by the Greeks to describe this region?

966) *In 313 AD,* Roman emperor Constantine issued the Edict of Milan.
*What did this edict grant?

967) *What regional capital,* which overlooks the Strait of Messina, offers a spectacular view of the Sicilian coast from Messina to Mount Etna?   a) Catanzaro b) Reggio di Calabria c) Melito di Porto Salvo

968) *Ancona, Pescara, Bari, and Brindisi* are Italian port cities located on what sea?

969) *Angelo "Charlie" Siringo* once arrested Billy the Kid and also

pursued such legendary outlaws as Butch Cassidy and The Sundance Kid. ***What famous detective agency did he work for?**

970) *His forebearers in Italy* invented the vegetable bearing their family name by crossing Italian rabe with cauliflower. (Hint: Deceased at the age of 87, he produced all but one of the 17 James Bond films to that time.) ***Who was he?**

971) *In 1908,* one of the worst natural disasters in modern European history took place when the Italian cities of Messina and Reggio di Calabria were destroyed with over 100,000 dead. (Hint: They are port cities located at the strait of Messina.) ***What destroyed these cities?**

972) *In 1224,* this Italian holy man and saint of the Catholic church was the first known person ever to receive stigmata—which occured two years before his death. Stigmata is the phenomenon of bleeding from the hands, feet, and side, which Christ suffered at the crucifixion.
*Who was he?

973) *Simply rememberd in Italian history* as The Four Days, the people of this Italian city during World War II launched an all-out offensive against the German occupying forces. They blew up tanks with home-made bombs and attacked German soldiers with knives and clubs, ultimately forcing the Germans to withdraw from their city.
*Identify the city of these valiant and heroic people.
a) Palermo b) Naples c) Reggio di Calabria

974) *During his first term as mayor,* crime in his city dropped 41 percent, the largest sustained decrease in the nation and the lowest rate in this city since the 1960's.
*Identify this Italian-American mayor or the city he presides over.

975) *Ella Tambussi Grasso* was the first American woman elected governor in her own right and the first Italian-American woman in Congress. ***Identify the state she so greatly served.**

976) *Leonard Riggio* is the founder and CEO of the largest book store chain in the U.S. The second largest is headed by Robert F. DiRomualdo. America's largest book publisher is chaired by Alberto Vitale. Steve Geppi is the owner of the world's largest distributer of English-language comic books—with 52% of the market share. Steven Florio is president of a major magazine publishing house that includes such titles as Vogue, Vanity Fair, Glamour and Gentlemen's Quarterly.

*Match the following companies with its chairman.
a) Barnes and Noble b) Random House c) Conde Nast
d) Diamond Comic Distributors, Inc. e) Borders

977) *In 1945,* Army colonel Henry A. Mucci, a graduate of West Point and a native of Bridgeport, Connecticut, led a force of 400 Army Rangers and Filipino guerrillas 30 miles behind Japanese lines to rescue 511 men (mostly American) held in a Japanese prison camp. They were the survivors of what infamous three-day, 65 mile forced march at the beginning of World War II?

978) *What pope* was known as The Warrior Pope and was responsible for creating the Vatican museum?

979) *What is the name* of the period known as "the golden age of Roman literature," which covered the reign of Augustus Caesar?

980) *Their art shows* influences from Greece, Egypt, Syria, Cyprus, and Mesopotamia, and it, in turn, influenced Roman art. The Greek historian, Herodotus, asserted that they came from Lydia in Asia Minor ***Who were these mysterious people who settled in north central Italy?**

981) *Joseph V. Toschi,* born in Lucca, Italy in 1915, arrived to San Francisco in 1928 at the age of fourteen. He is one of the foremost authorities in his field, and has developed methods and utilized long forgotten techniques employed during the ancient Egyptian and Renaissance periods. ***Identify the field of this brilliant innovator.** (Note: Authors step-father.)

982) *He was the son of a Florentine* leather craftsman. As a young man, he went to Paris and then to London, where he gained an appreciation of cosmoploitan culture, sophistication, and aesthetics. Returning to Italy, he opened his first retail store in Florence in 1920 at the age of thirty-nine.***Identify the man or his company that is synonymous with beautifully crafted artisan products.**

983) *Fabiola Fabia* was a wealthy Roman society woman of the 4th century AD. She is credited with establishing the first hospital and hospice in the Western world. She committed herself to the Christian concept of caring for the sick and the dying in a loving, charitable, and selfless way. ***What honor was bestowed upon Fabiola for her work by the Catholic Church?**

984) *Michelangelo* worked on this project from 1508 to 1512. It covered 6,000 square feet and included nine scenes from the Book of Genesis. ***What was it?**

985) *The Romans invented* the first cipher based on substitution— the so-called Julius Caesar method. What is the art of writing called which entails writing in or deciphering secret code?

986) *In what year did* Giovanni de Dondi create the first astronomical clock? In addition to the time, it showed the phases of the moon and the signs of the zodiac. a) 1152 AD b) 1291 AD c) 1364 AD

987) *In the early part* of the 16th century, Vincenzo Peruzzi of Florence was the first jeweler to cut this stone to make brilliants, by inventing the 58-facet form. ***What stone had he cut?**
a) Ruby b) Diamond c) Emerald

988) *The first pair* are reputed to have appeared in Pisa in 1291. The inventor is attributed to be a Dominican monk by the name of Alessandro Spina. ***What had he invented?**

989) *What did Albert Sacco, Jr.,* the chairman of the chemistry department at Worcester Polytechnic Institute in Massachusetts, do on the shuttle, *Columbia,* in 1995?

990) *Gaetano Lanza,* born in 1848 to Sicilian immigrants, founded the engineering department at what prestigious institution in Massachusetts, where he taught mechanical engineering for 36 years? An inventor, he developed the first wind tunnel in 1909.
*Identify the institution.

SPORTS

Sports

991) *He is the only driver in history* to win Daytona 500 (1967), Indy 500 (1969) and Formula One world championship (1978).(Hint: Son Michael is also a top driver.)   ***Who is he?**

992) *What Italian-American baseball player* is only the third player in baseball history to go directly to the major leagues from college baseball?

993) *The 1986* College Football National Championship came down to two teams.***Name either the Italian-American coach (Sports Illustrated, Sportsman of the Year) or the star quarterback (1986 Heisman Trophy Winner) who opposed him for this coveted title.**

994) *This Italian-American baseball player* hit two home runs his first two times at bat in World Series play. During the 1972 Series, he hit a total of four home runs to tie Babe Ruth's record. (Hint: Catcher for an American league team.)   ***Name him and his team.**

995) *Fireman Jim Flynn* (Andrew Chiarglione) was the only man ever to knock out this boxing great (Feb. 1916). (Hint: Was heavyweight champion from 1919 until 1926 when he lost title to Gene Tunney.)
                    *Can you identify his opponent?

996) *Italy's total Oylmpic* medal standings of 445 medals through the '96 Games, (Summer Games) ranks them in what position with other nations? (166 Gold, 135 Silver, 144 Bronze.)   a) 6th b) 10th c) 14th

997) *In his playing days,* he was one of the Seven Blocks of Granite at Fordham University. As a professional football coach, he was the personification of endurance in American sports. He has the second highest winning percentage in the NFL at .740.

*Name this legendary football coach.

998) *Body builder Angelo Siciliano* migrated to Brooklyn with his family in 1904. In 1922, he was named the *World's Most Perfectly Developed Man.* In 1929, he began a correspondence course to teach others how to develop their bodies. Most of us over the years have seen these advertisements of the 97 lb. weakling getting sand kicked in his face by the big bully. (Hint: Last name taken from ancient Greek titan who supported the weight of the heavens with his head and hands.)

*By what other name do we know this man?

999) *The 1965 home run king* in the American League, this promising baseball superstar's career was cut short by a devastating injury. (Hint: Played for the Boston Red Sox.)   ***Who was he?**

1000) *He managed Willie Mays* and the great Giant teams of the 60's. He ended his career as a manager of the 1979 Chicago Cubs. (Hint: Another name for hot dog.)   ***Who was he?**

1001) *The Italian community* of San Francisco's North Beach district produced three of the New York Yankees' most outstanding baseball players.   ***Name two of the three.**

1002) *In the late 1930's* this Italian-American revolutionized the game of basketball. He may have been the first to popularize the behind-the-back dribble, but he is known for making famous an even more startling innovation - the one-handed shot. He played college basketball at Stanford University where he was a three time All-American (1936-38).***Identity this Italian-American athlete who also pioneered the jump shot.**

1003) *Identify the great Hall of Fame* football player who played defensive end for the New York Giants from 1956 to 1964.

1004) *Known as hockey's Mr. Clutch,* he helped the Boston Bruins win the Stanley Cup in 1967 and was the first to break the 100 point barrier in 1969. He led the league in goals for six consecutive seasons, in points five times, and assists three times; and was voted MVP in both 1969 and 1974.   ***Who is this great Italian-American hockey player?**

1005) *He was The Voice of NFL films.* His narrations gave NFL

highlight films a sense of the dramatic that thrilled football fans of all ages. (Hint: Top televison news anchor for many years from Philadelphia.)
*Who was he?

1006) *This sport* is the second most popular team sport in Italy behind soccer. Next to the United States, its league offers the best competition in the world.   ***The sport is:**   a) Baseball b) Basketball c) Bowling

1007) *Italian World cup soccer teams* have won three world titles. Their last victory, in 1982 (cup play is every four years), caused dancing in the streets on both sides of the Atlantic.
*Who did the Italians beat in the championship final?
a) Germany b) Argentina c) Brazil

1008) *In 1925,* International Grand Prix racing began awarding a world championship title.
*Who was the first winner?
a) Alfa Romeo b) Lancia c) Ferrari

1009) *Known as much for his braggadocio* as his crackling fast ball, he once promised to strike out Johnny Bench four times in a game. Known as *The Count*, he was the National League Rookie of the Year in 1975, hit a home run in his first official major league at-bat, and pitched a no-hitter in 1976. (Hint: Broke in with the San Francisco Giants.)
*Who was this pitcher?

1010) *What Italian-American baseball manager* won five division titles and one World Series in the 1980's? (Hint: Claims his blood runs blue.)

1011) *This billiard legend,* who passed away in 1993, once pocketed 526 balls without a miss. He won the World Billiard Championship 15 straight times between 1942 and 1956.   ***Who was he?**

1012) *Born Angelo Merena, Jr.* in 1921, he has trained and managed fifteen world champions, including Mohammed Ali, Sugar Ray Leonard, and Jimmy Ellis.   ***Who is he?**

1013) *Born Harry Christopher Carabina,* he was a popular baseball radio announcer from 1945 until his death in 1997. He achieved celebrity status as the Chicago Cubs' radio announcer by singing, *Take Me Out To The Ballgame* with Wrigley Field Cub fans.
*Who was this popular baseball commentator?

1014) *With his sights set on Olympic gold,* this Italian-American won the 1986 World Figure Skating championship.   *Name him.

1015) *Chris Corchiani* of NC State, with 1,038 of them, is second only to Bobby Hurley of Duke in this all-time NCAA college basketball category.   *What is the category?

1016) *This Italian-American* is a two time world figure skating champion and an Olympic silver medalist.   *Who is she?

1017) *Named the 1984 Female Athlete* of the Year, she won an Olympic gold medal for women's all around gymnastics.
     *Who is this this dynamic Italian-American gymnist?

1018) *He was the first* of only four players to win all four Grand Slam golf titles in a career.   He was joined by Ben Hogan, Jack Nicklaus and Gary Player. *Who was this great Italian-American legend who is credited with inventing the sand wedge in 1931?

1019) *A. Bartlett Giamatti,* the distinguished past president of Yale University, became the 12th president of a 110-year-old national institution.   *Identify the institution.

1020) *Besides being Italian,* what do Yogi Berra, Roy Campanella, Joe DiMaggio, Tony Lazzari, Ernie Lombardi, Phil Rizzuto, and Tommy Lasorda all have in common?

1021) *What Italian-American baseball player* shares the record for most grand slams in one season? (He is a "true" gentleman and he did it for Baltimore in 1961.)

1022) *Along with three others,* he shares the record for hitting four consecutive home runs in a game.*Name this beloved Cleveland player.

1023) *There are only two catchers* who ever won a batting title, and this Italian-American did it twice. (Hint: .342 in 1938 with Cincinnati and .330 in 1942 with Boston.)   *Can you name him?

1024) *He was the 1985 Heisman Trophy* runner up, and quarterbacked Brigham Young University to a 28-14 victory in the 1985 Cotton Bowl. (Hint: An Italian saint who worked with youth.)
     *Name him.

1025) *He made Seton Hall* a college basketball power during his tenure as head coach. Moving on to professional basketball, he became head coach of the Golden State Warriors. (Hint: He was attacked by one of his players.) ***Who is he?**

1026) *Who was the first player* to earn over $100,000 a year via contract in 1949?

1027) *Nicknamed, The Scooter,* he was the American League MVP in 1950 and for many years a popular Yankee baseball announcer.
*Who is he?

1028) *It is known as the most grueling* and slowest of the Grand Prix circuit auto races. The race is run over 76 laps (156.4 miles) and involves an average of about 1,600 gear changes. The record time for the race, 1 hour 54 minutes, was held at one time by Riccardo Patrese.
*Name this famous race.

1029) *This famous boxing referee* officiated at seventy championship fights, including the first Ali-Frazier fight. ***Who is he?**
a) Arthur Mercante b) Dan Pecchio c) Lou Duva

1030) *The Italians introduced* this fencing sport to the world in the late 19th century. ***The sword used is:** a) foil b) epee c) sabre

1031) *This AFL star* led the league in scoring five times. He played for the Boston Patriots and is 19th on the all time NFL scoring list with 42 TD's, 176 FG's, and 350 PAT's. ***Who is he?**

1032) *He set all-time season records* for yards passing (5,084) and touchdown passes (48) in 1984, and passed for 4,000+ yards in five other seasons. ***Who is this great Italian-American quarterback who only has played for one professional team during his career?**

1033) *Who was the U.S. Open* golf champion in 1964? (Hint: He goes by the initials K.V.)

1034) *This Olympic event includes* riding, fencing, shooting and swimming. The Gold Medal winner in 1984 was Daniele Masala, of Italy, with 5,469 points. The Italian team won with 16,060 points, the highest number of points scored in any Olympic Games to date.
*What was the event?

1035) *A Heisman Trophy winner* from Penn State, he caught the last pass that Joe Namath completed as a pro football player in 1977. (Hint: He gave a memorable and moving acceptance speech when he received the Heisman trophy.) ***Name this former Los Angeles Ram.**

1036) *Six foot six and 260 pounds,* this Italian-born boxer defeated Jack Sharkey in 1933 to become heavyweight boxing champion of the world. ***Identify him.**

1037) *Born in 1940,* he was a seven-time Golden Glove Award winner and member of nine all-star teams. (Hint: Battled diabetes throughout his career.) ***Name this Chicago Cub third baseman.**

1038) *He was the captain* of the American hockey team that won the Gold Medal at the 1980 Winter Olympics, and also defeated the awesome Russian team. He was portrayed by Andrew Stevens in the 1981 TV movie, *Miracle On Ice*. ***Name him.**

1039) *Joe DiMaggio's batting average* during his fifty-six-game hitting streak was: a) .325 b) .389 c) .408

1040) *Many consider him the greatest* to ever have played the position of quarterback. He has the second highest all-time rating as a quarterback, at 92.3. He is third in completions with 3,409, and retired with 40,551 passing yards and 273 touchdown passes in a career that ran from 1979 through 1994. ***Who is this football legend?**

1041) *He was the past president* of the San Diego Padres. (Hint: Bees love him.) ***Name this respected baseball executive.**

1042) *What race car driver said,* "When somebody screws up in front of you at 200 miles per hour, man, school's out"?

1043) *1972 NFL Rookie of the Year,* this Steeler back went on to become the seventh leading all-time rusher in NFL history, with 12,120 yards and 91 touchdowns over a 13-year career. He also holds the Super Bowl rushing record of 354 yards. (Hint: His army followed him everywhere.) ***Name him.**

1044) *What famous baseball player* made this classic statement: "The game's not over till it's over"?

1045) *Known as Two Ton Tony,* what heavyweight boxer made this remark before his 1939 title bout with Joe Louis: "I'll moider de bum"?

1046) *After fining his star wide receiver* $500 for breaking curfew a second time, this legendary coach ended the conversation with this statement: "And the next time, it'll be $1,000. And if you find anything worth $1,000, let me know and I may go with you."

*Who was the coach?

1047) *Name the head basketball coach* at the University of North Carolina, who led the Wolf Pack to a National Championship in 1983.

1048) *In what weight division* was the popular 1960's boxer Willie Pastrano?   a) Featherweight b) Middleweight c) Light - Heavyweight

1049) *Name either the former* Italian-American head coach of the NFL's old Cleveland Browns or the head of football operations of the newly formed Cleveland Browns.

1050) *Italians seem to dominate this sport.* Alberta Vianello has 16 speed titles to her credit, and current record holders, in different categories, include Giuseppe Cantarella, Gianni Ferretti, and Alberto Civolani.   ***What is the sport?**

1051) *After announcing his retirement* as a player, he purchased the team (New York Cosmos). He is the holder of the NASL goal scoring record for a career: 195 goals through 1983. He also holds the single-season goal record of 34, and most goals scored in a single game, at 7.
*Who is he?

1052) *His double eagle* at the 1935 Augusta Nationals has endured as the single most spectacular shot in golf history.
*Name this famous Italian-American golf star.

1053) *He played middle-linebacker* for the Miami Dolphins when the team went undefeated in 1974, with a record of 17-0.
*Name this former player and current football commentator.

1054) *In 1936,* he won the American Open Golf championship with the lowest score ever made up to that time in a British or American Open championship. (Hint: He may have had a little *Saturday Night Fever* doing it.)   ***Name this Italian-American.**

1055) *Mike Getto* was the first Italian-American selected as an All-American in college football.   ***For what university did he play?**
a) Wisconsin b) Pittsburgh c) Colgate

1056) *This Italian-American baseball player* played first base for the 1985 World Champion Kansas Royals. (Hint: Nick name was Bye-Bye.)   ***Name him.**

1057) *This Italian-American* was the most prolific home run hitter in NCAA history, with 100 home runs in his college career. He hit a home run every seven times at bat. His other stats include a career .398

batting average, and 324 RBI's for 694 at bats. ***Who was this player?**

1058) ***This extremely successful*** college football coach has directed one of the nation's most respected and successful college football programs. He ranks fourth all-time in wins in Division 1-A with 298 through 1997. He has won two national championships, including five undefeated seasons. To date, he has won 18 bowl games.
*Name him and the school at which he coaches?

1059) ***Who was the National Collegiate Player*** of the Year in basketball from Stanford University in 1937?

1060) ***Name the Hall of Fame football player,*** who played fourteen seasons for the San Francisco Forty Niners without missing a game and was their number one draft pick in 1950.(Hint: Wore the number 73 and was a native of Lucca, Italy.)

1061) ***Tony DiCicco*** may not be the most famous coach for this sport in America, but he is by far the most successful. His 93-87 record in five years as head coach makes him the winningest coach in U.S. history. (Hint: Recently coached his team to a world title.)
*What sport does he coach?
   a) Women's National Volleyball Team
   b) Women's National Track Team
   c) Women's National Soccer Team

1062) ***An All-American back at Navy,*** he won the Heisman Trophy in 1960.
*Name him.

1063) ***They are the only two players*** (one of them an Italian-American) from the same college (University of San Francisco) to be inducted into the NFL Hall of Fame in the same year. ***Who are they?**

1064) ***Name the Italian-American owner*** of the San Francisco Forty Niner football team, who won five Super Bowls under his ownership.

1065) ***This All Pro defensive*** lineman's career spanned fifteen years. In 1977, he was named the NFL's Defensive Player of the Year. (Hint: Played for the Oakland Raiders.) ***Who is he?**

1066) ***Retiring from baseball*** with a .325 lifetime batting average, this Italian-American great led his American League team to nine World Championships in the thirteen years he played in the majors. During that career, he finished first, second, or third in the MVP voting six times. Most astonishing of all, in nearly 7,000 at-bats, he only struck out 369 times or 32 times per 600 at-bats.   ***Name this famous player.**

1067) *Often called the Will Rogers* of baseball because of his quips and observations of the game, this Italian-American is a familiar voice in broadcasting and is the author of the book, *Baseball is a Funny Game.* (Hint: Familiar face for many years on morning television.)***Who is he?**

1068) *Born Rocco Barbella,* any boxing fan will remember his famous fights with Tony Zale. Paul Newman starred in a movie of his life, *Somebody Up There Likes Me.****What is his better known name?**

1069) *What trophy* is awarded to the winners of the Super Bowl?

1070) *This former LA Ram quarterback* was the second quarterback in NFL history to pass more than 500 yards in a game. (509 yards: 1983)   ***Who is he?**

1071) *He was the first and only jockey* to ride two Triple Crown winners. His 17 victories in Triple Crown events— five Derbys, six Preaknesses, and six Belmonts—is a record that is unlikely to be broken. ***Who is the jockey who, beginning in 1931, won 4,770 races and more than \$30 million in purses?**

1072) *Dolph Camilli* led the National League in home runs in 1941. What team did he play for?

        a) Brooklyn Dodgers b) Cincinnati Reds c) Milwaukee Braves

1073) *What Italian-American* formerly owned the NBA's San Francisco Warriors?   (Hint: Ben Franklin would be proud.)

1074) *This New York Giant* tight end was instrumental in leading his team to a Super Bowl victory in 1986. (Hint: Bravo.)
          *Who is this inspirational and talented player?

1075) *This Italian-American billiard champion* is said to handle a billiard cue with the authority of Toscanini wielding a baton.
          *Name him.

1076) *Dino Meneghin,* with four Olympic appearances—including a bronze medal and ten championship titles—is one of Italy's most recognizable athletes and an Italian sports legend.
          *What sport did he play?
      a) Soccer b) Basketball c) Alpine skier

1077) *Martin Liquori,* a world class athlete, was among those who made this sport a National pastime in the United States.
Identify the sport.

1078) *Larry Pacifico* is the nine-time world champion in what weight lifting category?

1079) *Dominic J. (Nappy) Napolitano* spent fifty years coaching what sport at the University of Notre Dame?

1080) *He led Notre Dame* to the national college football championship in 1977, won three Super Bowl MVP awards, and was the Player of the Year in 1989. ***Who was this Italian-American player?***

1081) *In 1950 this DiMaggio brother* led the American league in stolen bases. ***Which one was it?***
a) Dom DiMaggio b) Joe DiMaggio c) Vince DiMaggio

1082) *Besides being named* American League MVP three times, he holds the record for most games without an error by a catcher.
Who was this Italian-American ballplayer?

1083) *Who was the last Italian-American* to win the lightweight boxing championship? (Hint: Nicknamed after an explosion.)

1084) *This Chicago Bear linebacker* played in 142 consecutive games, a record for the Bears. He played from 1966 to 1978.
Name him.

1085) *This great fighter* won titles in two weight classes: welter and middle. The Ring Fighter of the Year for 1957, he won, then later lost, the middleweight championship to Sugar Ray Robinson. Who was this tough Italian-American boxer with a big heart? (Hint: The opera *Carmen* was his favorite.)

1086) *Past winner of the PBA* national championship and Tournament of Champions, the highly successful Johnny Petraglia is associated with what sport?

1087) *He formed one half* of one of the greatest wrestling tag teams in the history of professional wrestling. Sicilian by birth, his family emigrated to Australia, and it was there that he learned his trade and earned the title of *"Man of a Thousand Holds."* Emigrating to the U.S. in the 1950's, he and his partner went on to break attendance records wherever they went, including the old Madison Square Garden in New York, where thousands were turned away when they fought the team of Argentina Rocca (another Italian) and Miguel Perez. (Hint: Team was named after a popular Australian animal.)**Name this wrestling great or give the name of his tag team.** (Note: Author is the proud nephew of this wonderful man.)

1088) *The talented, successful, and beautiful* Gabriela Sabatini of Argentina has made her mark in what sport?

1089) *He was the first to hit* two grand slams in the same game. (Hint: Hall of famer.)   *****Name this New York Yankee.**

1090) *Name the former Baltimore player* who was the first to hit grand slams in consecutive innings. (Hint: First baseman.)

1091) *He is the all-time World Series leader* in games, at-bats, hits and doubles. He was the American league MVP three times, in 1951, 1954, and 1955. He also managed pennant winning Yankees in 1964 and Mets in 1973.   ***Who is this great Italian-American ball player?**

1092) *Name the family* who has had the most sons in the baseball All-Star Game.

1093) *Cookie Lavagetto* played for what New York team?
            a) New York Giants b) New York Yankees c) Brooklyn Dodgers

1094) *Since 1983,* Tony LaRussa has received this honor three times.
                                            ***What is it?**

1095) *Born Alfred Manuel Pesano,* he had a successful career as a player and went on to become American League Manager of the Year four times (1974, 1976, 1980, 1981). His team won the World Series in 1977.   ***Who was he?**

1096) *One son is a major league infielder* and the other son played wide receiver for the Baltimore Colts.
            ***Name this Hall of Famer and his two sons.**

1097) *In 1982,* his club won a record 13 ball games at the beginning of the season. (Hint: National league team now known for their pitching.)
                         ***Name the team and its manager.**

1098) *He was the youngest player* to hit 100 home runs in his career. He was 22 years old when he accomplished this feat. Name this American league player. (Hint: Bean ball ruined his promising career.)

1099) *Only three bowlers* have ever won three consecutive professional tournaments. One of them was an Italian-American.

*He is:

a) Mike Limongello   b) Johnny Petraglia   c) Joe Berardi

1100) *He was the heart of the Oakland A's* teams that dominated the American League in the early 1970's

*Who was this outstanding 3rd baseman?

1101) *This distinguished gentleman* and his family were considered the nation's largest single investor in sports enterprises.

*Name him or his family.

1102) *What former Los Angeles Ram head coach* made this statement: "They say losing builds character. I have all the character I need"?

1103) *What great heavyweight* boxing champion said: "I have always adhered to two principles. The first one is to train hard and get into the best possible physical condition. The second is to forget all about the other fellow until you face him in the ring and the bell sounds for the fight"?

1104) *What coach made this statement* after turning down an offer to coach the NFL's New England Patriots: "What the hell's the matter with a society that offers a football coach a million dollars?"

1105) *The earliest literary reference* to this sport by the Roman poet Virgil in the Aeneid, was published after his death in 19 BC. Since the Renaissance (circa 1300 AD), Venice has held competitions in this sport.   ***What is it.**

1106) *George DiCarlo* won a gold medal in the 400 meter freestyle in Olympic record breaking time of three minutes 51.23 seconds.

*In what Olympic year did he do it?

a) 1972   b) 1976   c) 1984

1107) *James and Jonathan DiDonato* swam the 28 plus miles around this island in 9 hours and 42 minutes, using only the exhausting butterfly stroke.   ***What island did they swim around?**

1108) *Klaus Dibiasi* of Italy was a gold medalist in this sport at three consecutive Olympics' (1968, 1972, 1976) and a silver medalist at the 1964 Olympics.   ***What was his event?**

1109) *Wisconsin All American* and Heisman Trophy Winner in 1954, he went on to star for the Baltimore Colts, and scored the memorable winning touchdown in the sudden death NFL championship game against the NY Giants. (Hint: Brother of a well known Hollywood actor.)

*Who was he?

1110) *Ken Venturi,* well known Italian-American golfing great and TV golf commentator, won how many PGA championships during his career? a) 7 b) 11 c) 14

1111) This Italian-American baseball player holds the unbelievable baseball record of hitting safely in 56 consecutive baseball games. At age 19, he hit in 61 straight games for the Pacific Coast League's San Francisco Seals, a PCL record that still stands. ***Who was he?**

1112) *Born Rocco Francis Marchegiano,* he is the only undefeated heavyweight champion in ring history. His professional record was forty nine fights without a loss, with forty three by knockout.

*Name this boxing legend.

1113) *What football coach* is purported to have said, "Winning isn't everything, it's the only thing?"

1114) *Being one of the pivotal games* in football history, it proved the superiority of the T over other football formations. Among the players on the winning team were four Italian-Americans. They were guards George Musso and Aldo Forte, and fullbacks Gary Famiglietti and Joe Maniaci, who was also the place kicker. ***Identify either the professional team they played for, or the team they defeated in this 1940 NFL championship game.**

1115) *During the 1920's and 30's,* Henry Ciuci, Johnny Revolta, and Joe Turnesa starred in what sport?

a) Baseball b) Golf c) Auto racing

1116) *Giorgio Chinaglia,* a great soccer star in Europe for many years, and the holder of many offensive records in U.S. professional soccer, starred for what American team? (Hint: Team was located in New York.)

1117) *He was one of the premier relief pitchers* in the American League and had his greatest success with the New York Yankees. In 1986, he led the majors in saves, with 46. ***Who is he?**

1118) *He won the first Masters* Golf championship at Augusta.

1119) *Ben Abruzzo* was the first man to pilot this type of craft across both the Atlantic and Pacific oceans.   ***What was the craft?**

1120) *In 1954,* John Antonelli led the National League with a 2.29 ERA.   ***What team did he play for?**
                            a) St. Louis b) Cleveland b) NY Giants

1121) *Besides being Italian-American* and former Dodgers, what do Steve Sax and Mike Piazza have in common?

1122) *Two Hall of Famers* were opposing catchers in five World Series games between 1949 to 1956.   ***Identify these two ballplayers.**

1123) *Yogi Berra* was the first pinch hitter ever to do what in a World Series?

1124) *Fans of this sport* will immediately recognize these names for their contributions to this sport: Fangio, Ascari, Tarutfi and Castellotti.
                                  *Identify the sport.

1125) *Name the hero* of Italy's World Cup championship team of 1982.

1126) *In professional football,* what were the Morabito brothers known for?

1127) *Born Michael DiPiano,* he was the 1976 light heavyweight champion. By what name is he better known?

1128) *A five-time All-Star* during his 16-season National Hockey League career, almost all with the Chicago Blackhawks, this hockey goal keeper great was elected to the Hall of Fame in 1988. (Hint: You know his brother from the Boston Bruins.)   ***Who is he?**

1129) *Name two Italian-American* boxing champions that went by the same first name. (Hint: Knowing Sylvester Stallone could help.)

1130) *At age 13,* this gifted tennis player became the first seeded player to win a match at Wimbledon.   ***Who is she?**

1131) *Name one of the four* Italian-American winners of the Indianapolis 500 auto race in 1915, 1925, 1935 or 1969.

1132) *He was the first Indy 500 driver* to exceed the 100-mile per hour mark for an average speed of 101.34 miles per hour.
                     *Who was this Italian-American auto racer?

1133) *A former great* with the Oakland Raiders, he was AFC Player of the Year in 1967 and 1969. In 1967, he led the AFC in passing with 3,228 yards and 30 TD's. (Hint: Played college ball at Notre Dame.)
*Identify this strong armed quarterback.

1134) *Joe Amato* was the 1990 National Hot Rod Association champion and the first driver to surpass how many miles per hour?
a) 240 mph. b) 260 mph. c) 280 mph.

1135) *This Italian-American swimmer* won five Gold Medals, along with 1 Silver and 1 Bronze at the 1988 Summer Olympics and added 1 Gold and 1 Silver at the 1992 games for a grand total of nine medals in all. ***Who is this outstanding Olympian?**

1136) *High scoring* Alessandro Altobelli plays for what Italian national team?

1137) *Carmine Salvino* is one of the most colorful men in his sport, and was one of several who helped popularize it on a national basis.
*Name the sport.

1138) *Since 1976,* Nick Bolletieri has run a successful school for this sport in Bradenton, Florida. Many of today's top players are his graduates.
*Identify the sport he coaches.

1139) *Nino Benvenuti* was a champion in what sport in the 1960's?

1140) *Bruno Sanmartino* came to the United States from Italy after WW II, suffering from malnutrition. By 1963 he had become a world champion in this sport and held this title for eight years. 5'11" with a 58-inch chest, 21-inch biceps and 38-inch waist, at what sport did he excel?

1141) *This golfer,* with the Ladies' Professional Golf Association, won the Womens U.S. Open in 1969 and 1970. She had five tournament wins in 1980 and most consecutive holes without a bogey at 50. ***Who is she?**

1142) *This three time baseball MVP's career* ended when he was seriously injured and left paralyzed from an automobile accident. (Hint: Played on five pennant winners with Brooklyn Dodgers and 1 world series championship in 1955.) ***Who was he?**

1143) *Jerry Colangelo* became the first general manager of this new NBA team in 1968 at the age of 28, making him the youngest general manager in sports. (Hint: Also owns the major league baseball team named after a snake.)
*What successful NBA team is he president and owner of?

1144) *What American League player* received the most World Series checks?   a) Frank Crosetti b) Yogi Berra c) Tony Lazzeri

1145) *Bob Astromonte* was the last active player from this team when he retired in 1971.   ***What was the team?**

1146) *What year* were the Olympics held in Italy?

a) 1932 b) 1960 c) 1980

1147) *Begun in 1900* and originally called The International Lawn Tennis Challenge Trophy, Italy won this world title in 1976.
*Renamed,we now recognize the tournament by what name?

1148) *Winner of nine Emmy's,* he was the senior producer of ABC's Monday Night Football for many years.   ***Who is he?**

1149) *A former All-American* quarterback at UCLA, he was the 1967 Heisman Trophy winner.   ***Who is he?**

1150) *In the 1940's and 50's* this Italian-American pitched for all three New York teams and was the last pitcher to throw a no-hitter at Ebbets Field.   ***Who was he?**

1151) *Joe DeMaestri* replaced what Yankee shortstop after he was struck in the throat by a bad hop grounder in the 7th game of the 1960 World Series?

1152) *This Cardinal catcher* told the Anheuser-Busch advertising agency, owner of the ball club, that he would quit the game to devote full time to his rising popularity as an after dinner speaker if they would pay him $1,000 a month.   ***Who was this ballplayer?**

1153) *Who was the world's* Heavyweight Boxing champion in 1933?

1154) *A power hitting catcher,* he won the National League MVP award in 1971 when he led the league in batting, hits, total bases, and RBI's. After he retired, he went on to manage the Mets, Braves, and, in 1998, managed the New York Yankees to victory in the World Series.
*Who is he?

1155) *Italian Raimondo d'Inzeo* competed in a record eight Olympic games from 1948 to 1976, winning one Gold, two Silver and three Bronze medals.   ***Name the sport he participated in.**
a) Fencing b) Equestrian riding c) Archery

1156) *The highest average* race lap speed for a closed circuit was

146

214.158 mph. This record was held by what Italian-American for several years?

1157) *The 24-hour endurance Grand Prix* race at LeMans, France has been won a record nine times by this automobile company.
*Name the company.

1158) *In 1978,* Diane Ponza had the lowest average ever recorded to attain this feat of perfection. (Hint: Ball used has three holes in it.)
*What did she accomplish?

1159) *One of the premier relief pitchers* in baseball, he was the 1981 Cy Young Award winner and had 341 saves with 107 career relief wins during his stellar career. ***Name this former ace of the Oakland A's, Milwaukee Brewers, and San Diego Padres.**

1160) *Edoardo Mangiarotti* holds the record of 13 Olympic medals in this sport. (6 Gold, 5 Silver, 2 Bronze) He competed from 1936 to 1960. (Hint: He had an edge on the competition.) ***Name the sport.**

1161) *He was an outstanding running back* for the University of Alabama in the early 1970's and was known as the Italian Stallion.
*Who is he? a) Johnny Musso b) Frank Perachiotti c) Tony Sabatasso

1162) *This former pitching star* with the St. Louis Cardinals was the top National League pitcher in 1960, with a 21-9 record.
*Who was he?

1163) *Donna DiVerona* was a popular Olympian in what sport?

1164) *Alan Bonapane* held the record for throwing this object at a speed of 74 mph in 1980. ***What was it?**

1165) *William Turnesa* won it in 1938, and again in 1948. Sam Urzetta won it in 1950. (Hint: An amateur title.) ***What is it?**

1166) *The highest number* of world championship titles won in this sport is 15, held by Giacomo Agostini. In fact, Agostini is the only man to win two world championships in five consecutive years (1968-72). (Hint: Two wheels are involved.) ***What is the sport?**

1167) *In 1984,* Matt Guzzetta rode 2,443 miles from San Diego to Daytona Beach on 11.83 gallons of fuel, for a world record 214.37 miles per gallon. ***What did he ride?**

1168) *Nineteen year old Sal Durante* caught this famous record-breaking home run at Yankee Stadium on October 2, 1961. (Hint: Record held for 37 years until 1998.) ***Name the record and the hitter.**

1169) *Danny Nardico* was the only fighter ever to knock down this middleweight champion. ***Name this boxer.**
  a) Sugar Ray Robinson b) Jake La Motta c) Carmen Basilio

1170) *Born Guglielmo Papaleo,* he was the featherweight division champion two times during the 1940's. (1942-48, 1949-50) He won 73 consecutive bouts from 1940 to 43 and defended his title 9 times. His career record was 230-11-1 with 65 KOs. (Hint: You could say that he had a lot of pep and energy.)
  *Who was this great Italian-American champion?

1171) *In 16 events,* Italy has made five appearances in the finals over the years and has won three world titles. (Hint: World's favorite sport.)
  *Name this international sporting event?

1172) *Agnes Ion Robertson* was the first Italian-American woman to be chosen All American in this sport. ***Name the sport.**

1173) *What former welterweight* boxing champion said, "I can't concentrate on golf or bowling. I could concentrate in the ring, because someone was trying to kill me. Those bowling pins aren't going to hurt me"?

1174) *What Hall of Famer* made this famous quote: "You gotta be a man to play baseball for a living, but you gotta have a lot of little boy in you too"?

1175) *This All-Star second baseman* played for the Los Angeles Dodgers in the 1980's. (Hint: Last name is not Italian.) ***Who is he?**

1176) *"Hero? Vietnam vets are heroes.* The guys who tried to rescue our hostages in Iran are heroes. I'm just a hockey player." (Hint: Olympic team metalist.) ***Who said this?**

1177) *This former Chicago White Sox* pitcher of the 1940's is the only Italian born pitcher ever to play in the major leagues.
  *Name this player who was born in Lucca, Italy.
  a) Marino Pieretti b) Mike Ferretti c) John Candelaria

1178) *Who said,* "Football is blocking and tackling. Everything else is mythology"?

1179) *At sixteen,* she became the youngest Wimbledon semifinalist since 1887. ***Who is she?**

1180) *Because of his premature death,* the story of his life became a true inspiration to many.
*Name this valiant Chicago Bear running back.

1181) *In what sport are* Lou Carnaseca and Rolle Massimino head coaches?

1182) *A Hall of Fame defensive end,* he played in the Pro Bowl every year from 1955 to 1965, except 1958 when he broke his right ankle tackling Frank Gifford in Colts' 23-17 win over the Giants.
*Who is this great defensive player, whose career spanned 15 seasons starting in 1952. He was selected for the NFL's 75th Anniversary All-Time Team along with fellow Italian-American Ted Hendricks?

1183) *This former Oakland Raider* All Pro linebacker was selected to seven Pro Bowls and played in three Super Bowls during his career. (Hint: His nick name was The Stork.) ***Who is he?**

1184) *Sam Battistone* was the president and owner of what NBA team?
a) Utah Jazz b) New York Knicks c) Portland Trail Blazers

1185) *The Alpine World Cup,* instituted in 1967, has been won how many times by record holder Gustavo Thoeni of Italy?
a) 3 times b) 4 times c) 5 times

1186) *One of the earliest references* to this game came out of Italy where it was played (circa 1410), and went by the name of Calcio.
*What is the modern descendant of this game?

1187) *Johnny Addie was known as* The Voice for this sport, and is considered the most famous ring announcer ever. He announced over 200 world championships.   ***Name the sport he was associated with.**

1188) *As quarterback,* he led Notre Dame University to the National Championship in 1966. (Father is Irish, mother is Italian-American.)
*Who is he?

1189) *Sue Notorangelo* won the 1985 Race Across America championship by covering 4,000 miles from New York City to Long Beach, California. ***Identify her sport.**

1190) *Known as the Iron Horse* of Baseball Umpires," he was behind the plate when Don Larson pitched the only perfect World Series game. (Hint: Shared nickname with Herman Ruth.) ***Name this umpire.**

1191) *In 1974,* Buzz Capra led the National League with a 2.28 ERA. What team did he play for?   a) St. Louis b) Atlanta c) Los Angeles

1192) *Vito Voltagglo,* Stephen Palermo, Frank Pulli, Richard Stello and Terry Tata are associated with what sport?

a) Football b) Baseball c) Hockey

1193) *In 1917* (28) and 1919 (29) Ed Cicotte led the American League in victories and, in 1917, led the majors with the best ERA at 1.53.

*He played for:
a) Boston b) New York c) Chicago

1194) *In 1984, Italian Francesco Moser* broke the land speed record, which had stood since 1972. His time was 51.151 kph.

*What was his vehicle?

1195) *During these three seasons,* 1928, 29, and 30, this great college team was directed by Frank Carideo at quarterback (All American 1929-30) and powered by fullback Joe Savoldi.

*Name the famous college team they played for.
a) Michigan State b) Ohio State c) Notre Dame

1196) *In 1950,* two Italian-American pitchers led the majors with the best winning percentage in their respective leagues.
*Who had the best winning percentage, Vic Raschi of the Yankees, or Sal Maglie of the New York Giants?

1197) *Who followed* Perter Ueberroth as commissioner of baseball on September 8, 1988?

1198) *Who was the last Italian-American* (to date) to lead the majors in the RBI category?
a) Joe Torre b) Rocky Colavito c) Dante Bichette

1199) *Joe DiMaggio* led the American league in batting average in two consecutive seasons. What years were they?
a) 1939-40 b) 1946-47 c) 1949-50

1220) *In this event,* this quarterback has thrown for most yards at 1,142, most touchdowns at 11, and is 4-0.
*Identify the event and name the quarterback.

150

1201) *After 15 years,* Al Del Greco is 4th on what all-time NFL list?

1202) *In 1943,* quarterback Angelo Bertelli's Notre Dame team won a national title. ***What honor did Bertelli receive?**

1203) *Martin Gramatica* of Kansas State holds the record for the longest field goal without a kicking tee. ***How long was it?**
a) 55 yards   b) 59 yards   c) 65 yards

1204) *He is ninth* on the all-time post-season batting average list at .333.   List based on at least 70 at-bats. ***Who is he?**
a) Yogi Berra b) Joe DiMaggio c) Billy Martin

1205) *At age 15,* she won the U.S. Ladies Figure Skating Championships. After winning the World Championships in 1977 and 1980, she won the Silver Medal at the 1980 Olympics. Over the course of her skating career, she won 140 championships.
*Who is this great Italian-American skater?

1206) *What do these seven Italian-Americans* have in common: Alan Ameche (Wisconsin), Gary Beban (UCLA), Joe Bellino (Navy), Angelo Bertelli (Notre Dame), John Cappelletti (Penn State), Gino Torretta (Miami), and Vinny Testaverde (Miami)?

1207) *This Brooklyn-born* former football player and coach introduced the T-formation offense, which he used in 1956 to bring the New York Giants to their first NFL championship since 1938. In 1969, he coached the Washington Redskins to their first winning season in more than two decades. ***Who is he?**

1208) *He led the nation* in rushing his senior year at Wake Forest with 1,044 yards. He was drafted by the Chicago Bears where he gained 927 yards and caught 58 passes before his life was tragically cut short by cancer in 1970 at the age of 27. (Hint: Team mate and friend of football great, Gale Sayers.) ***Who was he?**

1209) *Nicknamed football's Iron Man,* he missed only one game in 14 years with the Los Angeles Rams and the New York Giants. He earned All-Pro honors seven times was was football's Player of the Year in 1962. (Hint: One could say that he had a robust career.)
*Who is this football hall of famer?

1210) *Remembered and honored* as the greatest Super Bowl drive of all time—eight complete passes in two minutes and thirty seconds—

was the miracle performed by what NFL legend? (Hint: 1984 Super Bowl.)

1211) *A successful and distinguished* college basketball coach, his .739 winning percentage (352-124) over fifteen years puts him fourteenth on the all-time coaches list. The author of three books, he left a successful tenure at Kentucky to coach the Boston Celtics.   ***Who is he?**

1212) *Joe Ciampi* and Geno Auriemma are extremely successful at what they do. Their winning percentages of .763 and .787 respectively prove it.   ***With what sport are they associated?**

1213) *Lou Duva* has trained and managed many great champions over his career.***What memorable Italian-American lightweight champion (1987 and 91), in the mold of Carmen Basilio, was under his guidance?**

1214) *In 1978,* Chicago businessman George Randazzo established this organization and impressive museum that recognizes and promotes the achievements of Italian-American athletes and their contributions to sports. ***Identify this organization that is headquardered in Chicago and has numerous branches across the United States.**

1215) *Buttercup Dickerson* was born in Tyaskin, Maryland in 1858. He was the first Italian-American to play baseball in the major leagues. His first game was July 15, 1878, when he was a starting outfielder for the Cincinnati club. He played for seven years and finished with a lifetime batting average of 284.   ***What was the name he was born with?**
a) Ronald Pezzolo b) Joe Bondanza c) Lewis Pessano

1216) *Phil Cavarretta* was the first Italian-American to manage a Major League baseball team. A former player, he managed this National League team from 1951 to 1954.   ***Identify the team.**

1217) *Former president* of the NFL San Francisco 49ers, he is now head of football operations for the "new" Cleveland Browns.
          *Who is this articulate and charming football executive?

1218) *Steve Mariucci* is the current head football coach (1999) of what perennial NFL football power?

ROMANS

Romans

1219) ***What prominent Roman*** became joint consul with Julius Caesar in 44 BC.? a) Pompey b) Marc Antony c) Octavius

1220) ***Who was*** the first Emperor of the Roman Empire?

1221) ***The emperor Vespasian*** started construction on a structure that would hold 55,000 people, but it was not completely finished until the time of his sons, Titus and Domitian ***What was the structure?**

1222) ***What Roman emperor*** was largely responsible for the evolution of the empire into a Christian state?

1223) ***What Roman emperor*** took control of the empire in 285 AD and instituted an immense program of legal, fiscal, and administrative reform that restored much of Rome's former strength?
a) Diocletian b) Marcus Aurelius c) Titus

1224) ***What people in Italy,*** from 800 BC to their decline in the 5th century BC, developed an elaborate urban civilization, particularly notable for its tombs? They ultimately were absorbed by Rome and their language is still largely undeciphered.

1225) ***He was one of the greatest men*** ever produced by the Roman Republic. He wrote vivid accounts of his conquest of Gaul and his civil war with Pompey. ***Identify this Roman.**

1226) ***What was the proclamation*** issued in 313 AD, granting permanent religious tolerance to Christians throughout the Roman

154

Empire? (Hint: An edict named after a major northern Italian city.)

1227) *Identify the wars* in which Rome and Carthage contested supremacy in the western Mediterranean in the third and second centuries BC.

1228) *What were the alleged last words* of Julius Caesar? (Hint: He was addressing a once loyal friend who had betrayed him.)

1229) *Identify the speaker* and translate the following Latin phrase, Veni, Vedi, Vici? (WAY-nee, WEE-dee, WEE-kee.) (Hint: Best-known Latin sentence of them all. Reported by Plutarch to have been uttered by this Roman commander by way of reporting his victory in 47 BC over Pharnaces, king of Pontus.)

1230) *What flower was named* for a Roman gladiators sword? (Hint: The name begins with the letter G.)

1231) *Caledonia was* the Roman name for what country?
a) England b) Belgium c) Scotland

1232) *The first was built* in 372 AD in Caesarea by St. Basile, the second was established in Rome a few years later. ***What were they?**
a) Universities b) Hospitals c) Orphanages

1233) *In ancient Rome*, women wore bandages wrapped around their feet and legs. ***What evolved from this tradition?**

1234) *Tradition holds* that Julius Caesar was born by what operation called a caeso matris utere? Translated from the latin this means, from the incised womb of his mother. ***What is the English word?**

1235) *The Romans were* the first to use this type of building material.
*What was it?

1236) *What assassination* took place on the Ides of March?

1237) *Name the Roman emperor* who built Castel Saint Angelo as his imperial mausoleum in the 2nd century AD. (Hint: Known for his wall.)

1238) *What Roman general* and politician instigated the plot against Julius Caesar and persuaded a reluctant Brutus to join the conspiracy?
a) Cassius b) Scripio c) Marc Antony

1239) *In ancient Rome*, this term referred to a magistrate of high rank. Today, it refers to an official examiner of printed or other materials, who may prohibit what he considers objectionable.

*What is the term that is still used today?

1240) *Of the seven hills* on which ancient Rome was built, name the one on which the capitol stood.

1241) *After a serious illness*, this Roman emperor went through a personality change which transformed him into a raging madman. His behavior eventually led to his assassination. ***Who was this emperor?**

1242) *Cannae is the name of* the famous battlefield in southeast Italy where what foreign general defeated the Romans in 216 BC? (Hint: He used elephants.)

1243) *What went into effect* on January 1st, 45 BC? (Hint: With some minor changes, it is still used today.)

1244) *Name the Roman emperor* who put aside his own son in favor of his wife's son as his successor; and then, when he had second thoughts, was poisoned by his wife.

1245) *She had a son* by Julius Caesar and three children by Marc Anthony.   ***Who was she?**

1246) *He was not only* considered Rome's greatest orator, but also one of its most articulate philosophers. ***Who was this noble Roman?**
a) Horace b) Cicero c) Virgil

1247) *St. Cecilia*, a Roman lady of the 3rd century, is the patron saint of the blind, and of musicians.   ***She is credited as the inventor of what musical instrument?**   a) Harp b) Organ c) Guitar

1248) *What ancient Roman game*, passed down through the centuries, still finds a home wherever Italians gather? (Hint: Kiss.)

1249) *The Romans built* elaborate baths at the natural hot springs located in this city in England. One of the most fashionable spas in the 18th century, it remains today a tourist attraction.

*Name this British city.

1250) *He succeeded Nero* as emperor, only to be killed because he refused to fulfill the expectations of his followers.   ***Who was he?**

1251) *In ancient Rome*, this term referred to the temporary supreme commander. In times of great national danger, the Senate would call upon

the consuls to appoint one who would hold office for no longer than six months. (Hint: Many can be found in Central and South America.)
*Identify the term that is still used today.

1252) *The Greek god* Dionysus was known by what other name in Roman mythology? (Hint: The god of wine and giver of ecstasy.)

1253) *Augustus Romulus* was the last of his kind.
*What was he?

1254) *Cicero and Julius Caesar* were initially friends but later became enemies. ***Is this statement true or false?**

1255) *The Romans sometimes* used the word as synonymous with Africa, sometimes for that section on the Mediterranean which included Carthage. (Hint: A modern day nation.) ***Identify the name.**

1256) *He was the ancient Italian* sky god and the supreme deity of Roman mythology. (Hint: One of the planets in our solar system.)
*Who was he?

1257) *Give the collective name* for the Roman emperors from Augustus through Nero.

1258) *Since 153 BC*, the first day of this Roman Deity's sacred month has marked the beginning of our calendar year. ***Identify this god.**
a) Jupiter b) Janus c) Janitarius

1259) *In biology*, the flowers and vegetation of a locality, and even intestinal bacteria, are named after this Roman goddess of flowers.
*What is her name?

1260) *Pyrrhic is an adjective* that describes a victory won at too great a cost. ***What was the original Pyrrhic victory that took place in 280 BC?**

1261) *Two Roman columns*, one still standing, marked the end of the Appian Way, which extended from Rome.
*In what Apulian city is this column located?
a) Bari b) Polignano a Mare c) Brindisi

1262) *Julius Caesar made this small*, 15-mile-long river famous when he crossed it in his campaign against Pompey, and committed himself either to conquer or to be slain. (Hint: The name of Francis Ford Coppola's best wine.) ***What is the name of this river?**

1263) *In the battle* of Adrianople (378 AD), the cavalry of the Visigoths rode down and over the Roman legions. This defeat brought about a major change in Roman tactics. ***What was different about it?**

1264) *What happened before* the Battle of Milvian Bridge (312 AD) that inspired the winning commander to go on to victory?

1265) *Name the Roman emperor* (161-180 AD) and stoic philosopher who was beset by internal disturbances and the gradual crumbling of the Roman frontiers.

1266) *Virgil states that* Roman youths would go into the fields and spend this day dancing and singing in honor of Flora, the goddess of fruits and flowers. ***What were they celebrating?**

1267) *A series of tales* in Latin verse by the Roman poet Ovid, collected in fifteen books, deals with mythological, legendary and historical figures. It shares a common title with a work by Apulelus, commonly known as the Golden Ass. ***Identify this work by Ovid.**

1268) *She was the goddess* of wisdom and patroness of the arts and trades, fabled to have sprung, with a tremendous battle cry, fully armed, from the head of Jupiter. ***Who was this Roman goddess?**
a) Minerva b) Juno c) Ceres

1269) *Who was the Roman procurator* (governor) of Judea in the first half of the first century?

1270) *The eight Roman magistrates* whose duty it was to administer justice were equivalents of today's Supreme Court justices. ***What was their proper title.**

1271) *The Roman empire* was inaugurated when Octavius received from the Senate the title Augustus. ***What year was this?**
a) 31 BC b) 27 BC c) 19 BC

1272) *In Roman history,* this unit was the imperial bodyguard. Organized by Augustus, it grew more and more powerful until many emperors were hardly more than its puppets. It survived to the time of Constantine the Great. ***Name this famous unit.**

1273) *Legend has it that* Rome was founded by Romulus in what year? a) 821 BC b) 753 BC c) 712 BC

1274) *The Latin initials* of the Roman Senate and People were inscribed on the standards of ancient Rome. ***What were these initials?**

1275) *In Roman mythology*, he is the god of love, the son of Venus and Mercury, and the counterpart of the Greek god Eros. (Hint: Today he is known for an arrow he shoots.) ***Name him.**

1276) *Who was the Roman emperor* at the time of Christ's crucifixion?

1277) *Name the Roman emperor* who completed the Colosseum and erected the famous triumphal arch that still stands today.

1278) *What was the outer garment* worn by Roman citizens when appearing in public?

1279) *What word was taken* from the name of a Roman goddess and is still figuratively applied to any woman of spotless chastity?

1280) *Name the first king of Rome*, who divided the year into ten months.

1281) *The Romans adopted* the arched ceiling and the squared temple foundation from whose architecture?

1282) *The giant ellipse*, enclosed by its dramatically repetitious tiers of arches, creates a unique visual impact. Rome's memorable attraction can surely lay claim to the title of history's most famous monument. ***Identify it.**

1283) *The Roman province* of Pannonia was very important because it connected both western and eastern halves of the Empire and insured Rome's overland communication routes. ***Identify the present day nation this former Roman province covered.**
a) Austria b) Hungary c) Croatia

1284) *What was terminated* by an order issued in Milan in 393 AD by Theodosius I, Emperor of Rome? a) Grain allowance for Roman citizens b) Praetorian Guard c) Olympic Games

1285) *What was the most* important feature of the Roman army?
a) Discipline b) Engineers c) Military tactics

1286) *Seen through Roman eyes*, his greatest offense, perhaps, was not his extravagance nor his cruelty, but his wild artistic vanity, which he indulged by appearing on stage as a singer and an actor, often wearing an unbelted silken robe.   ***Who was this Roman emperor?**

1287) *They were representatives* of the plebeian class during republican Rome, originally with no legal power. Later, however, they secured the power to summon the popular assembly and pass laws binding on the whole Roman state.   ***Name these Roman officials.**

1288) *Who were the famous* sons of the Roman war god Mars and the mortal woman Rhea Silvia, daughter of the king of Alba Longa?

1289) *The Romans referred* to the Cruithi tribes of central Scotland as the Painted People.   ***Who were these ferocious people who painted their faces, arms, and chests blue?**

1290) *In republican Rome*, a council of some 300 members was originally appointed by the consuls to advise them on questions of policy.   ***What was this council called?**

1291) *At one time*, Rome was a state in which the citizens elected their leaders and, after a prescribed period, those leaders would present themselves for reelection. ***What is this form of government called?**

1292) *This word originally* meant the sand that was thrown on the ground to soak up blood from gladiatorial combat. Today, it refers to an area where sporting activities take place.   ***What is the term?**

1293) *To take over the king's* duties after the expulsion of the last Roman king in 510 BC, one of two chief Roman magistrate offices was created. (Hint: Modern definition: an official appointed by a government to reside in a foreign city to represent its citizens there.)   ***Identify the title of the position which now served to replace the king.**

1294) *Julius Caesar reestablished* two enemy cities that had been completely destroyed by the Romans. Before their destruction, the cities had been major areas of commerce. One was in Greece and the other in North Africa.   ***Identify one of them.**

1295) *One of the most pleasing* buildings of ancient Rome was the, *Temple For All the Gods*. It was constructed in 125 AD, and is roofed by a magnificent hemispherical dome set upon a rotunda. It combines the Roman architectural genius for building strong domes with the grace of Greek columns.   ***Identify this temple.**

1296) *Roman emperors added* to their prestige by providing great entertainment for the masses. A particular structure, originally founded

160

by Tarquin the First (600 BC), was used in Rome for this purpose, although the permanent building, which held up to 250,000 spectators, was rebuilt in the time of Julius Caesar. ***What was this great Roman structure?**

1297) *For this Roman celebration*, which was held at the Colosseum, 2,000 gladiators and at least 230 wild animals were billed to die. ***What was this famous celebration that was held in 247 AD?**

1298) *The Romans constructed* a number of these structures around the eastern Mediterranean and built the first of their kind in western Europe, at what are now Dover and Boulogne, after the conquest of Britain (43 AD), to assist in crossing the English channel. ***What were they?**

1299) *Carthaginian rule of this* island was very harsh and oppressive tribute was levied. This may explain why, in 218 BC, the island gave up its garrison to invading Romans. In gratitude, the Romans granted the islanders the privileges of a municipium which, among other things, gave them control over their own domestic affairs. ***Identify this island.**

1300) *It was 280 miles long* and carried 8 million gallons of water into Rome every day. ***What was it?**

1301) *What Roman emperor* destroyed Jerusalem in 70 AD?

1302) *Though most religions* were tolerated by the Romans within the empire, what aspect of Christianity angered the Romans?

1303) *What Roman emperor* first persecuted the Christians by having them crucified and burned as torches to illuminate a public spectacle?

1304) *The worst persecution* of Christians came under what Roman emperor?   a) Hadrian b) Nero c) Diocletian

1305) *Through the strong* organization it inherited from the Romans, it became the repository of Roman and Greek culture.
*Identify this institution.

1306) *From the year 58 BC*, until the fall of the empire, a Roman citizen domiciled in Rome was entitled to something free of charge.
*What was it?

1307) *In 166 AD* what Roman emperor sent an embassy to China?
a) Marcus Aurelius b) Trajan c) Commodus

1308) *Stilicho was* a 4th century barbarian who became commander-in-chief of the Roman army.   ***From what tribe did he come?**

a) Vandals b) Goths c) Cimbri

1309) *The most important coin* of ancient Rome was made of silver and weighed 1/84 of a pound. (Hint: Its name starts with the letter D.)
*Identify this coin.

1310) *After the fall of Rome* and the western provinces, Rome's eastern provinces survived as the Byzantine empire, which lasted for how many more years? a) 250 b) 500 c) 1,000

1311) *The Roman empire is* distinguished from earlier states by the number of cities within the empire, their high level of development, and their relative size. ***By the late empire, the city of Rome had a population of how many people?** a) 500,000 b) 1,000,000 c) 1,500,000

1312) *The Roman province* of Dacia, in the Balkans, takes its modern name and its language from Rome. ***Name this country.**

1313) *In ancient Rome,* wine was used extensively in cooking, often in conjunction with a substance which gave even main dishes a rather sickly flavor. ***What was this substance?**

1314) *In what year* did Rome conquer Egypt?
a) 63 BC b) 31 BC c) 12 BC

1315) *In regard to taxation*, a Roman emperor told an overzealous tax collector of an eastern province, "Sheer my sheep, don't fleece them."
*Who was this emperor?
a) Tiberius b) Nero c) Nerva

1316) *The first major road* constructed by the Romans in 312 BC, linked Rome with the city of Capua. Later the road was lengthened to connect southern Italy to the Adriatic coast, making it over 360 miles long. This proved to be the nucleus of a system of firm-surfaced roads that eventually criss-crossed all Western Europe and much of North Africa.
*Name this road.

1317) *In 390 BC*, hordes of blond giants appeared out of the north. They sacked Rome and terrorized the area for months before they withdrew, only to return periodically. Other Latin towns found they needed Rome to aid their stand against the invaders. ***Who were these blond giants from the north whom Rome would come to dominate?**

1318) *The Carthaginians were* descendants of what ancient people who were considered to be the world's best sailors?

1319) *What was the name of Rome's* first province, a large island in the Mediterranean which she took from Carthage in the first Punic War?

1320) *Hannibal finally met* his match at Zama in 202 BC
*Who is the Roman general who defeated him?

1321) *Roman expansion* abroad was one of the reasons for the Republic's demise. (Hint: Having to do with the military.)
*Why was this?

1322) *The great eruption* of Mt. Vesuvius, that covered the thriving cities of Pompeii and Herculaneum, occurred in what year?
a) 59 AD b) 79 AD c) 89 AD

1323) *The Roman army* used Numidian auxiliaries extensively in what capacity?

1324) *What were Roman* cavalrymen obliged to supply at their own expense?

1325) *This Italian city* became the capital of the Western Roman Empire in 404 AD and, after the wars against the Goths, was made the seat of Byzantine government in Italy in 584.   ***Name the city.**
a) Venice b) Pesaro c) Ravenna

1326) *What city did* Emperor Augustus claim he found brick and left marble?

1327) *Who were the* legendary founders of Rome?

1328) *Name the leading thinker* of the early Christian Church whose greatest work, *The City of God*, was written as a philosophic meditation on the sack of Rome by the Visigoths in 410 AD.

1329) *Which Roman emperor* made his horse a senator?
a) Nero b) Caligula c) Galba

1330) *Romans referred* to the land around the Mediterranean as Mare Nostrum.   ***Translate.**

1331) *After whom* were most of our solar system's planets named?

1332) *Who led the revolt* of the Roman slaves and gladiators in AD 73? (Hint: Kirk Douglas starred in Hollywood's film version.)

1333) *What article of clothing* that Roman soldiers wore around their necks is still in fashion today?

1334) *Which Roman emperor* bet 400,000 sesterces on one roll of dice?   a) Nero   b) Vespasian   c) Titus

1335) *The Romans were* the first to play a game with a coin that they called "caput aut navis" (ship or chief). ***What is the game called today?**

1336) *The Romans were* the first to cultivate sea animals in a closed medium.   ***What do we call these closed mediums?**

1337) *Sister of Caligula* and mother of Nero, she had been the wife of emperor Claudius before she poisoned him. After many elaborate and thwarted attempts she was murdered by the new emperor, Nero.

                                        *What was her name?
                  a) Agrippina   b) Drusilla   c) Antonia

1338) *Flavius Marcus Apicius* was a Roman epicure in the time of Tiberius.   ***His name is still proverbial in all matters of gastronomy because of his book on the ways of tempting what?**

1339) *This hill fortress* in the Judaean desert was the last Jewish stronghold against the Romans when it was finally captured in 73 AD. (Hint: Inhabitants committed suicide rather than surrender.)

                                          *Identify the fortress.

1340) *Titus Pomponius Atticus* was a Roman man of letters who kept a staff of slaves whose work was to copy contemporary writings. This was one of the earliest enterprises of its kind.   ***What was it?**

1341) *Gaius Octavius* was the first emperor of Rome. By what name is he better known?

1342) *As one of the first two* consuls in Rome's history, what man is known as the founder of the Roman Republic? (Hint: Ancestor of one of Julius Caesar's assassins.)

1343) *"Laws are dumb* in the midst of arms," expounded which Roman orator?

1344) *Athletic games such as those* enjoyed by the Greeks in their Olympics, were not very popular in Rome. The Romans preferred another kind of sport, that featured four teams. The teams were named after four particular colors: Whites, the Greens, the Blues and the Red.

                                          *Identify the sport.

1345) *Name the Roman emperor* who split the Roman empire into East and West, each with a Caesar as vice regent.

1346) *Who was the speaker* of this famous eulogy? "This was the noblest Roman of them all; All the conspirators save only he, did that they did in envy of Great Caesar; He only, in a general honest thought, and common good to all, made one of them."

1347) *Name the Roman* who said, "The die is cast," as he led his army across the Rubicon into Italy.

1348) *On his march to Rome*, he saw a luminous cross in the sky, with the motto, *In hoc signo vinces* (by this sign conquer). ***Name the Roman who became emperor and gave new vitality to the empire.**

1349) *Because of his many works* and his mastery of Latin prose, this man was able to transform Latin from a blunt, utilitarian language of merchants and lawyers to a language that rivaled Greek in its capacity to convey the gamut of feelings and the fine distinction of ideas.
    *Who was this Roman orator, statesman, and man of letters?

1350) *This Roman general* had great success against Hannibal by employing wariness and caution rather than violence and defiance.
    *Who was he?

1351) *In Roman mythology*, a spirit presides over the birth of every man and woman and attends them throughout their lives.
    *Who is this spirit?

1352) *Who was the Roman* goddess of fortune or chance?

1353) *The strong defensive wall* around Rome was not built until 271 AD. ***What is its name?**
    a) The Aurelian Wall b) The Hadrian Wall c) The Trajan Wall

1354) *The poet Lucan* (Marcus Annaeus Lucanus) and the philosopher Seneca (Lucius Annaeus Seneca) were involved in a plot to overthrow this mad emperor. They were foiled, however, and both were ordered to commit suicide. ***Who was the Roman emperor they attempted to overthrow?**

1355) *In his attempt* to flee Rome, he was overtaken by bounty hunters who presented his head and right hand to his enemy, Antony, who had them placed on the rostrum in the Forum where he had first won his glory. ***Identify this Roman orator.**

1356) *How many wives* did Julius Caesar have?

a) one b) two c) three

1357) *The Roman empire* in the west ended when Romulus Augustus was banished by the barbarian Odocer in what year?

a) 456 AD b) 476 AD c) 492 AD

1358) *What society introduced* horse-drawn chariots to Italy circa 750 BC?

1359) *The Flavian emperors* of the first century are responsible for building what great Roman amphitheater?

1360) *What was* Stratagems?

1361) *What is the Latin name* for a reed that grew abundantly in the Nile valley and was used to make writing material? The stems were split in half, flattened and pasted together in layers at right angles to one another.

1362) *In its intellectual aspects*, the last years of the Roman republic are often referred to as what age?

1363) *Who inaugurated* the period of the Partnership of Emperors?

1364) *Name the Roman lyric* poet and satirist whose great poetic work was a four-book collection of odes called *The Carmina*. He was considered the master of stanzaic meter, just as Virgil was the incomparable master of the dactylic hexameter.

1365) *Which famous general* escaped extradition to Rome by committing suicide?

1366) *Name the Roman god* of the sea who became an important deity when Rome became a significant maritime power.

1367) *In Roman mythology*, who was the goddess of beauty and love, and one of the major characters in classical myth?

1368) *Which Roman ruler* forbade public gladiatorial combats in 264 AD?

1369) *The earliest recorded event* of this type occurred in Britain in 210 AD and was arranged by the Roman Emperor Lucius Septimius Severus.   ***What was the event?**

a) Horse racing b) Longbow archery competition c) Jousting tournament

1370) *In Roman law*, it was the sacred power originally wielded by the King and passed to the consuls after the founding of the Republic. Much later, it became an important ingredient of the legal basis of the power of emperors. ***Identify the term.**

1371) *Who were the professional* fighters required to fight to the death as part of Roman public entertainment?

1372) *The Roman circus was built* on the model of the Greek hippodrome. ***Name the first and largest of these structures.**

1373) *Who is considered* the first Christian martyr?

1374) *As the real center* of power of the Roman empire shifted eastward to Constantinople in the 4th century, Rome found a new role. ***What was it?**

1375) *According to legend*, the seventh king of Rome, Tarquin the Proud, antagonized the people by his despotic use of power. They deposed him and made their city a republic.
*In what year did Rome become a republic?
a) 701 BC b) 649 BC c) 509 BC

1376) *Hannibal was not the first* enemy commander to bring war elephants into Italy against Rome. In 280 BC, a king crossed the Adriatic from Greece with 25,000 soldiers and 20 elephants. He won two engagements before being defeated and sent back to Greece.
*Who was this king?

1377) *What Christian bishop* was killed in Rome on the 14th of February, AD 270?

1378) *Which Roman* governor tried Christ?

1379) *Which Roman* emperor does the king of diamonds represent?

1380) *The Romans played* what game with walnuts and hazelnuts?

1381) *Lucius Junius*, who established the Roman Republic, was the ancestor of what infamous conspirator?

1382) *The middle name* of the Roman poet Quintus Flaccus is the name he is universally known by. ***What is it?**

1383) *An ancient shepherd* named Faustulus relieved a she-wolf of the rearing of these twins. ***Name the twins.**

1384) *The eastern or Greek division* of the Roman Empire is known and identified by what other name?

1385) *What month of the year* was named after Julius Caesar?

1386) *Which Roman commander* never lost a campaign or left the field before the enemy?

1387) *This codification* is the foundation of the Roman law still used in many European countries. ***Identify this code.**

1388) *According to Plutarch*, which Roman leader ignored a soothsayer's warning to "beware the ides of March"—the day on which he was slain?

1389) *Vercingetorix was the great* Gaulic chieftain who was defeated at Alesia in 52 BC by which Roman general?

1390) *One Roman emperor felt* that the empire was getting too large and unwieldy. He stopped the expansion and tried to consolidate and fortify Roman lands. He was: a) Hadrian b) Caracalla c) Diocletian

1391) *Who was the Gothic King* and conqueror who plundered Rome in 410 AD?

1392) *Who was notorious* for his attacks upon Europe during the final stages of the Roman Empire? (Hint: He was known as *The Scourge of God*.)

1393) *How did the Romans improve* the Greek phalanx?

1394) *In 380 AD*, Christianity became the official religion of the Roman Empire under the reign of what emperor?
   a) Constantine b) Theodosius I c) Septimius Severus

1395) *During the days* of the Roman Republic, the poor majority were known as what?

1396) *Who was the ancient* Roman goddess of fertility?
   a) Tellus b) Isis c) Venus

1397) *During the days* of the Roman Republic, Rome was dominated by a native aristocracy referred to by what term?

1398) *Roman humor on a grand* scale is nowhere better represented than in this type of literary work, in which irony, derision, and wit are used to expose folly or wickedness. ***Identify the term which**

the Romans could rightly claim to have invented.

1399) *This was Rome's port city,* where merchant ships from around the world would unload their cargos.　　***The ancient city was:**
a) Orbetello b) Civitavecchia c) Ostia

1400) *In ancient Rome*, what was the center of business and social life of the city?

1401) *With the defeat of this enemy*, Rome gained its territories in Spain, Sicily, Sardinia, and Corsica.　　***Who was the enemy?**

1402) *Features of Roman life* that were borrowed from what people included gladiatorial combats and triumphs awarded to victorious generals.

1403) *Antony was defeated by* Octavian at what important battle?
a) Sirnmium b) Leptisa c) Actium

1404) *A standard bearing* this symbol was given to every legion. The legionnaires were meant to defend the sacred symbol to the death, and its capture by an enemy brought disgrace. (Hint: A symbol of the United States.)　　***What was the symbol?**

1405) *A Roman legion* contained how many men?
a) 2,500 b) 5,000 c) 6,000

1406) *Its codification* under the Eastern Emperor Justinian shaped it into the form used by medieval lawyers from the 12th century onwards.
*What did Justinian codify?

1407) *Gaius*, known by the nickname that referred to the little soldier boots he wore as a child, was murdered by the Praetorian Guard in 47 AD.　　***What is his well-known name?**

1408) *The reign of Trajan ushered* in a period of unprecedented prosperity and peace throughout the Roman empire.
*What was this period in Roman history called?

1409) *What was the traditional* Roman country house called?

1410) *They could be found* in any city of the Empire, and the most luxurious of them boasted marble walls.　　***What were they?**

1411) *The Romans' talent* for engineering shows in their spectacular system of bridge-like structures that transported water from remote sources, usually by gravity. ***Name this structure.**

1412) ***The earliest form of this musical*** instrument was found in Rome circa 50 BC. It is a woodwind instrument with a conical bore and a double reed mouthpiece. ***What is it?**

1413) ***The earliest known paved*** streets appeared in Rome around this time. ***The approximate date was:**
a) 210 BC b) 170 BC c) 73 BC

1414) ***What is*** the Pons Aemalius?

1415) ***What great genius*** of ancient science was killed when Roman legions conquered and sacked the Sicilian city of Syracuse in 212 BC?

1416) ***The Roman clepsydra*** took the form of a cylinder into which water dripped from a reservoir. Readings were taken against a scale with a float in the cylinder. An improved version appeared in Rome circa 159 BC. ***What was it?**

1417) ***Pictures made of small*** pieces of stone or glass were used to decorate the floors and walls of Roman villas.
*Identify this intricate art form.

1418) ***The great city*** of Florence was founded in what year?
a) 102 BC b) 62 BC c) 8 BC

1419) ***The excavation*** of Pompeii began by order of the king of Naples in what year? a) 1676 b) 1748 c) 1819

1420) ***Civis Romanus Sum!*** (I am a Roman citizen). Roman citizenship was given to every freeborn subject in the Empire.
*What year did this edict go into effect?
a) 49 AD b) 149 AD c) 212 AD

1421) ***Hymn singing*** was introduced in 386 AD by a Bishop of Milan who later was canonized. ***Who was this early doctor of the church?**
a) St. Ambrose b) St. Jerome c) St. Julian

1422) ***The primitive Roman calendar***, with its ten lunar months, was replaced in the 6th century BC with this dynasty's 12-month calendar. These people brought many innovations to Rome, including cult statues, temples, elaborate funeral rites, and a complicated method of divination employing the entrails of animals. ***Who were the people?**

1423) ***Archaeology and tradition*** agree that this hill was the site of

the earliest settlement in Rome.   ***What was the name of this hill?**
a) Capitoline Hill b) Aventine Hill c) Palatine Hill

1424) ***Appius Claudius*** built the first one in 312 BC. It was seven miles long and ran underground.   ***What was it?**

1425) ***Emperor Marcus Aurelius'*** son and successor fancied himself a latter day Hercules, and sometimes dressed the part.
*Who was this noted Stoic emperor's son?

1426) ***A native of Thrace,*** this man once served as a Roman legionnaire, but deserted to become a bandit. After his capture, he was forced to become a gladiator.
*Who was the slave who became a general?

1427) ***One of the universally acclaimed marvels*** of ancient Rome is a one hundred foot column which records this emperor's long and highly successful military career. It is adorned with 625 feet of continuous frieze figures.   ***To which emperor was this column erected?**
a) Vespasian b) Nerva c) Trajan

1428) ***What was*** the Forum Piscariun in ancient Rome?

1429) ***What is*** the term used for Roman numbers?

1430) ***Identify the word derived from Latin*** and used by the Romans to refer to a central hall or rectangular shaped open patio around which a Roman house is built.

1431) ***What great Roman philosopher*** made the following statement: "To be ignorant of what happened before you were born is to be ever a child. For what is the value of human life unless it is interwoven with past events by the records of history"?
a) Cicero b) Marcus Aurelius a) Horace

1432) ***They were not confined at home*** and many in the upper class were taught to read and write. Several flourished as poets during the reign of Trajan, and their position in society was much envied by others around the Mediterranean.   ***Who were they?**

1433) ***Give the Latinate*** singular form of the word trivia?

1434) ***What are*** the Quirinal and the Viminal?

1435) ***In 386 BC,*** when the invading Gauls were rampaging through Italy, the Capitoline Hill of Rome proved to be an excellent refuge. A

famous legend tells of the Gauls attacking the Capitoline citadel by night only to be foiled when an alarm awoke the sleeping Roman defenders.
*What was the alarm?

1436) *On his deathbed,* the first emperor of the Flavian line remarked, "Good Lord! I must be turning into a god!" He was ridiculing the contemporary practice of deifying emperors after they died.
*Identify this Roman emperor.
a) Titus b) Vespasian c) Galba

1437) **What major tribe** was one of the earliest to join and be assimilated by the Latini?　　　　　a) Sardi b) Tyrrheni c) Sabines

1438) *Before the Roman Forum was built,* that area between the Palatine and the Esquiline hills was used for what purpose?

1439) *What musical instrument* did Nero supposedly play when most of Rome was destroyed by fire in A.D. 64?
a) Lyre b) Violin c) Harp

1440) *It took Rome 600 years* to fully conquer what area?
a) North Africa b) Italian peninsula c) Asia minor

1441) *After the defeat of Carthage and Syria,* what last country stood in Rome's path of total domination of the Mediterranean?

1442) *What Roman weapon* was known as the pila?

1443) *Roman sailors nicknamed it* "the raven" because of its similatity to a beak.　　　　　***What was it?**

1444) *The Roman consul Marius* eliminated this practice, which offered a great temptation to the enemy and slowed down his army. He made legionnaires carry essential supplies on their backs and, because of this, legionnaires became known as Marius's mules.
*What did Plarius eliminate?

1445) *The people of what country* were called the *Helvetii* by the Romans?

1446) *In what architectural specialty* did the Romans excel?

1447) *What are the most* enduring relics of Rome's power?

1448) *Alesia is the site* of what Roman general's great victory?

1449) *Can you give the term* for the professional commissioned officers of the Roman army?

1450) *Besides carrying catapults* and other siege machines, what was the main weapon of the Roman war galley?

1451) *How did the* Praetorian guard get its name?

1452) *A fire service* and night police were established for the fourteen districts of Rome.
*What Roman emperor was responsible for this?
a) Augustus b) Trajan a) Hadrian

1453) *What did the Romans call* their certificate of citizenship? (Hint: Today we receive one upon graduation.)

1454) *What famous Roman* orator described the Sicilians as, "an intelligent race, but suspicious."

1455) *Generally completed by 126 AD,* it is seventy-three miles long, ten feet wide and fifteen feet high. In its final form, it had regularly spaced milecastles and turrets every two miles for patrolling garrisons, and sixteen forts located at strategic points. The area was evacuated by the Romans in 383 AD. ***What is this structure?**

1456) *What was the* weakest link in the Roman army?

1457) *The Romans utilized* two methods to capture a fortified position.
*Can you name one of them?

1458) *The Romans made them* out of marble or bone. (Hint: Used in gambling.) ***What were they?**

1459) *A Roman elected to this position* supervised a city's food supply, traffic and entertainment. ***What is the term?**
a) Quaestor b) Aedile c) Praetor

1460) *The Roman infantry employed* a formation that utilized 27 men, formed into four rows, with shields turned upward in such a way as to completely protect and cover the formation against enemy spears and missiles. (Hint: It looked like a particular amphibian.)
*What was this type of formation called?

1461) *Besides his gladius* (sword) and dagger, what other weapon was carried by a Roman legionary?

1462) *Identify the term* used by the Romans to describe a "fast-food" shop where poorer Romans could purchase hot meals.

a) Thermoplium b) Tepidarium c) Caldarium

1463) *What is the word* for a raised platform round the arena of an amphitheater.

1464) *From this date forward,* after the Carthaginian navy was defeated, Rome never lost command of the sea.
*What year was this?
a) 301 BC b) 241 BC c) 194 BC

1465) *What was* the Roman quinquereme?

1466) *How did Nero* meet his end?
a) Execution b) Suicide c) Old age

1467) *In 168 BC,* whose legendary phalanx was cut to pieces by the Romans at Pydna in Greece?

1468) *What were the Hastati,* Principles, Triarti, and the Velites of the Roman republic?

1469) *What was* the Roman groma?

1470) *True or false:* Wine was always watered down. It was considered bad manners to drink wine undiluted.

1471) *At the beginning of the* 2nd century AD, this Roman emperor invaded Dacia and built Rome's finest military bridge, across the Danube at the Iron Gates. It was 1500 meters long and built on 20 massive stone piers 50 meters high and 20 meters wide.
*Who was the Roman emperor?
a) Galba b) Nerva c) Trajan

1472) *Although Roman engineering feats* were absolutely astounding, they really excelled in what type of military construction?

1473) *Name the hill in the city of Rome* on which the royal palaces were built during the days of the Roman Empire.

1474) *What did the* dextrarium iunctio (joining of hands) ceremony signify?

1475) *The primary policy* of the Roman emperors during the 1st century AD was to: a) consolidate existing territories b) expand the frontiers of the empire as much as possible c) consolidate the west and expand into the east

1476) *It is the name given* for the pre Etruscan civilization of Italy.
*Identify the term.
a) Vetulonian b) Gabian c) Villanovan

1477) *It is said that while the Romans* were establishing their empire, more of these people died in battle than all the other peoples of the empire put together. ***Who were they?**

1478) *In ancient Rome,* a wet sponge attached to a stick was used in lieu of what modern day convenience?

1479) *The eastern Roman empire* finally fell when Constantinople was conquered by the Muslim leader of Turkey, Sultan Mehmet II.
*This occurred in the year:
a) 1399 b) 1453 c) 1492

1480) *What was the name* by which the Celts of Northern Italy and France were known to the Romans?

1481) *This Roman poet* and philosopher wrote a poem called *The Nature of the Universe,* which explained in length the workings of the universe and denied that the gods of Rome had any interest in the affairs of men. ***Who was he?**

1482) *The Roman system* of roads eventually covered more than 53,000 miles. (Note: A Roman mile is a thousand paces, or 4,800 feet in length.) ***Each mile of a Roman road was marked by what?**

1483) *Within a legion,* Roman centurions were in command of units called centuries. ***How many men made up a unit?**
a) 50 b) 80 c) 100

1484) *Identify the term* which described the arena in which chariot races took place.

1485) *What is the word* meaning an oblong building of ancient Rome that served as a court or place of assembly? (Hint: Used today to describe a large church.)

1486) *Only a Roman citizen* could join the army as a legionnaire. Noncitizens were permitted to join as aides or helpers to the legionnaires.
*What were they called?

1487) *A bulla is:* a) a type of ox b) a lucky charm c) a gladiatorial opponent

1488) *Roman women* used what product to soften and moisturize their skin?   a) Asses' milk b) Olive oil c) Crushed ant egg paste

1489) *What was a strigil* used for in ancient Rome?
          a) A missile for a catapult b) An instrument for torture
          c) A tool for scraping off dirt when bathing

1490) *When consulting a haruspex* in ancient Rome, you would be: a) Consulting with an architect b) Having your eyes tested
          c) Discovering the will of the gods

1491) *What Byzantine ruler* of the Eastern Empire (527- 565 AD) regained much of Rome's lost territory?

1492) *The walls of wealthy Romans* were usually covered by this art form. The artist covered the wall to be painted with a smooth layer of new plaster and while it was still damp, painted in the background. When this dried, he added the foreground and the finishing touches. The artists paints are made from plant and animal dyes and thickened with egg whites.
                    *****Name this ancient art form.**

Answers to Questions
1 through 1492

Food, Music, & Entertainment

1) Rossano Brazzi
2) Andrea Bocelli
3) Nicolo Paganini
4) Anne Bancroft
5) Ernest Borgnine
    (Ermes Effron Borgnino)
6) Vermouth
7) Zabaglione
8) Polenta
9) Frank Capra
10) Vittorio De Sica
11) Arturo Toscanini
12) Perry Como (Pierino Roland Como)
13) Lina Wertmuller (Arcangela Felice Assunta Wertmuller von Elgg)
14) Richard Conti
15) Crisp bread sticks
16) Vic Damone (Vito Rocco Farinola)
17) Giuseppe Verdi
18) Bobby Darin
19) La Boheme
20) Saffron
21) Virna Lisi
22) Mario Lanza
23) Gina Lollobrigida
24) Neapolitan songs
25) Butter
26) Vince Edwards - TV's *Ben Casey, M.D.*
27) Sophia Loren
28) Fabian Forte
29) Marcello Mastroianni
30) Dino De Laurentiis
31) Roberto Rossellini
32) Tony Franciosa
33) La Scala
34) Connie Francis
35) Bacala or Pesce Stocco
36) Ben Gazzara
37) Giacomo Puccini
38) Peter Gennaro
39) c) Umbrellas
40) Risotto alla Milanese
41) Luchino Visconti
42) Frankie Laine
43) Opera
44) Wladziu Valentino Liberace
45) The Venetians
46) Dean Martin (Dino Crocetti)
47) Mario Del Monaco
48) Vincent Gardenia
49) Vincente Minnelli
50) Pesto
51) Anna Moffo
52) Sal Mineo (born Salvatore)
53) Allegro
54) Liza Minnelli
55) Lucrezia Borgia
56) Frank Zappa
57) *Il Trovatore*
58) Nicolas Cage
59) Tempo
60) Ragu
61) Enrico Caruso
62) *The Godfather / Godfather Part II*
63) Enzio Pinza
64) Stephen Segal
65) Tony Danza
66) Fish stew
67) Lorenzo Da Ponte
68) Giancarlo Menotti
69) Vittorio Gassman
70) Ray Liotta

71) Danny De Vito
72) Sophia Loren
73) *Carrie*
74) Its chocolate
75) *The Deer Hunter*
76) Chianti
77) Federico Fellini
78) John Travolta */Urban Cowboy*
79) b) Harry Warren
80) The artichoke
81) Vittorio De Sica
82) Pizza parlor
83) *The Rose Tattoo*
84) Russ Columbo
85) The pasta is cut on an implement called a *chitarra* (guitar)
86) Jimmy Durante
87) Joe Bonaparte
88) Zoetrope Studios / Niebau Coppola
89) Giacomo Puccini / Tosca
90) Enrico Caruso
91) A liqueur that is a potent digestive, flavored with herbs
92) Aida
93) *Cinderella*
94) Cavalleria Rusticana
95) Pizza Margherita
96) Extravaganza
97) Renata Tebaldi
98) Penny Marshall
99) Prima donna
100) Al dente means *to the tooth*, or that it must remain slightly resistant to the tooth. Neither too soft nor too sticky.
101) James Bond series
102) *Fiorello* / Fiorello La Guardia
103) Judy Canova
104) Toma
105) A sparkling wine
106) *La Dolce Vita*
107) Frank Capra
108) Sophia Loren / *Two Women*
109) Anthony Caruso
110) *Calabria*
111) c) Historical pageants
112) *Serpico, Godfather II, Dog Day Afternoon, and Justice For All.*
113) *The Godfather*
114) Sylvester Stallone / *Rocky*
115) a) Apulia
116) *The Buddy Holly Story*
117) Western Europe's oldest film school (1935)
118) Jake La Motta
119) a) Eduardo Ciannelli
120) The Pizza
121) Joe Pesci
122) Frank Sinatra
123) Susan Sarandon (Susan Abigail Tomalin)
124) Vittorio De Sica
125) Sardinia
126) Spaghetti westerns
127) Bobby Darin
128) The Marx Brothers
129) James Darren
130) Truffles
131) Mandolin
132) c) Wily Coyote
133) Zucchini
134) Bill Conti
135) Panettone
136) Louis Prima
137) Walter Lantz
138) They are: snails Milanese style and frog legs in butter and wine.
139) Aldo Ray (Da Re)
140) Cecil B. DeMille and D. W. Griffith
141) b) *Jagged Edge*
142) Robert Alda / Alan Alda
143) *Mondo Cane*
144) *Last Tango in Paris*
145) Fish
146) Connie Stevens
147) Roberto Benigni
148) Victor Buono
149) Mario Lanza
150) Genoa
151) *The Pride and the Passion* / Sophia Loren

152)	Claudia Cardinale	195)	(c) Sardinia
153)	Anna Magnani	196)	Giacomo Puccini (1858-1924)
154)	Sylvester Stallone	197)	Coloratura
155)	Nino Rota	198)	c) Trumpet
156)	*The Deer Hunter*	199)	Antonio Lucio Vivaldi
157)	Frank Sinatra	200)	Piedmontese fonduta
158)	Europe's largest film studio		(fondue)
	complex	201)	Luciano Pavarotti
159)	Brenda Vaccaro	202)	Andante
160)	Panforte	203)	Giuseppe Verdi
161)	Rudolph Valentino	204)	Arturo Toscanini
162)	Cesare Danova	205)	Ministrone
163)	Dom DeLuise	206)	Falstaff
164)	b) *The Italians*	297)	Basso
165)	Lazio (Rome)	208)	Sophia Loren
166)	Robert De Niro	209)	Oratorio
167)	a) Castrato soprano	210)	Ossobuco Milanese
168)	Brian De Palma	211)	a) Anna Maria Alberghetti
169)	Tom Conti	212)	Martin Scorsese
170)	A meal that begins at midday	213)	Don Ameche (Dominic Felix
	and often continues far into		Amici)
	the night	214)	Silvana Mangano
171)	a) Don Giovanni	215)	Polenta
172)	c) Romeo and Juliet	216)	Giacomo Puccini
173)	Libretto	217)	Frankie Avalon (Francis
174)	Morgana King		Thomas Avallone)
175)	Gaetano Donizetti	218)	Solo
176)	Beniamino Gigli	219)	Anne Bancroft (Anna Maria
177)	Vittorio De Sica		Louise Italiano)
178)	Argentina	220)	Rice and peas
179)	*Karate Kid / Karate Kid II /*	221)	Tony Bennett
	Karate Kid III	222)	Talia Shire (Talia Rose
180)	Sausage		Coppola)
181)	b) *Cobra*	223)	Sonny Salvatore Bono
182)	Niccolo Paganini	224)	Enrico Caruso
183)	Gioacchino Rossini	225)	Genoa
184)	Clint Eastwood	226)	Rudolph Valentino
185)	c) Apulia	227)	Ernest Borgnine (Ermes
186)	a) Roberto Onegna		Eferon Borgnino)
187)	Annette Funicello	228)	Sylvester Stallone
188)	b) La Presa di Roma	229)	*Madame Butterfly*
189)	Soprano	230)	Pastas
190)	Sicily	231)	Al Pacino (Alfredo Pacino)
191)	c) Italo Calvino	232)	Beverly D'Angelo
192)	Italy's first sound motion	233)	Naples, Italy
	picture	234)	b) 1914
193)	*La Gioconda*	235)	Beef steak
194)	Mario Lanza	236)	Falsetto

179

237)	Jimmy Durante (James Francis Durante)	281)	*Serpico*
238)	Finale	282)	*Petrocelli*
239)	Frank Fontaine	283)	Captain Francis Furillo
240)	Bouillabaisse	284)	Dixieland jazz / Original Dixieland Jazz Band
241)	Mario Lanza	285)	Gorgonzola
242)	Libretto	286)	a) *Gaslight*
243)	a) ABC	287)	Dean Martin
244)	Garlic	288)	(b) 1944
245)	Wine	289)	*Pinnochio*
246)	a) Claudio Monteverdi	290)	Polenta
247)	b) Giulio Caccini	291)	Frank Sinatra
248)	b) 1972	292)	*Columbo* (Peter Falk)
249)	Larry Minetti	293)	*The Tonight Show*
250)	Cookies shaped into images of saints and knights.	294)	Frederic Chopin
		295)	Raddicchio rosso
251)	a) Cesare Siepi	296)	Scott Baio
252)	John Cazale	297)	Liberace
253)	Jack Valenti	298)	Bozo the Clown
254)	Simone Signoret	299)	Liza Minnelli
255)	Fruit cake	300)	a) Pear
256)	Don Pasquale	301)	Al Capone
257)	Madonna	302)	Stanley Tucci
258)	*Pagliacci*	303)	*Baretta*
259)	Lou Costello	304)	Hanna-Barbera Productions
260)	Armand Assante	305)	Lucca
261)	Rudolph Valentino	306)	Michelangelo
262)	*Tosca*	307)	Pat Cooper
263)	Franco Zeffirelli (Franco Zeffirelli-Corsi)	308)	Giancarlo Giannini
		309)	Leonardo DiCaprio
264)	Ballerina	310)	Campania - Naples
265)	Sicily	311)	Marcello Mastroianni
266)	Carlo Ponti	312)	Liguria
267)	Ed Marinaro	313)	Vince Lombardi
268)	La Strada	314)	Louis Prima
269)	Pasta	315)	A wine
270)	c) Sicily	316)	*Cavalleria Rusticana*
271)	Pizza	317)	Mary Elizabeth Mastrantonio
272)	a) *Marechiare*	318)	a) Holland
273)	Rocky Marciano	319)	Perry Como
274)	a) ABC	320)	Cheeses
275)	Cocoa	321)	Al Martino
276)	Mrs. Colombo	322)	Music conservatories
277)	b) Drum	323)	Guy Lombardo
278)	A hand extrusion machine for making pasta	324)	Score
		325)	True
279)	Al Molinaro	326)	Figaro
280)	Panettone		

327) Giovanni Pierluigi
     DaPalestrina
328) Falsetto voice
329) Joe Mantegna
330) Blood of Judas
331) Gioacchino Rossini
332) (a) 1911
333) *That Midnight Kiss, The Toast of New Orleans, The Great Caruso, Because You're Mine,The Student Prince* (voice only),*Serenade, The Seven Hills of Rome, For the FirstTime.*
334) Pier Angeli
335) Olive oil
336) Maria Muldaur (Maria Grazia Rosa Dominica D'Amato)
337) *From Russia with Love*
338) Connie Francis
339) Robert Blake
340) b) Milan
341) John Travolta
342) b) Cindy Lauper
343) c) *The Sheik*
344) Sausage (made with pork, seasoned with pepper, garlic, salt, and spices.)
345) Salami
346) Jerry Colonna
347) *Your Show of Shows*
348) Giuseppe Verdi
349) David Caruso
350) a) Umbria - Marche
351) *Life with Luigi*
352) *La Traviata*
353) Rene Russo
354) Beniamino Gigli
355) A ribbed noodle
356) Ron Luciano
357) *Happy Days*
358) Quentin Tarantino
359) Mira Sorvino
360) a) Vincenzo Bellini
361) Sinatra
362) Frank Langella
363) Frank Sinatra

364) James Farentino
365) *E.T.* (The extra-terrestial)
366) Father Guido Sarducci
367) Finocchio's
368) Joey
369) Her operatic singing
370) *The Hulk*
371) a) L'Avventura
372) Sophia Loren
373) Jon Bon Jovi
374) a) Mario Monicelli
375) Penthouse
376) The Federal Express commercials
377) *Divorce Italian Style*
378) $1.00
379) Henry Mancini
380) *Romancing The Stone / Back To The Future*
381) Garry Marshall
382) Baby Octopus
383) *Patton*
384) *Peter Gunn* / Henry Mancini
385) Grappa
386) Caesar salad
387) Italian cheeses
388) Amaretto
389) Manicotti
390) Emmy for best day-time actress
391) Paul Sorvino
392) Parmesan cheese
393) Guy Williams
394) To produce a thin checkerboard cookie
395) *The Sopranos*
396) Prickly pear
397) Galliano
398) Bernadette Peters
399) Sophia Loren
400) Henry Fonda
401) Antonio Stradivari
402) It was created by Italian immigrants in America who were told by social workers to eat a starch and a meat together at dinner. In Italy, meatballs are served as a

second course, but never with pasta.

403) *Il Postino* (The Postman)
404) Bruce Springsteen
405) Costa Cruise Lines
406) a) Peroni - Brewery founded by Francesco Peroni in 1846
407) Chianti region between Florence and Siena in Tuscany.
408) Bobby Rydell (Roberto Ridarelli)Joanie James (Joan Babbo)Frankie Valli (Frank Castelluccio)

Art, Science & Literature

409) Galileo Galilei
410) The compass
411) Gusto
412) Luigi Palma De Cesnola
413) United States in Washington D.C.
414) c) Donatello
415) The canal lock
416) Ghetto
417) a) Raphael
418) Leonardo Fibonacci
419) Marco Polo
420) Beniamino Bufano
421) Antonio Stradivari (1644-1737)
422) Shorthand
423) Quota
424) *Captain Blood* and *Scaramouche*
425) Virgil
426) The Decameron
427) Giovanni Cimabue
428) Gabriele D'Annunzio
429) Motto
430) Elizabethan period (Concepts of courtesy)
431) Venus
432) Nitroglycerin
433) Giulietta e Romeo (Romeo and Juliet)

434) c) Duccio Di Buoninsegna
435) Manifesto
436) The typewriter
437) *Gerusalemme Liberata* (Jerusalem Delivered)
438) Gardening
439) Laura
440) a) Lodovico Ariosto
441) The staff
442) Ballot
443) Fra Angelico
444) Enrico Caruso
445) Luigi Pirandello
446) Contraband
447) The invention of the barometer
448) Venetian glass
449) (a) 3
450) Baroque
451) Fra Bartolommeo (1472-1517)
452) *The Garden at Fenzi-Contini*
453) Guglielmo Marconi
454) Confetti
455) Enrico Fermi
456) Galileo Galilei
457) Alessandro Volta
458) Sophia Loren
459) The Venetian School
460) Song of Devine Love
461) The Name of the Rose
462) Forerunner of the modern-day condom
463) Influenza
464) The Trevi fountain
465) The submachine gun
466) Mario Puzo /*The Godfather*
467) Giovanni Boccaccio
468) a) Charles Botta
469) Incognito
470) Sandro Botticelli
471) a) Otello
472) Imbroglio
473) Filippo Brunelleschi
474) Stucco
475) c) Padua
476) The espresso machine
477) Guglielmo Marconi

478)	Lava	526)	St. Augustine
479)	Leonardo Da Vinci	527)	a) Bernard DeVoto
480)	Charles A. Ponzi	528)	The universal joint
481)	Joe Palooka	529)	Fresco
482)	a) Raphael	530)	Nobel Prize in literature
483)	*Bread and Roses*	531)	Botany
484)	Fra Lippo Lippi	532)	A marine compass
485)	a) Carlo Levi	533)	Scenario
486)	Inferno (Hell)	534)	Decameron
487)	The Last Supper	535)	c) Antonello Da Messina
488)	Anti-anthrax serum	536)	*Metamorphoses* or *The*
489)	Autopsy		*Golden Ass*
490)	Mural	537)	William Shakespeare
491)	b) Marcello Malpighi	538)	Gore Vidal
492)	The Merchant of Venice	539)	a) 11th century
493)	Humanism	540)	Cupola
494)	Giotto	541)	Merchant of Venice
495)	Artificial ventilation	542)	Constantino Brumidi
496)	The medical thermometer	543)	Enrico Fermi
497)	Propaganda	544)	Alessandro Volta / The word
498)	The Renaissance		is volt
499)	Bravo	545)	Campanile
500)	Italic	546)	Syphilis (name of a shepherd
501)	Italophile		from Greek mythology who
502)	The watermark		angered the gods)
503)	Terrazzo	547)	Sandro Botticelli
504)	Dante Alighieri	548)	Filippo Brunelleschi / Il
505)	a) 1780		Duomo
506)	b) Pescara, Abruzzo	549)	Giorgione
507)	Leonardo Da Vinci	550)	Eyeglasses
508)	Galileo Galilei	551)	The syringe
509)	Fiasco	552)	Copperplate engraving
510)	Vincenzo Lancia	553)	a) Giorgio Aldine
511)	Francesco Redi	554)	Portico
512)	Neil Armstrong	555)	Julius Caesar
513)	c) Anthony Pescetti, Ph.D	556)	*Christ in Concrete*
514)	St. Peter's, Rome	557)	*Mona Lisa*
515)	Lawrence Ferlinghetti	558)	Ghiberti - Sculptor /
516)	Virgil		Ghirlandaio - Painter
517)	Video magnetic tape	559)	Three-way light bulb
518)	Chemistry	560)	Guglielmo Marconi
519)	a) Marconi monument	561)	St. Thomas Aquinas
520)	a) 1546	562)	Cameo
521)	Dilettante	563)	Niccolo Machiavelli
522)	b) Giovanni Morgagni	564)	Playwriting
523)	(b) Playwrights	565)	Florence
524)	b) Stanislao Carnizzaro	566)	lb.
525)	Replica	567)	Seven Jacuzzi brothers from

183

Pomone, Italy. Joseph, Frank, Valeriano, Rachele, Candido, Giocondo, and Gelindo. Whirlpool bath.

568) c) Ovid
569) a) Benito Mussolini
570) Perfume (Eau de Cologne)
571) Volcano
572) Their tombs
573) The Lincoln Memorial
574) 1) Gallo-Italian
    2) Corsican
    3) Venetian
    4) Central Italian
    5) Tuscan
    6) Southern Italian
575) Gay Talese
576) 1) Machiavelli
    2) Lorenzo de' Medici
577) Verona
578) Dante Gabriel Rossetti
579) Torso
580) a) Niccolo Tartaglia
581) Infantry
582) Michelangelo
583) Milan
584) b) Giorgio Vasari
585) Archeology
586) Mr. Coffee
587) Algebra
588) Studio
589) Cryptography
590) *Mona Lisa*
591) Bellini
592) Capelletti and Montecchi
593) Terracotta
594) The canals of Mars
595) Leonardo da Vinci
596) c) Camillo Golgi
597) Charcoal makers
598) Caravaggio
599) Galileo
600) Marcello Malpighi
601) Regiment
602) Aeneas
603) William Shakespeare
604) c) Ralph J. Menconi
605) a) Leone Battista Alberti

(1404-1472)
606) c) Dr. Salvador Luria
607) The hang glider
608) (b) 1895-1915
609) General
610) c) 1986
611) Electroconvulsive therapy (ECT) or electroshock therapy
612) Umbrella
613) Agostino Beccari
614) Decameron
615) a) Luigi Porta
616) Michelangelo
617) Christina Geogina Rossetti
618) Leonardo da Vinci
619) (b) 6
920) Tempura
621) Helicopter
622) The camera obscura
623) Coffee
624) Galileo Galilei
625) c) Renato Dulbecco
626) Porcelain
627) The decline and fall of the Roman Empire
628) a) Leonardo da Vinci
629) a) Cholera
630) Guglielmo Marconi
631) b) 1598 to 1647
632) Full-Wheel bicycle
633) Avogadro's Number
634) Giambattista Basile
635) b) Luigi Galvani
636) St. Bonaventure
637) R.A. Scotti
638) A leg
639) Raffaele Bombelli
640) c) Arezzo
641) a) Francesco Grimaldi
642) The cookbook
643) b) St. Francis of Assisi
644) a) Bologna
645) The piano
646) Agostino Bassi
647) Galileo Galilei
648) Offshore drilling
649) a) Living, Loving, and

184

Learning
650) a) Martial
651) The Pantelegraph
652) The American eagle
653) Enrico Fermi
654) Video
655) Mario Puzo
656) Archimedes
657) Canzone
658) Arrigo Boito
659) Vincenzo Bellini
660) He wrote the first Catholic novel, *Father Rowland, A North American Tale*
661) c) Alessandro Monzoni
662) a) Girolamo Fabrizio
663) Masaccio
664) Giotto di Bondone
665) His autobiography
666) AIDS virus (In 1978, he discovered and isolated the virus that is linked to leukemia)

History, Geography, & Business

667) b) Mario Cuomo, former governor of New York
668) The Island of Elba
669) A.P. Giannini
670) National Italian-American Foundation
671) Republic of San Marino
672) Venezuela
673) a) Fiorello LaGuardia 1934-46 New York
b) Robert Maestri 1936-46 New Orleans
c) Angelo Rossi 1931-44 San Francisco
674) a) Count Camillo Benso Cavour (1810-1861)
675) Thomas Jefferson
676) b) St. Ambrose
677) c) Joseph and Rosario Di Giorgio / Di Giorgio Corp.
678) Christopher Columbus

679) Bertolli Olive Oil
680) Giuseppe Garibaldi
681) b) San Francisco
682) The Lombards - Region of Lombardy
683) c) 550,000
684) Niccolo Machiavelli (1469-1527)
685) Congressional Medal of Honor
686) c) 1.6 million
687) c) 90% (25% were from Sicily)
688) b) Etruscans
689) John Cabot (Giovanni Caboto)
690) Benito Mussolini
691) Sardinia
692) Naples
693) Giuseppe Mazzini
694) Gallo (Earnest and Julio)
695) a) Corsica
696) c) Roma
697) Marco Polo
698) b) Poker
699) Sicilian Vespers
700) The Itali
701) a) 5th
1) German 2) English 3) Irish 4) African American 5) Italian (26 million Americans of Italian heritage.)
702) The Saracens (Arabs)
703) a) Columbus
704) Giovanni Da Verrazano
705) Geraldine Ferraro
706) New Founde Lande (Newfoundland)
707) Yale University
708) The Apennines
709) a) Federal Bureau of Investigation
710) Ethiopia
711) 1) Ligurian Sea
2) Tyrrhenian Sea
3) Ionian Sea
4) Adriatic Sea

185

712)	The oldest public art museum	752)	Ferdinand Magellan
713)	Pompeii and Herculaneum	753)	U.S. Senate
714)	b) Augusta, Georgia	754)	New City
715)	Mt. Vesuvius	755)	c) 1880
716)	New Amsterdam (Today over 700,000 Italian- Americans resideint Brooklyn.)	756)	Florence, Pisa
		757)	Peter Rodino, U.S. congressman, New Jersey
717)	a) Sicily	758)	Chicago
718)	President Abraham Lincoln	759)	Fiorello La Guardia
719)	Judge John Sirica	760)	a) Genoa
720)	Spanish Armada	761)	Latin
721)	c) General Pietro Bodoglio	762)	Renaissance
722)	1) Capital punishment 2) Torture	763)	Leonardo Da Vinci and Galileo Galilei
723)	Antonin Scalia	764)	b) Dell Publishing Company
724)	Spain	765)	a) 500
725)	Venice	766)	New York Stock Exchange
726)	a) Enrico Tonti	767)	The fork
727)	Ottoman Turks	768)	Admiral Corporation
728)	Germany	769)	A bikini
729)	Britannia	770)	c) National Italian-American Foundation
730)	St. Francis of Assisi, San Francisco	771)	Jeans
		772)	Joseph Alioto
731)	President Calvin Coolidge	773)	Napoleon Bonaparte (Buonaparte)
732)	Capri		
733)	Giovanni Casanova	774)	Tenth and Last
734)	Arkansas, Louisiana	775)	West Coast of Sicily the Tyrrhenian Sea
735)	Italian Swiss Colony		
736)	Catherine De Medici	776)	Joe DiMaggio
737)	A.P. Giannini	777)	Ghirardelli Chocolate Company
738)	Lee Iacocca		
739)	Milan	778)	Admiral Andrea Doria
740)	Planters Nut Company	779)	c) Rome
741)	Coast of Sardinia	780)	1) Angelo Rossi 2) Joseph Alioto 3) George Moscone
742)	The Order Of The Sons Of Italy		
		781)	The Vatican
743)	Andrea Doria	782)	Mario Savio
744)	The garment industry	783)	The Red Brigades
745)	Ice cream	784)	Rome
746)	c)Luigi Palma Di Cesnola	785)	The Trevi fountain
747)	Lucrezia Borgia	786)	Mt.Vesuvius
748)	St. Frances Cabrini	787)	The Irish
749)	Art - 1) Michelangelo 2) Raffaelo 3) Da Vinci	788)	Capri
		789)	b) New Orleans
750)	a) Fairbanks	790)	The Lido
751)	Sebastian Cabot	791)	Del Monte Corporation

792)	Italian card games	835)	c) Four
793)	Wine making	836)	a) Ladies Garment Workers'
794)	The Lion (Il Leone)	837)	La Scala, located in Milan
795)	c) Paris	838)	c) France
796)	Avignon, France 1321	839)	b) Lombardy
797)	Peter Rodino	840)	Judge John Sirica
798)	The Tiber	841)	Dr. Maria Montessori /
799)	Vermont		Montessori School
800)	Fascism	842)	Benito Mussolini
801)	c) Austria	843)	a) 3,845
802)	The Leader	844)	Trieste
803)	The kitchen	845)	a) New York
804)	a) ABC	846)	Padua
805)	Romance languages	847)	Cremona
806)	b) Magenta	848)	Pisa
807)	Peasants	849)	b) 1944
808)	Verranzano-Narrows Bridge	850)	The Renaissance
809)	League of Nations	851)	Galileo Galilei
810)	Congressional Medal of	852)	Filippo Mazzei
	Honor	853)	c) Siena
811)	Ferrari and Maserati	854)	Antonio Meucci
	Automobiles	855)	b) Abruzzo
812)	c) 25%	856)	Turin (Turino)
813)	The Dolomites	857)	Sardinia
814)	Americo Vespucci	858)	a) Mario Biaggi
815)	Pistol (Town of Pistoia)	859)	Vincent Impellitteri
816)	False, President	860)	Sardinia
817)	Henry Ford	861)	The Battle of the Little
818)	Republic		Bighorn, where General
819)	King of Italy		George Armstrong Custer
820)	b) Chicago		and his Seventh Cavalry
821)	Nikita Khrushchev		were massacred.
822)	Al Smith	862)	b) Bologna
823)	a) Lancia	863)	b) The Lawrence Strike
824)	Sacco and Vanzetti	864)	The Neapolitan Coast of
825)	Charles J. Bonaparte		Campania
826)	b) Communist Party	865)	b) Calabria
827)	The Metropolitan Opera	866)	Chef Boyardee
	Company	867)	b) Venice
828)	a) Mississippi	868)	Giuliano Della Rovere (Pope
829)	The Tocci brothers were two		Julius II)
	boys down to the sixth rib,	869)	Melvin Belli
	but only one below	870)	b) Food - pasta
830)	a) Salt	871)	Jacqueline Kennedy
831)	b) Thomas Jefferson	872)	Secretary of Transportation
832)	b) Francis Ford Coppola	873)	Italian cowboy
833)	The Counter Reformation	874)	Ellis Island
834)	a) Brenner Pass	875)	Naples

187

876)	Mafia and Cosa Nostra	911)	Saracens
877)	France	912)	b) Jesuit
878)	Conza - Blimpie	913)	c) Giuseppe Garibaldi
	DeLuca -Subway Sandwich	914)	c) Sicily
879)	Giuseppe Garibaldi	915)	b) The Italian government
880)	China	916)	b) Cape Cod
881)	c) 1,070,000	917)	c) Italian Swiss Colony
882)	Francis Spinola	918)	Ferdinand and Isabella
883)	de' Medici	919)	c) Ravenna
884)	Joe DiMaggio and Marilyn	920)	The Alps
	Monroe	921)	San Marino and Vatican City
885)	Mafia	922)	Southern Pacific
886)	Turkey (1911-12) Italo/	923)	c) Genoa
	Turkish War	924)	Lorenzo de' Medici
887)	b) Suetonius	925)	Florentine dialect
888)	b) 1788	926)	Galileo
889)	a) The Lateran Treaty	927)	The Etruscans
890)	The National Enquirer	928)	The Roman Empire
891)	c) New Orleans	929)	Opera
892)	Louis J. Freeh	930)	Gianni Versaci
893)	Don S. Gentile (Dominic	931)	Cesare Borgia
	Salvatore Gentile)	932)	Giuseppe Verdi
894)	U.S. Ambassadors Peter F.	933)	c) St. Rocco
	Secchia,former U.S.	934)	Piedmont, Val D'Aosta,
	ambassador to Italy. The		Lombardy, Trentino-Alto
	following current U.S.		Adige, Veneto, Friuli-
	ambassadors since 1998.		Venezia Giulia, Liguria,
	Foglietta (Italy);		Emilia-Romagna,Tuscany,
	Lino (Albania);		Umbria, Le Marche, Latium,
	Rosapepe (Romania);		Abruzzo, Molise, Campania,
	Tufo (Hungary).		Apulia, Basilicata, Calabria,
895)	Austria		Sicily, and Sardinia.
896)	Monte Cassino	935)	Tuscany
897)	Alcohol	936)	Shipbuilding
898)	a) Rhode Island	937)	Italian National Anthem
899)	San Salvador	938)	b) 1.55 billion
900)	Sebastian Cabot	939)	56,000,000
901)	Emperor Halie Selassie	940)	b) 1922
902)	New York	941)	Treaty of Versailles
903)	Geraldine Anne Ferraro	942)	Frank Rizzo
904)	Brooklyn	943)	Radio Flyer, Inc. Radio Flyer
905)	Benito Mussolini		wagon
906)	Peter W. Rodino	944)	The crossword puzzle
907)	First Italian-American	945)	Pope (Pope Pius XII)
	Daily Newspaper in U.S.	946)	a) Destroyer
908)	a) 1850	947)	Corsica
909)	Archimedes	948)	b) 1454
910)	c) Arizona	949)	b) Milan

950) a) Genoa
951) Tammany Hall
952) Albania
953) c) June 1943
954) Anno Domini (In the Year of Our Lord)
955) The Papacy
956) Radio signals
957) Lombardy
958) Mezzogiorno
959) Their ships
960) a) National Security Council
961) Rome
962) St. Peter's Basilica Vatican City
963) Florence
964) The Middle East
965) Magna Grecia (Greater Greece)
966) Granted Christians the freedom to worship
967) b) Reggio di Calabria   968) Adriatic Sea
969) Pinkerton Detective Agency
970) Albert R. "Chubby" Broccoli
971) Earthquake and tidal wave
972) St. Francis of Assisi
973) b) Naples
974) Mayor Rudolph W. Giuliani New York City
975) Connecticut
976) Riggio - Barnes and Noble
      DiRomualdo - Borders
      Vitale - Random House
      Geppi - Diamond Comic Distributors
      Florio - Conde Nast
977) Bataan Death March (70,000 started the march)
978) Pope Julius II
979) The Augustine Age
980) The Etruscans
981) Art restoration (canvas paintings)
982) Guccio Gucci / Gucci
983) Sainthood / St. Fabiola
984) Sistine Chapel

985) Cryptography
986) c) 1364 AD
987) b) Diamond
988) Spectacles
989) Besides conducting scientific experiments, he was the first man of Italian descent to fly to the moon.
990) Massachusetts Institute of Technology (MIT)

Sports

991) Mario Andretti
992) Pete Incaviglia
993) Joe Paterno / Vinny Testaverde
994) Gene Tenace / Oakland A's
995) Jack Dempsey
996) a) 6th
997) Vince Lombardi
998) Charles Atlas
999) Tony Conigliaro
1000) Herman Franks
1001) 1) Tony Lazzeri-Second base
      2) Frank Crosetti-Short stop
      3) Joe DiMaggio-Centerfield
1002) Hank Luisetti
1003) Andy Robustelli
1004) Phil Esposito
1005) John Facenda
1006) Basketball-or as it is referred to in Italy, "Basket"
1007) West Germany, 3-1
1008) a) Alfa Romeo
1009) John Montefusco
1010) Tommy Lasorda
1011) Willie Mosconi
1012) Angelo Dundee
1013) Harry Carry
1014) Brian Boitano
1015) Most Assists, Bobby Hurley of Duke has Record at 1,076.
1016) Linda Fratianne
1017) Mary Lou Retton (Rettoni)
1018) Gene Sarazen (Eugenio Saraceni)

189

1019)	Commissioner of Major League Baseball	1061)	c) Women's National Soccer Team
1020)	Members of Baseball's Hall of Fame	1062)	Joe Bellino
1021)	Jim Gentile (5)	1063)	Gino Marchetti and Ollie Matson
1022)	Rocky Colavito	1064)	Edward DeBartolo, Jr.
1023)	Ernie Lombardi, 1938 .342 / 1942 .330	1065)	Lyle Alzado
1024)	Robbie Bosco	1066)	Joe DiMaggio
1025)	P.J. Carlesimo	1067)	Joe Garagiola
1026)	Joe DiMaggio	1068)	Rocky Graziano
1027)	Phil Rizzuto	1069)	The Vince Lombardi Trophy
1028)	The Monaco	1070)	Vince Ferragamo
1029)	Arthur Mercante	1071)	Eddie Arcaro
1030)	(c) Sabre	1072)	a) Brooklyn Dodgers
1031)	Gino Cappelletti	1073)	Franklin Mieuli
1032)	Dan Marino	1074)	Mark Bavaro
1033)	Ken Venturi	1075)	Willie Mosconi
1034)	The Modern Pentathlon	1076)	b) Basketball
1035)	John Cappelletti	1077)	Running
1036)	Primo Carnera	1078)	Power lifting
1037)	Ron Santo	1079)	Boxing
1038)	Mike Eruzione	1080)	Joe Montana
1039)	(c) .408	1081)	a) Dom DiMaggio
1040)	Joe Montana	1082)	Yogi Berra
1041)	Buzzie Bavasi	1083)	Ray Boom-Boom Mancini
1042)	Mario Andretti	1084)	Doug Buffone
1043)	Franco Harris	1085)	Carmen Basilio
1044)	Yogi Berra	1086)	Bowling
1045)	Tony Galento	1087)	Al Costello (Giocomo Costa) The Fabulous Kangaroos
1046)	Vince Lombardi	1088)	Women's tennis
1047)	Jim Valvano	1089)	Tony Lazzeri
1048)	c) Light-Heavyweight	1090)	Jim Gentile
1049)	Sam Rutigliano / Carmen Policy	1091)	Yogi Berra
1050)	Roller skating	1092)	The DiMaggios (Vince, Joe, and Dom.)
1051)	Giorgio Chinaglia	1093)	Brooklyn Dodgers
1052)	Gene Sarazen (Eugenio Saraceni)	1094)	Manager of the Year
		1095)	Billy Martin
1053)	Nick Buoniconti	1096)	Yogi Berra / Dale Berra / Tim Berra
1054)	Tony Manero		
1055)	Mike Getto - Tackle, University of Pittsburgh	1097)	Atlanta Braves / Joe Torre
		1098)	Tony Conigliaro
1056)	Steve Balboni	1099)	b) Johnny Petraglia (1971)
1057)	Pete Incaviglia	1100)	Sal Bando, Oakland A's
1058)	Joe Paterno, Penn State	1101)	Edward DeBartolo, Sr.
1059)	Hank Lusetti	1102)	Ray Malavasi
1060)	Leo Nomellini	1103)	Rocky Marciano

1104) Penn State / Joe Paterno
1105) Rowing
1106) (c) 1984
1107) Manhattan
1108) Platform diving
1109) Allan Ameche
1110) Ken Venturi
1111) Joe DiMaggio
1112) Rocky Marciano
1113) Vince Lombardi
1114) Chicago Bears defeated the Washington Redskins 73-0.
1115) b) Golf
1116) New York Cosmos
1117) Dave Righetti
1118) Gene Sarazen (Eugenio Saraceni)
1119) A hot air ballon
1120) New York Giants
1121) Both were Rookies of the Year. Sax in 1982 and Piazza in 1993.
1122) Yogi Berra - N.Y. Yankees - Roy Campanella - Brooklyn Dodgers
1123) Hit a home run
1124) Auto racing
1125) Paolo Rossi
1126) They were the original owners of the NFL San Francisco 49'ers
1127) Mike Rossman
1128) Tony Esposito
1129) Rocky Marciano / Rocky Graziano
1130) Jennifer Capriati
1131) Ralph DePalma - 1915, Peter DePaola - 1925, Kelly Petillo - 1935, Mario Andretti - 1969
1132) Peter DePaola
1133) Daryl Lamonica
1134) c) 280 mph.
1135) Matt Biondi
1136) Its World Cup Soccer Team
1137) Bowling
1138) Nick Bolletieri Tennis Academy
1139) Middleweight Boxing Champion
1140) World Federation Wrestling Champion
1141) Donna Caponi-Young
1142) Roy Campanella
1143) Phoenix Suns
1144) a) Frank Crosetti (23)
1145) Brooklyn Dodgers
1146) b) 1960
1147) The Davis Cup
1148) Chet Forte
1149) Gary Beban
1150) Sal Maglie
1151) Tony Kubek
1152) Joe Garagiola
1153) Primo Carnera
1154) Joe Torre
1155) b) Equestrian riding
1156) Mario Andretti
1157) Ferrari
1158) With a 112 average, she bowled a perfect 300 game
1159) Rollie Fingers
1160) Fencing
1161) a) Johnny Musso
1162) Ernie Broglio
1163) Swimming
1164) A Frisbee
1165) U.S. Amateur Golf Championship
1166) Motorcycling in the 350cc and 500cc class
1167) A motorcycle
1168) Roger Maris' 61st home run
1169) b) Jake LaMotta
1170) Willie Pep (Guglielmo Papaleo)
1171) World Cup Games (Soccer)
1172) Basketball
1173) Carmen Basilio
1174) Roy Campanella
1175) Steve Sax
1176) Mike Eruzione, captain of the gold medal U.S. Olympic hockey team
1177) a) Marino Pieretti
1178) Vince Lombardi

1179) Gabriela Sabatini
1180) Brian Piccolo
1181) College Basketball,
Carneseca - St. John's
Massimino - Villanova /
UNLV
1182) Gino Marchetti
1183) Ted Hendricks
1184) a) Utah Jazz
1185) b) 4 times
1186) Soccer
1187) Boxing
1188) Terry Hanratty
1189) Marathon bicyclist
1190) Babe Pinelli
1191) b) Atlanta Braves
1192) Baseball umpires
1193) c) Chicago White Sox
1194) A Bicycle
1195) c) Notre Dame
1196) Sal Maglie at .818 (18-4) tops
Vic Raschi at .724 (21-8)
1197) A. Barlett Giamatti
1198) c) Dante Bichette 1995 - 128 -
Joe Torre 1971 - 137 - Rocky
Colavito 1965 - 108
1199) a) 1939-40
1200) Super Bowl / Joe Montana
1201) Most points scored at 1,260
1202) The Heisman Trophy
1203) 1998 - c) 65 yards
1204) c) Billy Martin
1205) Linda Fratianne
1206) Heisman trophy winners
1207) Vince Lombardi
1208) Brian Piccolo
1209) Andy Robustelli
1210) Joe Montana
1211) Rick Pitino
1212) Women's college basketball
1213) Vinny Pazienza
1214) National Italian-American
Sports Hall of Fame
1215) Lewis Pessano
1216) Chicago Cubs
1217) Carmen Policy
1218) San Francisco 49'ers

Romans

1219) Marc Antony (Marcus
Antonius 82-31 BC)
1220) Augustus (63 BC - 14 AD)
1221) The Colosseum
1222) Constantine I
1223) Diocletian (245-316 AD)
1224) The Etruscans
1225) Julius Caesar
1226) Edict of Milan
1227) Punic Wars
1228) Et Tu, Brute?
1229) Julius Caesar (I came, I saw,
I conquered.)
1230) Gladiolus
1231) c) Scotland
1232) b) Public hospitals
1233) Stockings
1234) Caesarian section
1235) Cement
1236) The assassination of Julius
Caesar
1237) Hadrian
1238) a) Cassius
1239) Censor
1240) Capitoline Hill
1241) Caligula
1242) Hannibal
1243) The Julian calendar which,
with some minor changes, is
the one we use today.
1244) Claudius I
1245) Cleopatra (The last
Macedonian queen of Egypt)
1246) b) Cicero
1247) b) Organ
1248) Bocce
1249) Bath
1250) Galba
1251) Dictator
1252) Bacchus
1253) Last of the Roman emperors
in the West (476 AD)
1254) True

1255)	Libya	1291)	A republic
1256)	Jupiter	1292)	Arena
1257)	Julian Emperors	1293)	Consul
1258)	b) Janus	1294)	Corinth, Carthage
1259)	Flora	1295)	The Pantheon
1260)	Pyrrhus, King of Epirus, defeated the Romans at Heraclea in modern day Basilicata,but suffered ruinous losses, hence the expression, Pyrrhic victory.	1296)	The Circus Maximus
		1297)	Rome's 1,000th Anniversary (247 AD)
		1298)	Lighthouses
		1299)	Malta
		1300)	Aqueducts
1261)	c) Brindisi	1301)	Titus
1262)	The Rubicon	1302)	Their refusal to worship the emperors
1263)	The introduction of heavy, mounted troops with horse and man adorned in scale armor.	1303)	Nero
		1304)	c) Diocletian
		1305)	The Christian (Catholic) church
1264)	Constantine had a vision which revealed to him that, as a Christian, he would be victorious	1306)	A monthly grain allowance
		1307)	a) Marcus Aurelius
		1308)	a) Vandals
1265)	Marcus Aurelius	1309)	Denarius
1266)	First day of spring, May Day	1310)	c) 1,000 yrs.
1267)	Metamorphoses	1311)	c) 1,500,000
1268)	a) Minerva	1312)	Romania
1269)	Pontius Pilate	1313)	Honey
1270)	Praetor	1314)	b) 31 BC
1271)	b) 27 BC	1315)	a) Tiberius
1272)	Praetorian Guard	1316)	The Appian Way
1273)	b) 753 BC	1317)	The Gauls (Celts)
1274)	S.P.Q.R.	1318)	The Phoenicians
1275)	Cupid	1319)	Sicily
1276)	Tiberius	1320)	Scipio Africanus
1277)	Titus	1321)	The army and its leaders became the dominant factor in politics
1278)	Toga		
1279)	Vestal, from the virgin goddess Vesta	1322)	b) 79 AD
		1323)	As cavalry units
1280)	Romulus	1324)	Their horses
1281)	The Etruscans	1325)	c) Ravenna
1282)	Colosseum	1326)	Rome
1283)	b) Hungary	1327)	Romulus and Remus
1284)	c) Olympic games	1328)	St. Augustine of Hippo
1285)	b) Its engineers	1329)	b) Caligula
1286)	Nero	1330)	Our Sea
1287)	Tribunes	1331)	Roman gods
1288)	Romulus and Remus	1332)	Spartacus
1289)	Picts (Pictae)	1333)	The tie
1290)	The Senate		

1334)	a) Nero		church in the west
1335)	Heads or tails / coin flip	1375)	c) 509 BC
1336)	Fish tanks	1376)	Pyrrhus
1337)	a) Agrippina	1377)	St. Valentine
1338)	An appetite	1378)	Pontius Pilate
1339)	Masada	1379)	Julius Caesar
1340)	A publishing house	1380)	Marbles
1341)	Augustus Caesar	1381)	(Marius Junius) Brutus
1342)	Lucius Junius Brutus	1382)	Horace
1343)	Cicero	1383)	Romulus and Remus
1344)	Chariot racing	1384)	Byzantine Empire
1345)	Diocletian	1385)	July / Julius Caesar
1346)	Marc Antony	1386)	Julius Caesar
1347)	Julius Caesar	1387)	Justinian Code
1348)	Constantine	1388)	Julius Caesar
1349)	Cicero	1389)	Julius Caesar
1350)	Quintus Fabius	1390)	a) Hadrian
1351)	Genius	1391)	Alaric
1352)	Fortuna	1392)	Attila the Hun
1353)	a) The Aurelian Wall	1393)	By turning it into a legion
1354)	Nero		which allowed for much
1355)	Cicero		greater mobility.
1356)	c) 3 - Cornelia, Pompexa,	1394)	b) Theodosius I
	and Calpurnia	1395)	Plebians
1357)	b) 476 AD	1396)	a) Tellus
1358)	The Etruscans	1397)	Patricians
1359)	The Colosseum	1398)	Satire
1360)	One of the first Roman books	1399)	c) Ostia
	on military tactics. It was	1400)	The Forum
	written by Sextus Julius	1401)	Carthage
	Frontinus, provincial	1402)	The Etruscans
	governor of Britian circa 75	1403)	c) Actium
	AD.	1404)	A silver eagle
1361)	Papyrus	1405)	c) 6,000
1362)	The age of Cicero	1406)	Roman law
1363)	Diocletian	1407)	Caligula
1364)	Horace	1408)	Pax Romana
1365)	Hannibal	1409)	Villa
1366)	Neptune	1410)	Baths
1367)	Venus	1411)	Aqueducts
1368)	Constantine	1412)	Oboe
1369)	Horse racing with Arabian	1413)	b) 170 BC
	horses imported by Romans	1414)	The first stone bridge
1370)	Imperium		in Rome, circa 179 BC.
1371)	Gladiator	1415)	Archimedes
1372)	Circus Maximus in Rome	1416)	Water clock
1373)	St. Stephen	1417)	Mosaics
1374)	As the center of the Christian	1418)	b) 62 BC

1419)	b) 1748 AD	1460)	Tortoise formation
1420)	c) 212 AD	1461)	A javelin
1421)	a) St. Ambrose	1462)	a) Thermopolium
1422)	The Etruscans	1463)	Podium
1423)	c) Palatine Hill	1464)	b) 241 BC
1424)	An aqueduct	1465)	Standard Roman War Galley
1425)	Commodus	1466)	He committed suicide
1426)	Spartacus	1467)	The Macedonian Phalanx, losses - 100 Romans 20,000 Macedonians
1427)	c) Trajan		
1428)	Fish market		
1429)	Roman numerals	1468)	The four types of legionary (soldiers who made up a Roman legion, up to the 2nd century BC)
1430)	Atrium		
1431)	a) Marcus Tullius Cicero (108-43 BC)		
1432)	Roman women	1469)	An ancient surveying instrument
1433)	Trivium		
1434)	Two of the seven hills of Rome	1470)	True
		1471)	c) Trajan
1435)	The honking of the sacred geese of Juno	1472)	Siege works
		1473)	The Palatine Hill
1436)	b) Vaspasian	1474)	Marrage ceremony
1437)	c) Sabines	1475)	a) Consolidation
1438)	A cemetery	1476)	c) Villanovan
1439)	Lyre	1477)	The Celts
1440)	Conquest of Italy	1478)	Toilet paper
1441)	Macedonia	1479)	b) 1453
1442)	The javelin	1480)	Gauls
1443)	A naval boarding plank	1481)	Lucretius
1444)	The baggage train	1482)	A milestone
1445)	Switzerland	1483)	b) 80
1446)	Bridge building	1484)	Circus
1447)	The great military roads	1485)	Basilica
1448)	Julius Caesar	1486)	Auxiliaries
1449)	Centurions	1487)	b) A lucky charm
1450)	Its underwater ram, located at the front of the ship.	1488)	a) Asses' milk
		1489)	c) A tool for scraping off dirt when bathing.
1451)	It was named after the Praetorium, the area of the camp where the general's tent was pitched.	1490)	c) Discovering the will of the gods.
		1491)	Justinian
		1492)	Fresco
1452)	a) Augustus		
1453)	Diploma		
1454)	Cicero		
1455)	Hadrian's Wall		
1456)	c) The cavalry		
1457)	Blockade / Assault		
1458)	Dice		
1459)	b) Aedile		

Web Page Listings:

Now, with the World Wide Web, you can access information and have it appear before your eyes in a matter of seconds. For example, if you want to go to the Uffizi Gallery in Florence, you don't have to telephone your travel agent and book an airline ticket and hotel reservation. You can now simply sit down in front of your computer and type in: **www.televisual.it/uffizi/** and you are there! This fantastic web site has an index listing the various rooms, artists, and works housed in the museum. Briefly, the Uffizi Gallery, founded in Florence in 1581 by the De Medici family, is one of the oldest museums in the world. This web site contains pictures, comments, biographies, and a glossary of artistic movements and techniques. You may even register to download full-screen high resolution pictures.

If you are not aware, there are many Italian and Italian-American related web sites on the Internet that encompass a host of subjects from opera to genealogy. Every day new sites are added and it would be impossible to keep up with them or list them all in a static, published text; but to get you started, I have listed several web sites that I have found most interesting and informative. One good thing about web sites are the links they list, which can direct you to still more important and related web sites. Here are a few that I know you will find interesting. If you know of any outstanding sites, please email me at **heritage@dellnet.com** with the address so I can include it in the next printing of this book. **http://www.geocities.com/Athens/Acropolis/1709/Alfano1a.htm** This is one of the earliest web sites I found and perhaps one of the best. Mr. Alfano has performed a great service to the Italian-American community and I commend him. His listed links are a great resource for Italian-Americans interested in learning more about their heritage:

http:homepage.interaccess.com/~arduinif/index.htm Another interesting and equally valuable site is the Arduini and Pizzo family web site created by Mr. Frank Arduini. Both Mr. Arduini and Mr. Alfano have brought to light valuable information that can help tens of thousands understand their Italian roots better.

Here are several other addresses that you may find of interest:

For the opera fan: **www.opera.it/English/**

The Italian Genealogy Homepage:

Genealogy assistance: **www.italgen.com/**

Italian Genealogical Group : **www.italiangen.org/contact.htm**

Italy on the Web:
www.geocities.com/Athens/1809/index.html

The Italian Heritage Society of Indiana:
www.italianheritage.org/

The Italian Consulate**:**
www.crl.com/~conitdet/links.htm

Business finder, people finder, email search and travel guide for Italy
http://in100.infospace.com/_1_198640292_info/index_int.htm

***Vincero Enterprises: Authors web site for this book.
www.italianheritage.net

The excellent service I used to help me research both my father's and mother's families in Italy:

Genealogical Search Services.

Mr. & Mrs. Norman Moyes at:
www.itsnet.com/~gss

POINT - http://members.aol.com/pointhompg/home.htm

PIE   - www.cimorelli.com/pie/piesani.htm

Italian-American Organization Web Sites

Keep our Italian customs and traditions alive and vibrant by participating in an Italian-American organization in your area. Here are the web page listings of some of the major Italian-American organizations in the United States that may have a local chapter in your area.

1) The National Italian American Foundation (NIAF)
www.niaf.org/

2) Order Sons of Italy in America (OSIA)
www.osia.org

3) UNICO
www.uniconat.com/

4) FIERI-Young Italian-Americans to age 39
www.fieri.org/

Participate in your Heritage in the Second Edition

After reading the material in this book, if you believe I have overlooked a noteworthy Italian or Italian-American person, event, or invention, I encourage you to send me the information. If it is included in the next edition, your name will appear in a special contributor's section. You have a wonderful opportunity to participate to the "heritage awareness" of our Italian-American community. Email, write, telephone, fax or carrier pigeon your information to:

Leon J. Radomile
c/o Vincero Enterprises
11 East Blithedale Ave.
Mill Valley, CA 94941
Telephone - 1-800-715-1492
FAX - (415) 883-4115
Email address: heritage@dellnet.com

Some more outstanding Italian-American Web-Sites

http://abruzzo2000.com/
Sicily@www.sicily.infcom.it
www.daddezio.com/italgen.html
Italian Tribune - **www.italiantribune.com/100001Opening-HomePage.htm**
The Italian web ring: **www.angelfire.com/ny/maryg/ring/htm**
Italian language courses: **www.cyberitalian.com/**

*Remember - if you have a great Italian-American web site, please send it to me for inclusion in the next edition.

Italian Dessert Recipes
*To eat (mangiare) while reading this book.

One of my store's customers, who is of Italian descent, asked me if I planned to have any Italian recipes listed. It took me only an instant to decide that she had a great idea. What type of an Italian book would this be, anyway, if it didn't have at least a couple of Italian recipes? Thank you, Kathleen Gigliotti-Fenger, for your idea and contribution. That evening, I telephoned my mother and asked her to select two of her favorite dessert recipes for the book. They should represent our Italian home regions of Abruzzi and Sicily, I told her. Following are the two dessert recipes my mother selected. Try them—you won't be sorry. **(If you have a great recipe, sent it to me, maybe the next book will be on great Italian-American recipes.)**

Abruzzi Black Cake

4 oz. (4 sqs.) unsweetened chocolate
1/2 cup butter
5/8 cup flour

1/2 cup sugar
3 eggs, separated
3/4 cup chopped filberts

Melt chocolate over hot water. Cream butter, add sugar, and continue beating until creamy. Add egg yolks and beat until well blended. Add melted, cooled chocolate, and beat well for 2 minutes. Beat egg whites until stiff but not dry. Fold into chocolate mixture. Combine nuts and sifted flour and fold gently into batter. Pour into 8 inch square pan lined with waxed paper, and bake in moderate oven 350°F until a toothpick inserted into cake comes out clean and cake shrinks from side of pan, 35 to 40 minutes. Cool cake in pan, and frost with chocolate frosting.

Sicilian Cream Tart
Cassata All Siciliana

1 sponge cake, 9-inch
1-1/2 lb. ricotta
6 tablespoons rum

1/4 cup chopped candied cherries
1/2 teaspoon cinnamon

1/2 cup powdered sugar

1/2 cup chopped toasted almonds

2 oz. grated sweet chocolate

Slice cake into 3 layers. Or, use a commercial sponge cake which may be bought in layers. Sprinkle layers with rum.

Crush ricotta very fine with hands or potato masher, add sugar, and beat 3 minutes, until creamy. Stir in remaining ingredients until well blended. Spread over sponge cake layers, using a half-inch of filling on each layer. Spread top and sides with the following frosting:

1/4 cup butter

2 egg whites

2 1/2 cups powdered sugar

1 teaspoon almond extract

Cream butter with 1 cup sifted confectioners sugar. Beat egg whites until stiff, and gradually beat into egg whites the remaining 1 1/2 cups powdered sugar. Fold egg whites into butter mixture, and add the almond extract.

Cover sides and top of Cousteau evenly with the frosting. Store in refrigerator until ready to serve. Serves 10.

105 Italian-American Festivals in 30 States Around the Country to Enjoy

A special thank you to Dona De Sanctis of the National Italian American Foundation, for supplying me with the directory of Italian-American festivals.

City	Month	Contact
California		
Lodi	June	John Ferro (219)368-3077
Oakland	Sept.	Richard Vannucci (510)581-9139
Sacramento	Aug.	Ital. Cultural Society (916)Italy-00
San Diego	Oct.	Marco Li Mandri (619)493-4433
San Jose	Oct.	Sal Scrivano (408)293-7122
Santa Barbara	Aug.	Italian Club (805)565-2968
San Rafael	Aug/Sept	(Film) Lido Cantarutti (415)456-4056
Santa Rosa	Sept.	J. Mancini-Mitchell (707)542-5245
Stockton	Aug.	Mike Turbetti (209)931-3529
Sutter Creek	June	Chris Formularo (209)267-0206
Visalia	Oct.	Ida Romanazzi (209) 732-0823
Colorado		
Denver	Aug.	Potenza Lodge (303)477-1722
Connecticut		
New Haven	June	St. Anthony's (203)624-1418
New Haven	June	St. Andrew's (203)865-9846
Norwich	Sept.	Frank Jacaruse (860)889-0864
Straford	Aug.	Daniel L. Capozzi (203)574-2832
Middleberry	Sept.	Jenny Johnsky (203)574-2832
Waterbury	July	Carmine Raneri (860)576-8981
Waterbury	Aug.	Roberto Mancini (860)274-2302
Wesport	July	Peter T. Romano (203)227-0595
Delaware		
Wilmington	June	St. Anthony's (302)421-3790
Florida		
Melbourne	March	Frank A. Cona (407)768-1560
Ft. Walton Beach	Oct.	Vito Marinelli (850)678-2725
Palm Coast	Oct.	Alphonse Ripandelli (904)445-1893
Venice	Feb.	Carl Sellitti (941)493-6344
Vero Beach	Oct.	Jerry Giordano (407)562-9170
Illinois		
Benld	May	Jerry Saracco (217)835-2689
Berwyn	Sept.	Joe Camarda (773)736-3766
Blue Island	Aug.	St. Donatus (708)755-2982
Chicago Heights	Aug.	Luciano Panici (708)755-2982
Chicago	June	Heart of Italy (773)625-0506
Melrose Park	July	Lady of Mt. Carmel (708)344-4140
North Lake	July	Mary Scalera (708)562-5530
Chicago	July	Tony Napoli (847)537-3365
Farmington	Sept.	Chamber of Commerce (309)245-2441
Roskford	Aug.	Noe Marinelli (815)885-2150

Springfield	Sept.	Claudio M. Pecori (217)788-2450
Stone Park	Aug.	Italian Cultural Center (708)345-3842
Stone Park	May	Joe Bruno (630)350-7822

Louisiana

Harvey	Sept.	Fr. Tom Ruekert (504)340-1962
New Orleans	Sept.	Gasper J. Schiro (504)486-6936

Maine

Portland	Aug.	St. Peter's Church (207)797-5954

Massachusetts

Boston	July	Edna (617)635-3911
Boston	Aug.	Lenny Gilardi (508)283-7716
Boston	Aug/Sept	20 different festivals (617)523-2110
East Boston	July	Lisa Capogreco (617)561-3201
Lawrence	Sept.	Raymond E. DiFiore (978)794-5762
Worcester	July	Father Bafaro (508)797-4546

Michigan

Grand Rapids	Aug.	Al Forte (616)942-7354
Sterling Heights	Aug.	M. Reno Garagiola (810)751-2855

Minnesota

Chisholm	July	Jill Verichak (800)372-6437

Missouri

St. Louis	Oct.	Marianne Peri Sack (314)837-8830

Nebraska

Omaha	July	Joe Citro (402)341-9562

Nevada

Reno	Oct.	Eldorado Hotel 1-800-648-5966

New Jersey

South Orange	Oct.	Pat Gagliardi (516)223-7138
Bayonne	Aug.	Rev. Donald Di Pasquale (201)436-8160
Hammonton	July	Fr. Joseph (609)561-3012
Hoboken	July	St. Ann's (201)659-1116
Holmdel	Sept.	PNC Bank Arts Center (732)442-9200
North Wildwood	June	Main Street Org. (609)729-6818
North Wildwood	June	Vince Piccirilli (609)522-8395
Oakhurst	Aug.	Henry Schepiga (732)229-5996

New York

Bronx	June/July	Msgr. John A. Ruvo (718)295-3770
Brooklyn	July	Mt. Carmel Church (718)384-0223
Glen Cove	July	James Suozzi (516)671-1796
Glen Cove	Aug.	Ida Corvino Milletich (516)6761625x101
Hempstead	Sept.	Jeanie Werner (516) 463-6580
Manhattan	Sept.	San Gennaro Society (212)577-2000
Scotia	Aug.	Bobby Mallozzi (518)355-1144
Syracuse	Sept.	William Salomone (315)437-2058
Utica	Sept.	St. Anthony's Church (315)732-1177
Watertown	July	St. Anthony' Church (315)782-1190
Watertown	Sept.	Italian American Club (315)782-1080
Valhalla	July	Sal Cantatori (914)993-9333

Ohio

Canton	June	Sam Coletti (330)494-0886
Columbus	Oct.	Msgr. Mario Serraglio (614)294-5319
Lowellville	July	Al Boggia (330)536-6978
Cuyahoga Falls	July	Martin Testa (330)296-8154

Oklahoma

McAlester, S.E.	May	Italian Festival Foundation (918)426-2055

Oregon

Portland	Aug.	Lucia DiFabo (503)284-6989

Pennsylvania

Erie	June	Robert Casillo (814)864-1703
Erie	March	Ronald J. DiVecchio (814)456-6304
Erie	June	Ronald J. DiVecchio (814)456-6304
Erie	Aug.	Ronald J. DiVecchio (814)456-6304
Erie	Aug.	Michael Barzano (814)455-8563
Old Forge	Sept.	Louis Ciuccio (570)562-0181
Pittsburgh	Oct.	Italian Consulate (412)391-7669
Scranton	Sept.	Carlo Pisa (570)343-9624
Crabtree	July	Rizzi DiFabo (724)836-4323
Dunmore	Aug.	Rev. Antony Tombasco (570)344-1239
Edensberg	May	Joseph J. Bentvegna (570)344-1239

Rhode Island

Newport	Oct.	23 America's Cup Rd. Newport, RI 02840
Westerly	July	111 High St. Westerly, RI 02840

Tennessee

Nashville	Sept.	(615)255-5600x251 or 217

Washington

Walla Walla	Oct.	Carmela Destito-Buttice (509)529-1509

West Virginia

Clarksburg	Sept.	Rosalyn Queen (304)622-7314
Wheeling	July	(304)233-2771

Wisconsin

Kenosha	Aug.	(414)652-2771
Kenosha	July	Fr. John Richetta (414)652-7660
Milwaukee	July	Paul Iannelli (414)223-2180 (414)223-2193

To order additional copies for family and friends.
(A great gift)

Telephone orders to: **1-800-715-1492**

Mail orders to: **Vincero Enterprises**
11 E. Blithedale Ave.
Mill Valley, CA 94941

Place orders through our web page: **www.italianheritage.net**

FAX orders to: **(415) 883-4115**

Single copies price	$14.92
California residents 7.25%	1.08
Postage & Handling	2.50
Total	$18.50

Quantity shipping:		
1 to 5	$ 2.50
6 to 10	$ 4.00
11 to 24	$ 6.00
25 to 100	$10.00
101 to 1,000	$25.00
over 1,000	to be determined

*Books shipped via U.S. mail or UPS

Payment can be made with:
Visa, Mastercard, Discover, American Express,
personal or business **checks,** or **money orders.**

Bibliography

Eric Amfitheatrof, *The Children of Columbus.* Boston, Little, Brown, 1973.

Attenzione Magazine, issues: October 1981 through April 1987. New York, Adams Publications.

Barone, Arturo, *Italians First! An A to Z of Everything Achieved First by Italians.* Third Revised Edition. Kent, England: Renaissance Books, 1999.

Barraclough, Geoffrey, *The Times Atlas of World History.* Maplewood, New Jersey, 1979

Barzini, Luigi, *The Italians.* Tenth Printing. New York: Atheneum, 1964.

Benet, William Rose, *The Reader's Encyclopedia,* Second Edition. New York, Harper & Row, 1965.

Benton, William, Publisher, *Encyclopedia Britannica.* Chicago, Il., 1966.

Boni, Ada, *Italian Regional Cooking.* Italy, Bonanza Books, 1969.

Brownstone, David and Irene Franck, *Timelines of War.* Boston, Little, Brown, 1996.

Catanzaro, Angela, *The Home Book of Italian Cooking.* New York, Fawcett, 1957.

Cipolla, Gaetano, *What Italy Has Given To The World.* New York, Legas, 1994.

Cross, Milton, *Complete Stories of the Great Operas.* New York, Boubleday, 1952.

Dahmus, Joseph, *Dictionary of Medieval Civilization.* New York, Macmillan, 1984.

De Sanctis, Dona, editor, *Ambassador Magazine.* Rome, Italy Italy Magazine, 1989 through 1999.

De Sanctis, Dona, editor, *The NIAF News*, Publication of the National Italian American Foundation, Inc. Washington D.C. 1989 through 1999.

Durant, Will, *The Renaissance: A History of Civilization in Italy from the Birth of Petrarch to the Death of Titian—1304-1576.* New York, Simon & Schuster, 1953.

Duckett, Eleanor Shipley, *The Gateway to the Middle Ages: Italy.* New York, Dorsett Press, 1938.

Ganeri, Anita, *How Would You Survive As An Ancient Roman?*

Danberry, CT., Grolier, 1995.

Giordano, Joseph, editor, *The Italian-American Catalog*. New York 1986.

Giscard d'Estaing, Valerie-Anne, *The World Almanac Book of Inventions*. New York, World Almanac, 1985.

Grant, Michael, *History of Rome*. New York, Charles Scribners & Sons, 1978.

Greenfield, Jeff, *Television: PrimeTime-News-Sports*. New York, Abrams, 1980.

Timetables of History. New York, Simon & Schuster, 1979.

Harkness, John, *The Academy Awards Handbook*. Updated 1999 Revised Edition. New York, Pinnacle Books, Fifth Edition, 1999.

Iorizzo, Luciano J., and Salvatore Mondello, *The Italian-Americans*. New York, Twayne, 1980.

Janson, H.W., *History of Art. A Survey of the Major Visual Arts from the Dawn of History to the Present Day*. New York, Prentice-Hall, 1969.

Katz, Ephraim, *The Film Encyclopedia,* Third Edition. New York, Harper Collins, 1998.

Kendall, Alan, *The World of Musical Instruments*. London, Hamlyn, 1972.

Levey, Judith S. & Agnes Greenhall, editors, *The Concise Columbia Encyclopedia*. New York, Columbia University Press, 1983.

Meserole, Mike, *Ultimate Sports Lists*. New York, DK Publishing, 1999.

Michael, Paul, *The Academy Awards: A Pictorial History*. Fifth edition, New York, Crown Publishers, 1982.

Moquin, Wayne, and Charles Van Doren, editors, *A Documentary History of the Italian-Americans*. New York, Praeger, 1974

Morison, Samuel Eliot, *The Great Explorers: The European Discovery of America*. New York, Oxford Press, 1978.

Nelli, Humbert S., From Immigrants to Ethnics: *The Italian-Americans*. New York, Oxford University Press,1983.

Ogrizek, Dore, editor, *The World In Color: Italy*. New York, Whittlesey House, 1950.

Rolle, Andrew, *Troubled Roots*. Chicago, Free Press, 1980.

Scarpaci, Vincenza, *A Portrait of The Italians in America*. New York, Scribner, 1982.

Spignesi, Stephen, *The Italian 100. A Ranking of the Most Influential, Cultural, Scientific, and Political Figures, Past and Present*. Secaucus,

New Jersey: Citadel Press Book, 1998.

Pescosolido, Carl A., and **Gleason, Pamela,** *The Proud Italians - Our Great Civilizers.* Washington D.C.,Latium Publishing, 1991.

Sports Illustrated, *1999 Sports Almanac.* New York, Bishop Books, 1999.

Stirton, Paul, *Renaissance Painting.* New York, Mayflower Books, 1979.

Denise Dersin, editor.*What Life Was Like When Rome Ruled The World.* Richmond, Virginia, Time-Life Books,1997.

Wenborn, Neil, *The 20th Century: A Chronicle In Pictures.* London, Hamlyn, 1989.

Woolf, Henry, Editor,*Webster's New Collegiate Dictionary.* United States, 1973.

Index

A

ABC #243, #274, #804
Abruzzo #506, #855, #934
Abruzzo, Ben #1119
Accolti, Bernardo #534
Acker, Jean #161
Actium #1403
Addie, Johnny #1187
Admiral Corporation #768
Adriatic Sea #711, #968
Aedile #1459
Aeneas #602
Aeneid #602
Agostini, Giacomo #1166
Agricolo #495
Agrippina #1337
Aida #91
AIDS virus #666
Airoldi, Giuseppe #944
Al dente #100
Alamanni, Luigi #438
Alaric #1391
Albania #952
Alberghetti, Anna Maria #211
Alberini, Filoteo #188, #608
Alberti, Leone Battista #589, #605
Albertazzie, Colonel Albert F. #880
Albert, King Charles #894
Alberto, Peter Caesar #716
Alcohol #897
Alda, Alan #142
Alda, Robert #142
Aldine, Giorgio #553
Alesia #1389, 1448
Alfa Romeo #1008
Alfano, Franco #216
Algebra #587
Alighieri, Dante #504
Alioto, Joseph #772, #780
Allegro #53
Alps, The #920
Altobelli, Alessandro #1136

Alzado, Lyle #1065
Amaretto #387
Amato, Joe #1143
Ambrose, St. #676
Ambrosio, Arturo #332
Ameche, Alan #1109, #1206
Ameche, Don #213
Amerighi, Michelanglo #598
Andante #202
Andretti, Mario #991, #1042, #1131,#1156
Angeli, Pier #334
Anno Domini #954
Anti-Anthrax Serum #488
Antonelli, John #1120
Antonini, Luigi #836
Antonioni, Michelangelo #371
Antonius, Marcus (Marc Antony) #1219,#1346,#1403
Apennines, The #708
Apicius, Flavius Marcus #642, #1338
Appetite #1338
Appian Way #1316
Apuleius, Lucius #536
Apulia #115, #185, #934
Aqueduct #1300, #1411, #1424
Aquinas, St. Thomas #561
Arabian horses #1369
Arcaro, Eddie #1071
Archeology #585
Archimedes #656, #909, #1415
Arena #1292
Aretinus, Guido #539, #640
Arezzo #640
Argentina #178
Ariosto, Ludovico #440
Arizona #910
Arkansas #734
Armani, Gorgio #930
Armati, Salvino #550

208

Bertelli, Angelo #213, #1206
Bertolli Olive Oil #679
Bertolucci, Bernardo #144
Barziza, Decimus et Ultimus #774
Biaggi, Mario #858
Biaggini, Benjamin #922
Bianchi, Daniela #337
Bichette, Dante #1198
Bicycle #632
Bigolo #278
Bikini #769
Bini, Lucio #611
Biondi, Matt #1135
Biondo, Plavio #627
Biringucci, Vannoccio #518
Blake, Robert #339
Blimpie #878
Blockade #1457
Blood of Judas #330
Boccaccio, Giovanni #426,#467, 614#
Bocce #1248
Bocelli, Andrea #2, #275
Bodoglio, General Pietro #721
Boiardi, Ettore #866
Boitano, Brian #1014
Boito, Arrigo #658
Bolletieri, Nick #1183
Bologna #644, #862
Bombelli, Raffaele #639
Bon Jovi, Jon #373
Bonapane, Alan #1164
Bonaparte, Charles J. #825
Bonaparte, Napoleon #773
Bond, James #101
Bono, Sonny (Salvatore) #223
Borders Books #976
Borgia, Cesare #931
Borgia, Lucrezia #55, #747
Borgnine, Ernest #5, #227
Bosco, Robbie #1024
Botany #531
Botta, Charles #468
Botticelli, Sandro #431,#470,#547
Bouillabaisse #240
Bozo the Clown #298
Brabantio #471
Brandi, Raffaele Esposito #95

Bravo #499
Brazzi, Rossano #1
Bread and Roses #483
Brenner Pass #834
Bridge building #1446
Brindisi #1261
Briscola #792
Britannia #729
Broccoli, Albert R. #970
Broglio, Ernie #1162
Brooklyn #904
Brother Cipolla #426
Brumidi, Constantino #542
Brunelleschi, Filippo #473, #548,#605
Brutus, Lucius Junius #1342
Brutus, Marius Junius #1381
Bufano, Beniamino #420
Buffone , Doug #1084
Buitoni, Giovanni #870
Bulla #1487
Buonaparte, Napoleone #930
Buoniconti, Nick #1053
Buono, Victor #148
Buontalenti, Bernardo #745
Buscagilia, Leo #649
Butter #25
Byzantine Empire #1384

C

Cabiria #234
Cabot, John #689,#751,#959
Cabot, Sebastian #751, #900
Cabrini, St. Frances #748
Caccini, Giulio #247
Julius Caesar #555, #1225, #1229, #1236, #1347, #1388, #1385, #1386,#1379, #1389, #1448
Caesarian Section #1234
Cage, Nicolas #58
Cagliari, #860
Calabria #110, #865, #934
Caligula #1241, #1329, #1407
Calpurnia #1356
Calvary #1456
Calvino, Italo #191

Doria, Andrea #743
Drummer #277
Dulbecco, Renato #625
Dundee, Angelo #1012
Durante, Jimmy #86, #237
Durante, Sal #1168

E

E.T. #365
Earthquake #971
Eastwood, Clint #184
Eco, Umberto #461
Edict of Milan #966, #1226
Edwards, Vince #26
Egypt #1314
Eisenhower, Dwight D. #721
Elba, The Island of #668
Electroconvulsive Therapy
(ECT) #611
Electroshock Therapy #611
Elizabethan Concepts of
Courtesy #430
Ellis Island #874
Emilia-Romagna #934
Emperors #1302
Engineers #1285
Ennius, Quintus #516
Eruzione, Mike #1038, #1176
Esposito, Phil #1004
Esposito, Tony #1128
Esposito, William #892
Espresso machine #476
Et tu, Brute? #1228
Ethiopia #710
Etna, Mt. #967
Etruscans, The #1224,#1281,
#1358,#1402,#1422
Extravaganza #96
Eyeglasses #550

F

Fabia, Fabiola #983
Fabrizio, Girolamo #662
Fabulous Kangaroos, The #1087
Facenda, John #1005

Fairbanks #750
Fallopius, Gabriele #462, #662
Falsetto #236, #328
Falstaff #206
Famiglietti, Gary #1114
Fangio #1124
Fanzoni, Giuseppe #652
Farentino, James #364
Fardella, Enrico #882
Farinelli #167
Farnese, Alessandro #720
Fascism #800
Faustulus #1383
Federal Bureau of Investigation
#709
Federal Express #377
Fellini, Federico #77
Fendi #930
Fenzi-Contini, #452
Ferdinand #918
Ferigno, Lew #370
Ferlinghetti, Lawrence #515
Fermi, Enrico #455, #543, #653
Ferragamo, Vince #1070
Ferrari automobile #811, #1157
Ferrari, Ludovico #587
Ferrari, William #286
Ferraro, Geraldine Anne
#705,#903
Ferre, Gianfranco #930
Ferrero, Eduardo #882
Ferretti, Gianni #1050
Fiasco #509
Fibonacci, Leonardo #418
Ficco di India #396
Figaro #326
Filiberto, King Emanuele #275
Finale #238
Fingers, Rollie #1159
Finiguerra, Masa #552
Finocchio club #367
Fish #140
Fish market #1428
Fish stew, #66
Fish tanks #1336
Fiume #428
Flaccus, Quintus #1382
Flora #1259

Giova, Flavia #532
Giovane Italia #693
Giovanni, Don #171
Giraldi, Cinzio #603
Giuliani, Mayor Rudolph W. #974
Giulietta e Romeo (Romeo and Juliet) #433
Gladiator #1371
Gladiolus #1230
Gladius #1461
Goering, Herman #893
Godfather, The #62, #113, #248, #466
Godfather, The Part II #62, #112
Golden Ass, The #536
Golgi, Camillo #596
Gorgonzola #285
Grain allowance #1306
Gramatica, Martin #1203
Grappa #385
Grasso, Ella Tambussi #975
Graziano, Rocky #1068, #1129
Griffith, D. W. #140
Grimaldi, Alberto #184
Grimaldi, Francesco #641
Grimaldi, Joseph #368
Groma #1469
Guaragna, Salvadore #79
Gucci, Guccio #982
Gucci, Maurizio #930
Guccione, Bob #375
Guidi, Tomasso di Giovanni #663
Gusto #411
Guzzetta, Matt #1167

H

Hadrian #1237, #1390
Hadrians Wall #1455
Hall of Fame, baseball #1020
Hang Glider #607
Hanna-Barbera Productions #132,#304
Hannibal #1242, #1365,#1376
Hanratty, Terry #1188
Happy Days #357
Harris, Franco #1043

Haruspex #1490
Harvey, William #600, #662
Hastati #1468
Heisman Trophy, The #1202, #1206
Helipoter #621
Hendricks, Ted #1183
Herculaneum #713
Herodotus #980
Hills of Rome 1434
Historical pageants #111
Holden, William #87
Holland #318
Honey #1313
Horace #1364, #1382
Horse #1324
Hulk, The #370
Humanism #493
Hungary #1283

I

Iacocca, Lee #379, #738
Ice cream #745
Il Duomo #548
Imbroglio #472
Immigrant group #686,#687, #881,#755
Immigration Act of 1924 #843
Impellitteri, Vincent #859
Imperium #1370
Incaviglia, Pete #992, #1057
Incognito #469
Infantry #581
Inferno #486
Influenza #463
Ionian Sea #711
Irish, The #787
Isabella #918
Itali, The #700
Italian card games #792
Italian government, The #915
Italian Swiss Colony #735, #917
Italians, The #164
Italic #500
Italophile #501

Liguria #312, #934
Ligurian Sea #711
Lincoln Memorial #573
Lincoln, President Abraham #718
Lino, Marisa #894
Lion, The #794
Liotta, Ray #70
Liquori, Martin #1077
Lisi, Virna #21
Litrico, Angelo #821
Loggia, Robert #141
Lollobrigida, Gina #23
Lombardi, Ernie #1023
Lombardi, Gennaro #82
Lombardi, Vince #313, #997, #1046,#1113,#1178,#1207
Lombardo, Guy #323
Lombards, The #682
Lombardy #934,#839,#957
Longino, Andrew Houston #828
Loren, Sophia #27, #72, #108,#151,#228,#372,#399,#458
Lou Retton, Mary #1017
Louisiana #734
Lucan #1354
Lucca #305
Lucci, Susan #390
Luciano, Ron #356,
Lucky charm #1487
Lucretius #1481
Luisetti, Hank #1002
Luria, Dr. Salvador #606
Lusetti, Hank #1059
Lyre #1439

M

Macchio, Ralph #179
Macedonia #1441
Macedonian Phalanx #1467
Machiavelli, Niccolo #563, #576, #684,#931
Madame Butterfly #229
Madonna #257
Maestri, Robert #673
Mafia #876, #885
Magellan, Ferdinand #752

Magenta #806
Maglie, Sal #1150, #1196
Magna Grecia #965
Magnani, Anna #83, #153
Malavasi, Ray #1102
Malpighi, Marcello #491, #600
Malta #1299
Mameli, Goffredo #937
Mancini, Henry #379, #384
Mancini, Ray Boom-Boom #1083
Mandolin #131
Manero, Tony #1054
Manfredo #626
Mangano, Silvana #214
Mangiarotti, Edoardo #1160
Mangione, Chuck #198
Maniaci, Joe #1114
Manicotti #389
Manifesto #435
Mantegna, Joe #329
Maravia, Alberto #458
Marbles #1380
Marche, Le #350, #934
Marchetti, Gino #1063, #1182
Marciano, Rocky #273 ,#1103, #1112,#1129
Marconi Monument #519
Marconi,Guglielmo #453, #477, #519,#560,#630,#644,#956
Marechiare #272
Marinaro, Ed #267
Marine compass #532
Marino, Dan #1032
Mariucci, Steve #1218
Marius #1444
Marotta, Vince #586
Marriage ceremony #1474
Marsala #265
Marshall, Garry #381
Marshall, Penny #98
Martial #650
Martin, Billy #1095, #1204
Martin, Dean #46, #287
Martini, Major Anthony #795
Martini, John #850
Martino, Al #321
Matthew #959
Marx Brothers, The #128

N

Ravenna #919, #1325
Ray, Aldo #139
Red Brigades, The #783
Redi, Francesco #511, #640
Reggio di Calabria #967, #971
Regiment #601
Renaissance, The #498,#762, #850
Rene Russo #353
Renzetti, Joe #116
Replica #525
Republic #818, #1291
Revolta, Johnny #1115
Rhode Island #898
Rice and peas #220
Rigatoni #355
Rigbelli, Gennaro #192
Riggio, Leonard #976
Righetti, Dave #1117
Rambaldi, Carlo #365
Risotto Alla Milanese #40
Rizzo, Frank #942
Rizzuto, Phil #1027
Robertson, Agnes Ion #1172
Robustelli, Andy #1003, #1209
Rocca, Argentina #1087
Rocco, St. #933
Rocky #114
Rodino, Peter W. #757,#797,#906
Rogallo, Francis #607
Roma #696
Roman emperors #1253
Roman Empire, The #627, #928
Roman gods #1331
Roman law #1406
Roman numerals #1429
Roman war galley #1465
Roman women 1432
Romance languages #805
Romania #1312
Rome #514, #779, #784, #961,#985 #1146,#1326,#1413
Rome Anniversary #1297
Romeo and Juliet, #172
Romulus #1273,#1280, #1288
Romulus and Remus #1383, #1288,#1327
Rosapepe, James #894

Rose Tattoo #83
Rossellini, Roberto #31, #153
Rossetti, Christina Geogina #617
Rossetti, Dante Gabriel #578
Rossi, Angelo #673, #780
Rossi, Paolo #1125
Rossi, Pietro #917
Rossini, Gioacchino #183, #331
Rossman, Mike #1127
Rota, Nino #155
Rowing #1105
Rubicon #1262
Rutigliano, Sam #1049
Rydell, Bobby #408

S

S.P.Q.R. #1274
Sabatini, Gabriela #1088, #1179
Sabatini, Rafael #424
Sabines #1437
Sabre #1030
Sacco, Alberto Jr. #989
Sacco, Nicola #824
Saffron #20
Salami #345
Salimbeni, A. #629
Salo Republic #905
Salt #830
Salvino, Carmine #1137
Salvio, Mario #782
San Francisco #681
San Gennaro Festival #875
San Marino, Republic of #671, #921
San Salvador #899
Sanmartino, Bruno #1140
Santo, Ron #1037
Santoni, Dante #188
Santoria, Dr. #496
Saracens, The #702, #911
Sarandon, Susan #123
Sarazen, Gene #1018, #1052, #1118,
Sardinia #125, #195,#691,

Index

Stello, Richard #1192
Stevens, Connie #146
Stock Exchange #867
Stockings #1233
Stone bridge #1414
Stradivari, Antonio #400, #421
Stratagems #1360
Strigil #1489
Strike, The Lawrence #863
Stucco #474
Studio #588
Submachine gun #465
Subway sandwich #878
Suetonius #887
Suicide #1466
Surveying instrument #1469
Switzerland #1445
Sword #1478
Syphilis #546
Syringe #551

T

Tagliocozzi, Gasparo #520
Talese, Gay #575
Tasso, Torguato #437
Tammany Hall #951
Tarantino, Quentin #358
Tarquin #1296, #1375
Tartaglia, Niccolo #580
Tarutfi #1124
Tata, Terry #1192
Tebaldi, Renata #97
Tellus #1396
Tempo #59
Tempura #620
Tenace, Gene #994
Tenth and Last #774
Terence #523
Terracotta #593
Terrazzo #503
Testaverde, Vinny #993, #1206
Tetrazzini, Luisa #369
Theodosius I #1394
Thermometer, The Medical #496
Thermopolium #1462
Thoeni, Gustavo #1185

Tiber River, The #798
Tiberius #1276, #1315
Tie #1333
Tiro #422
Tidal wave #971
Titus #1277, #1301
Tocci #829
Toga #1278
Toilet paper #1478
Toma #104
Tombs #572
Tonight Show,The #293
Tonti, Enrico #726
Torchi, Joseph V. #981
Torre, Joe #1097, #1154, #1198
Torretta, Geno #1206
Torricelli, Evangelista #447
Torso #579
Tortoise formation #1460
Tosca #89, #262
Tosti, Francesco Paolo #272
Toscanini, Arturo #11, #212
Toschi, Filippo #679
Toschi, Joseph V. 981
Traetta, Philip #322
Trajan #1408,#1427, #1471
Travanti, Daniel #283
Travolta, John #78, #341
Treaty of Versailles #428
Trentino-Alto Adige #934
Trevi Fountain, The #464,
#785
Triarti #1468
Tribunes #1287
Trieste #844
Trifolau #130
Trivium 1433
Troisi, Massimo #403
Trotti, Lamar #288
Trovatore, Il #57
Truffles #130
Trumpet #198
Tucci, Stanley #302
Tufo, Peter #894
Turin #856
Turkish War #886
Turnesa, Joe #1115, #1165
Turri, Pellegrini #436

World War II veterans #812

Y

Yale University, #707
Your Show Of Shows #347

Z

Zabaglione #9
Zaccaro, John #903
Zappa, Frank #56
Zeffirelli, Franco #172, #263
Zenetti, Daniela #930
Zoetrope Studios #88
Zucchini #133